Toddlers Together

Toddlers

The Complete Planning Guide For A Toddler Curriculum

Together

By Cynthia Catlin

Illustrated By Karen Theusen

gryphon house

Beltsville, Maryland

Copyright © 1994 Cynthia Catlin

Published by Gryphon House, Inc.
10726 Tucker Street, Beltsville, MD 20705

Cover Design: Graves, Fowler & Associates
Cover Photo: Nancy Alexander

Library of Congress Cataloging-in-Publication Data

Catlin, Cynthia, 1962–
    Toddlers together : the complete planning guide for a toddler
curriculum / by Cynthia Catlin ; illustrated by Karen Theusen.
        p. cm.
    Includes index.
    ISBN 0-87659-171-3 : $24.95
    1. Education, Preschool—Activity programs. 2. Education,
Preschool—Curricula. I. Title.
LB1140.35.C74C38   1994
372.21—dc20   94-21491
                                                               CIP

Table of Contents

Chapter 6—For Toddlers in Summer: June, July and August

Chapter 7 —For Toddlers Celebrating: Holidays, Birthdays and Special Occasions

Dedicated to

Mama for her foundation,
Papa for his pride,
Ron for his patience
and
Alan for his inspiration.

—Cynthia Catlin

Dear Teacher,

I am a toddler.
I am a super snooper.
I search and check
everything within my reach
and often beyond.
I am curious,
too curious at times.
I declare my independence,
often quite loudly.
I know I can do it,
all by myself.

But,
Please stay close.

I need you there,
to help keep me
from hurting myself
when I am too curious.
I need you
to encourage me,
and allow me
to try to do it by myself,
and to help when I can't,
or when I get frustrated.

I need you
to hug and cuddle with me.
If I do something you don't like,
Tell me.
Show me a better way.
Please don't reject me.
Please be patient.
I have really only been in this world a short while.

The world
and its ways
are still so very, very new to me.

—from a toddler

Introduction

The term "toddlers" typically describes children between one and three years of age. They are longer infants but not yet preschoolers typically refers to children between one and three years of age. This group includes children who are walking and beginning to talk to those interacting with peers and asking endless questions at an age when curiosity is high, all toddlers literally plunge headfirst into life.

Teaching toddlers is a challenge for they love to test the world around them—the physical environment as well as the adults caring for them. A toddler will vacillate between wanting to be close and wanting to be autonomous. The caregiver must be fully present and connected with toddlers when they feel dependent, yet allow the children to move away and explore on their own when they are ready to be independent.

Teachers of toddlers must become one of the group, playing and interacting with them to guide their early attempts at socializing with peers and to model appropriate use of materials. Providing for this age group is physically demanding. Ask any parent or teacher of a toddler at the end of the day! To fully enjoy teaching children from one to three years of age, one must be dedicated to the challenges as well as the joys of being with toddlers.

Despite the demands, teaching children under three is extremely rewarding. They want and need lots of hugs and cuddling. It is fulfilling to observe and be a part of the tremendous growth and development that occurs between 12 and 36 months of age. While the children may not remember specific teachers or activities, they will take with them a curiosity and an "I can do it!" attitude as they begin their lifelong journey of learning. Toddlers live for the moment; every experience offers a new awareness for them. Adults need only to watch toddlers, and find joy in the children's innocence, to rekindle their own curiosity and excitement about life.

Unfortunately, one and two year olds are often misunderstood in terms of their unique characteristics and needs. Environments and activities for toddlers have often been geared more towards infants or resemble a "push down" of a preschool class. Expecting toddlers to stay involved in activities not stimulating enough or, conversely, too advanced for their developmental abilities tends to lead to frustration for both the child and the caregiver. Toddlers have specific needs and characteristics unique to their stage of development that must be taken into consideration when planning for children under three.

The ideas in this book come from ten years of experience teaching toddlers, providing first hand knowledge of the characteristics of the age and a belief in the special nature of teachers who choose to teach one and two year olds. The underlying premise emphasizes teacher involvement and what is appropriate for children from one to three years of age. Many of the activities have suggestions for modifying the activity for younger toddlers, for older toddlers, or for differing developmental levels within a group. The references to ages are guidelines only, not rigid classifications. Each teacher knows her/his children, their capabilities and what will work with them better than any outsider.

Children under three are actively acquiring language so all activities include sample vocabulary and many also include chants or simple songs with familiar tunes to use with the toddlers to promote their language development. Since toddlers are primarily in the sensory-motor stage of development, the activity ideas emphasize the senses and physical activity as much as possible. Resources may be limited, so suggestions are provided for materials that can be made from inexpensive or disposable items. As any parent of a toddler will confess, their child probably prefers the boxes and miscellaneous household items over the expensive toys they have bought!

All of the activities are meant to be used with the children individually and in small groups during their play time, while other choices are available, and not as a whole group. One and two year olds do not learn well, if at all, in situations involving the entire group. Rather, toddlers learn best through their independent explorations and interactions with their caregivers, who can promote their learning by initiating activities based on the children's play behaviors and interests.

Considering that children under three master skills through repetition and will repeat actions over and over, most of the activities have suggestions for extending the ideas for variety and additional learning. With appropriate learning experiences for toddlers that they will find truly enjoyable, at the end of each activity they will wholeheartedly say, "Again!"

Helpful hints for teachers of toddlers

The role of the teacher

Stay involved and interact fully with the toddlers on their level—on your knees, on the seat of your pants, with a lap available and yet ready to move as needed elsewhere.

Take care of yourself. Find a classroom activity that relaxes you and do it often, whether it be singing, dancing or building towers with the children. Toddlers do pick up on your non-verbal cues and stress level easily. It is as though they have a "mood antenna." Stressed out teachers lead to anxious toddlers with crying and/or aggression bound to follow. Leave your worries from home outside the classroom door each morning and face them at the end of the day. Connect with the toddlers, enjoy their simple joys and get a reprieve from the burdens of adulthood as you enter the "for-the-moment" nature of toddlers.

Daily schedule

Routine tasks of diapering, toilet learning, mealtimes, hand washing, etc. take up a large amount of time when caring for toddlers. Turn these tasks into optimal teaching times filled with language stimulation. Caregiving routines offer a perfect opportunity for a few moments of one-to-one interaction with each child.

Keep in mind that toddlers do not function well in a large group with all required to do the same activity. This leads to frustration for the toddlers and especially for the teachers when they spend all of their energy keeping the children together as a group. There may be a few times when all the children must stay together, such as mealtimes or leaving the room. Keep these situations to a minimum and try to make them as toddler-oriented as possible by talking with the children or singing songs and doing fingerplays.

Plan for a "Wow!" activity each day as one of the choices offered that will make the toddlers think "Wow, this is neat. I want to do it again!" The children can choose to join in, just watch or even not participate at all. The "Wow!" activity may be teacher-initiated and require more supervision than the other free choice materials that are also available. This book is filled with a number of potential "Wow!" activities.

Provide lots of opportunities to have the toddlers do things "all by myself." Even the youngest toddlers can help put away a blanket or bring their diaper to the changing area. Older toddlers can actually help with some "chores" like wiping the table or carrying supplies outside for an activity. Toddlers do enjoy helping out, so let them be your "special helpers" throughout the day to build their self-esteem and independence.

A consistent daily schedule is important as toddlers thrive with familiarity and routines. When the children know what to expect next, they feel secure. Toddlers can also guide their own behavior when they have a consistent routine and, thus, can be more independent.

Toys and materials

All toys and materials used by children under three must be larger than a certain size (approximately two inches in length by one inch diameter) so as not to be a choking hazard. Simple devises to check the size of objects can be purchased from most school supply stores or distributors for a nominal cost. Check all items used with toddlers.

Try to have duplicate or very similar toys to avoid problems with sharing. Toddlers are very much in the "mine" stage. It is easier to redirect children's interest to a comparable toy rather then making them wait and share, which many have difficulty doing.

Place the toys and materials at the children's level to allow them to choose on their own what they want to explore. As the toddlers leave these items to play with something else, do try to have them return the toys to the proper shelf or area. Toddlers can learn to help clean up with encouragement.

Use shelves rather than toy boxes. Putting all the materials in toy boxes or baskets only teaches the toddlers to "dump." But, sorting the materials into similar categories such as books, manipulatives, cars, etc. on separate shelves helps toddlers develop their organizational skills.

Hang pictures at the toddlers' eye level so they can examine them. With some guidance and patience at first, toddlers will learn to leave the pictures up on the wall. Cover the pictures with clear contact paper or laminate them to add durability. Use pictures from magazines and calendars, posters from conference exhibitors, etc. Do hang the children's artwork beyond their reach as it is not easily replaced. Change the materials, books and pictures periodically for variety and to relate to different themes.

Make sure the room is not overstimulating. The shelves and walls do not need to be filled to the brim with pictures and materials. Tone down bright colors with neutral materials or wood. Be aware of too much stimulation especially during the holidays and special events when even adults can feel overwhelmed. However, the room does need an ample supply of toys, books and pictures to make it a place that invites the children to play and learn.

Room arrangement

Offer at least three different types of materials or activities, such as books, dolls and stuffed animals, hats, simple manipulatives, cars and climber, in distinct areas for young toddlers to have choices.

Set up the classroom in basic learning centers for older toddlers, such as book/cozy corner, blocks and vehicles, home living and dress-up, manipulatives and puzzles, discovery space, sensory table, music/art area and a large motor/movement section as space permits.

Establish a location in the room to be a "snuggly spot" with cardboard or teacher-made books, puppets, stuffed animals, pillows, soft materials, etc. for the children to "get away" and relax as they need. The area should be away from high traffic or loud activities but still have adequate supervision. Toddlers need the opportunity to have quiet or "down time."

Arrange the shelves and structures so that you can see easily into all the areas of the room, especially while on your knees or sitting. Toddlers do require close supervision and the teacher must be able to see the children at all times, even when busy changing a diaper.

Be critically aware of your room arrangement and how it affects behavior. Avoid wide open spaces as they invite children to run. Yet, too cramped space can lead to aggression. Materials unsafe or not for the children to use must be out of reach and out of sight. Cluttered space leads to dumping and random behaviors. Examine your room arrangement when a child continually behaves in a challenging way rather than blaming the child for his or her actions. Reflect on why the behavior could be happening or how it can be prevented. Keep in mind that children often behave in response to the environment. Adjust the room arrangement, planning, schedules, activities, etc. as needed. It is definitely much easier to change the environment than it is the child.

To ponder today and often

Walk in your room on your knees! This helps you see how the room looks from the toddler perspective. Keeping this toddler perspective, ask yourself:
Does it feel safe?
Does it allow me to play and explore on my own?
Is this room inviting and oriented to my interests?
Is it a place where I would want to stay all day?

Look at yourself as a teacher. Through the heart of a toddler, ask yourself:
Do I relate to the children on their level?
Am I nurturing and understanding of the toddlers' individual and unique needs?
Am I available to them, and yet do I let them go off and learn on their own?
Would I want to be a toddler under my care?

For Toddlers Together:
Adjusting and Interacting

Young children begin to move beyond the parent-child relationship during the toddler years. Encourage this transition with activities to enhance the toddlers':
- ◆ *Adjustment to the Group*
- ◆ *Awareness of Others*
- ◆ *Early Interactions With Others*

My Family

Looking at pictures of family members helps toddlers keep a mental image of those most familiar to them. This sense of security is important as toddlers are adjusting to a new room full of strangers.

Skills encouraged

social-emotional
language

Language to use with toddlers

family
special
mother
father
brother
sister
names
grandparent
pet
home
work

Materials

photos of the children and
   their families
scissors
construction paper
glue or tape
posterboard
clear contact paper

To do

1. Have the parent bring in one or two pictures of the child with his parents, siblings, grandparents, special caregiver or pet.

2. Attach the picture to posterboard or construction paper for sturdiness. Cover the picture with clear contact paper or laminate it.

3. Place the picture in or near the child's cubby area, or add it to a permanent display of photos of the children and their families. Be sure to display the photos at a toddler's eye level.

4. Talk with the toddler about who is in the picture, their name, what they like to do with that person, etc.

5. When the child seems sad during the day, encourage him to look at the photograph of those he loves.

To do again

Ask the parent to attach a photo key ring with a picture of family members to the child's diaper bag. When learning about families, ask each parent to send a small "brag book" photo album filled with five to ten pictures for the child to show his teacher and friends at school. Look at the "Family Brag Books" often with the children.

Teaching Hints

Although it is tempting to avoid using the words "mommy" or "daddy" with a toddler who is having a difficult adjustment a new situation, it is best to be up front with the child about his parents. Gently explain to him "Yes, your dad will come back when he finishes teaching at his school." Simple, matter-of-fact comments reassure the toddler and help build trust between the child and caregiver.

My Friends

Pictures of real people fascinate toddlers, especially pictures of people they know at home and playmates at school. Use photographs of the children at school and from home to make a class photo album and to display on the walls.

To do

1. Take pictures of the children playing in the room and outside. Make sure to have a picture of each child, preferably doing one of their favorite activities.

2. Put the pictures together into a "Class Photo Album." An album from a store can be used, or a book can be made easily with posterboard, contact paper and book rings.

3. Look at the class book often with the toddlers. Talk with them about who is in the picture, what they are doing, etc. Be sure to include a photo from nap time, as it surprises the children to see themselves sleeping on their mats.

4. Use pictures of the children involved in daily activities as "learning center labels" in the room. For example, take a picture of the children washing their hands, looking at books, playing with dolls, painting, putting away their blanket in their cubby, etc. Glue the photo to a piece of construction paper for backing and cover with clear contact paper. Put the picture up in the center or the area of the classroom where that action takes place.

5. Take pictures of the children at special events and playing throughout the year. Put the photos up, at toddler eye level, for the children and parents to enjoy. Add the pictures to the class album when you are finished displaying them.

To do again

At different times during the year, take pictures of the children or have the parents send a picture from home related to the theme, such as with their favorite stuffed animal or pet, as a baby, playing outside, etc. Attach the photos to posterboard to put up on the wall at the toddler's eye level. Use the photos to talk about the topic with the toddlers.

Teaching hints

Parents enjoy seeing pictures of their child just as much as the toddlers do. Allow the children to take turns taking the class photo album home for their families to enjoy. At the end of the year, save the class album for your keepsake!

Skills encouraged

social-emotional
language

Language to use with toddlers

Who is this?
What are they doing?
names of children and
 family members
picture
friends
family
school
home

Materials

photos of the children at
 home and at school
posterboard
scissors
construction paper
glue or tape
contact paper
yarn or book rings
photo album

My Blanket!

When they are away from their parents, toddlers find security in special attachments to objects such as blankets, dolls or stuffed animals. Spend time exploring these security objects, as they can be as important in the lives of toddlers as their family members!

Skills encouraged

social-emotional
language

Language to use with toddlers

song
snuggle
blanket
special
friend
colors
warm
different
stuffed animals
secure

Materials

receiving blankets or baby
  quilts
stuffed animals

To do

1. Have a blanket day when each toddlers brings a favorite blanket. Have extras on hand in case someone forgets.

2. Talk to each child about his or her special blanket. Let them hold or sit on their blanket while you read a story.

3. Encourage the toddlers to "snuggle" with their blankets as you sing the following song with them to the tune of "My Bonnie Lies Over the Ocean."

   My blanket is my friend.
   My blanket is so special.
   My blanket keeps me warm.
   So don't take my blanket away.
   Chorus:
   Blanket, blanket, it belongs to me, to me!
   Blanket, blanket, blanket belongs to me.

4. Change the words as follows to use the song and blankets as a gross motor activity.

   My blanket goes up high.
   My blanket goes down low.
   My blanket goes all around,
   And it can go every which way!
   Chorus:
   Blanket, blanket, it dances with me, with me!
   Blanket, blanket, blanket dances with me.

5. Make up other songs from familiar tunes about blankets. The following is sung to the tune of "Mary Had a Little Lamb."

   Rhonda has a boat blanket, boat blanket, boat blanket.
   Rhonda has a boat blanket,
   That she sleeps with every night.

To do again

Use other security objects that the children may be attached to in the above songs. Include stuffed animals, dolls or burp rags! Toddlers can be attached to some very unusual items!

Teaching hints

As toddlers adjust to the room, encourage them to keep their special attachment objects in their bags or cubbies until nap time. Children who are carrying their security objects around may get frustrated when others touch the item, or may spend more time snuggling with their special object than playing or interacting with others.

Let's Rock

The rocking motion of this activity works wonders with toddlers new to a group during the first few minutes after the parent has left. It provides a perfect opportunity for comforting one-on-one interaction.

1+

What to do

1. While holding the toddler in your lap, rock back and forth or side to side while quietly repeating the following chant, said in a gentle, sing-song style.

   We are rocking
   Rocking, rocking
   Rocking to and fro.
   I am rocking
   You are rocking
   Back and forth we go.

2. Repeat the chant as long as the child desires.

3. As you rock the child, encourage the toddler to rock a doll or stuffed animal while singing the song with you.

To do again

Older toddlers can rock one another. One child sits in front of the other while the one in the back puts his arms around the child. The children can sing the "Rocking, rocking" chant as they move side to side. This is a perfect way to establish friendships and early nurturing behaviors.

Teaching hints

Use this song to comfort or calm down any child who seems out of control from frustration, or is over-excited. The rocking motion is very soothing for most children and even teachers.

Skills encouraged

social-emotional
motor skills

Language to use with toddlers

rocking
back and forth
I
you
we
lap
sit
hold you
comfort
together

Materials

none needed

Love Somebody

A chant about caring for individual children enhances the formation of the teacher-child relationship when a toddler is new to the group. The children's special attachments can also be chanted about to emphasize loving feelings with even the youngest of toddlers.

Skills encouraged

language
social-emotional

Language to use with toddlers

love
somebody
names
who
song
rhythm

Materials

none needed

To do

1. While holding or working individually with a child, chant the following verse with a definite rhythm:

   Love somebody, yes I do
   Love somebody, yes I do
   Love somebody, yes I do
   Love somebody and I'll tell you who.
   I love Shirley, yes I do.
   I love Shirley, yes I do.
   I love Shirley, yes I do.
   I love Shirley, and now I've told you who.

2. Substitute the names of other children who are playing nearby.

3. Repeat the verse and sing about the child's favorite object or snugly:

   Shirley loves something soft, yes she does.
   Shirley loves something soft, yes she does.
   Shirley loves something soft, yes she does.
   Shirley loves something soft and I'll tell you what.
   Shirley loves her cat pillow, yes she does.
   Shirley loves her cat pillow, yes she does.
   Shirley loves her cat pillow, yes she does.
   Shirley loves her cat pillow, and I told you what.

Teaching hints

Since this is a rather long chant, it is best done with one child at a time or with a small group, while the other children are playing. It is also a perfect chant to say during one-on-one times like diaper changes.

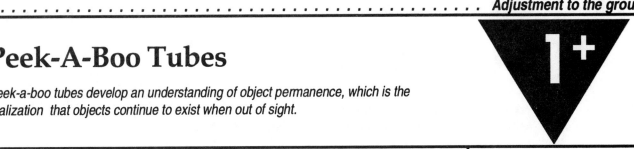

Peek-A-Boo Tubes

Peek-a-boo tubes develop an understanding of object permanence, which is the realization that objects continue to exist when out of sight.

To do

1. Obtain at least two clear 35-mm film canisters or other small, clear containers such as those from seasonings or plastic boxes. The two plastic containers will need to be exactly the same size.

2. Put a small pompom or other small soft object inside one of the containers.

3. Place the second container or film canister on top with the two open ends forming a seam.

4. Glue the two ends together with a hot glue gun, or use thick colored tape to secure the seam.

5. Completely cover one of the clear containers with contact paper or colored tape. Leave the other half uncovered in order to see the pompom.

6. Allow the toddlers to explore the "peek-a-boo" tubes. Show the younger toddlers how to move the tube back and forth to make the pompom disappear and reappear.

7. Talk with the toddler about the pompom hiding and then coming back into sight. Say "peek-a-boo" when it reappears and "uh-ohh" when it disappears.

Teaching hints

The peek-a-boo tubes fascinate younger toddlers, so it is best to have more than one available.

Skills encouraged

object permanence
fine motor

Language to use with toddlers

see
hidden
inside
turn
look
peek-a-boo
tube
where
pompom

Materials

contact paper
colored tape
clear film canisters
small clear containers
pompom or other small
  soft item
hot glue gun

Surprise!

Hiding familiar objects helps the toddlers develop the awareness that objects continue to exist even when out of sight. This is an important understanding for toddlers who are adjusting to being away from their parents.

Skills encouraged

object permanence
language
social-emotional
sensory development

Language to use with toddlers

hidden
surprise
what
see
feel

Materials

adult's tube sock
plastic jar or gift tin
familiar small objects
drawstring bag
tissue box

To do

1. Take the lid off the gift tin or plastic jar and slide it into the sock with the open end facing out. The sock should fit completely over the container and have approximately a two inch overhang.

2. Hide a special toy or object inside the container. Change the objects occasionally for variety or to relate to a particular theme.

3. Show the toddler how to put her hand inside to feel the object.

4. With older toddlers, ask "What could it be?" and other open ended questions to promote curiosity and language. For example, with a stuffed animal, "What do you feel?" "Is it soft like a bunny, or hard like a block?" "Could it be a carrot or a stuffed mouse?"

5. Show surprise when the child removes the object. Talk to the toddler about the special features of the object.

6. Make several surprise cans with different objects hiding inside and allow the toddlers to explore them.

To do again

Use a drawstring bag, a small square tissue box or even a paper sack as surprise containers.

Teaching hints

The toddlers' interest in this activity will be promoted by the teacher's playfulness in questioning and display of excitement with the surprise. Use the containers to spark interest in objects related to a theme. Play a little guessing game by describing the object, and then showing it as a surprise.

Boo Boxes

Peek-a-boo activities help toddlers adjust to being away from their parents by helping them understand that objects continue to exist when they cannot be seen. Boxes and tops with pictures can be made into simple peek-a-boo fun.

To do

1. Collect a variety of sturdy boxes, such as those from jewelry stores, cigar boxes or school boxes. For variety, match boxes can be used with older toddlers.

2. Cut pictures from magazines to fit inside the bottoms of boxes. Pictures of children, families and animals tend to be the most popular with toddlers. Use pictures from a variety of ethnic groups and family groups.

3. Tape the picture to the inside bottoms of the boxes.

4. Cover the outside of the boxes with patterned contact paper if desired.

5. Put the top down on the boxes.

6. Put the boxes out for the toddlers to explore on their own.

7. Talk with the children about the pictures inside. Encourage them to play a simple peek-a-boo with the pictures by opening and closing the lids.

To do again

Make a "Boo Box" for each child. Ask the parents to send a picture of themselves or their family for the inside of the box.

Skills encouraged

object permanence
fine motor

Language to use with toddlers

box
open
close
inside
hidden
look
picture
peek-a-boo
surprise
mommy
daddy

Materials

small, sturdy boxes
magazine pictures
contact paper
glue
scissors

Picture, Picture on the Wall

Peek-a-boo is an all-time favorite activity of toddlers. Pictures on the wall covered with a piece of fabric allow toddlers to play peek-a-boo on their own.

Skills encouraged

fine motor
object permanence
language

Language to use with toddlers

lift
fabric
see
hidden
underneath
peek-a-boo
picture

Materials

pictures
posterboard or
  construction paper
contact paper
scissors
glue or tape
fabric squares

To do

1. Collect pictures from magazines. Relate the pictures to a theme if possible. Pictures of animals, children, babies and families are always popular with toddlers.

2. Mount the pictures on posterboard or construction paper for sturdiness. Cover with clear contact paper or laminate.

3. Cut the pieces of fabric in sizes that will cover the pictures with at least a two inch margin on each side.

4. Attach the pictures to the wall or bulletin board at a toddler's eye level.

5. Cover the picture with the fabric piece. Attach the fabric to the wall at the top edge only, so that it can be lifted.

6. Encourage the toddlers to look under the fabric piece for a peek-a-boo surprise.

7. To keep the toddlers interested, change the pictures periodically.

To do again

Use photographs of the children in the class underneath the fabric pieces.

Teaching hints

When looking for pictures of people in magazines, choose ones with individuals from different ethnic backgrounds, in non-sexist occupations and roles and/or various family groupings.

Lift the Flap Books

Lift the flap books promote toddlers' concept of object permanence and fine motor skills. Simple and sturdy homemade versions can be made inexpensively with greeting cards.

To do

1. Collect a variety of birthday, get well, new baby, Christmas, Hanukkah, etc. cards with pictures that would interest toddlers. Used cards are fine. Encourage parents to donate their old cards.

2. If the cards do not have any pictures inside them, add stickers, small magazine pictures, or a drawing related to the outside of the card.

3. Cut the posterboard into equal squares, eight by eight inches or a larger size that will accommodate your largest card.

4. Glue one card onto each side of the squares of posterboard.

5. Save two pieces of the posterboard for the front and back covers. The two covers can be left blank or decorated with stickers or pictures as desired.

6. Cover each side of the posterboard pieces with clear contact paper. Laminating machines will not usually work with the thickness of the posterboard and two cards.

7. Slice the top, bottom, and right edges of the card with a utility blade so it can be opened and closed.

8. Put the pieces of posterboard together in order like a book with a front and back cover.

9. Punch two holes on the left side of each piece of posterboard.

10. Thread yarn or book rings through the holes and put the book together.

11. Let the toddlers look at the book. Encourage them to open and close the cards to see what is inside.

12. Make up a simple story with the cards if possible. Or just talk to the toddlers about the pictures on the outside and the hidden ones inside the card.

Skills encouraged

fine motor
language
object permanence
pre-reading/emergent
  literacy

Language to use with toddlers

look
book
open
close
What is inside?
picture
cards

Materials

greeting cards
posterboard
scissors
hole punch
thick yarn or book rings
clear contact paper
utility blade
stickers
small pictures

1⁺

Our Names

A simple chant of names can be used to help teachers and toddlers learn each other's names in a fun and casual way.

Skills encouraged

language
social interaction

Language to use with toddlers

clap
name
beat

Materials

none needed

What to do

1. Chant to the syllables of each child's and teacher's name. Clap to the beat of the chant. Say the chant in a sing-song fashion:

   Marc, Marc
   That is his name.

2. Use the chant to describe what the children are wearing, playing with or even eating:

   Blue, blue
   Marc is wearing his blue sweater.
   Reading, reading
   Marc is looking at a book
   Water, water
   Marc is drinking water.

To do again

Use the chant with older toddlers to help them learn their full names. Send the words home for the parents to use with their children. For example:

Marc Alexander, Marc Alexander
That is your full name.

Teaching hints

Most toddlers do not have the patience for long group times so it is best to do these chants during the children's play, mealtimes or during transitions.

Mary Had a Little Lamb

These variations on a traditional song provide individual recognition which promotes positive self-esteem. They can also be used to learn each others' names.

To do

1. Change the words of the following traditional song to include the children's names and clothing or special features.

   Sing to the tune of "Mary Had a Little Lamb."

   > *Tommy has light blonde hair,*
   > *Light blonde hair, light blonde hair.*
   > *Tommy has light blonde hair,*
   > *And that makes Tommy special.*
   > *Tommy wears his engineer hat,*
   > *Engineer hat, engineer hat.*
   > *Tommy wears his engineer hat,*
   > *To keep him toasty warm.*

2. Use the verse with other children's names. Let older toddlers tell you what they want you to sing about them.

3. Change the verse to sing about what the individual children may be doing in their play as well.

   > *Tommy plays with wooden blocks,*
   > *Wooden blocks, wooden blocks.*
   > *Tommy plays with wooden blocks,*
   > *To build a wooden house.*

To do again

Hold up a picture of the child while singing about their hair or eyes, etc.

Skills encouraged

social-emotional
language

Language to use with toddlers

song
sing
name
clothing
hair
eyes
color
special

Materials

photos of the children

Say Cheese!

Toddlers practice interacting with their peers as they pretend to take pictures of each other. The old cameras also offer a fun way for toddlers to refine their fine motor skills as they push the buttons.

Skills encouraged

social skills
fine motor
imaginative play

Language to use with toddlers

picture
look
smile
see
push
button
camera
friends

Materials

old cameras—instamatic
and Polaroid work well

To do

1. Send a note home to parents asking for old cameras, preferably instamatic and Polaroid, to help you acquire a collection. Make sure all batteries have been removed.

2. Place old cameras out for the children to explore.

3. Pretend to take pictures of the children with the cameras to model the interaction.

4. Encourage the toddlers to take pictures of each other.

5. Add the cameras to an area with dress-up clothes and hats.

Teaching hints

Younger toddlers will prefer to explore the camera and its buttons at first. Toddlers more familiar with cameras and picture-taking will enjoy posing for each other.

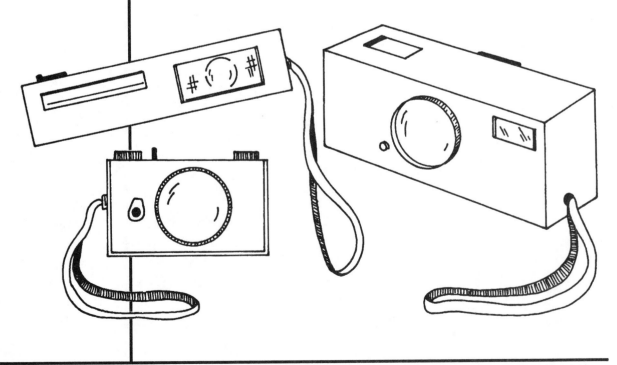

We're Not Babies!

All too soon for their parents, toddlers will proclaim emphatically that they are no longer babies and start to declare their independence. Yet, they are fascinated with babies. Taking care of baby dolls will bring out the most nurturing side in many toddlers.

To do

1. Look at pictures of babies. Have the parents bring in pictures of the children as babies to put up in the room. Emphasize with the toddlers that they used to be babies.

2. Provide baby dolls, small blankets and a doll bed.

3. Encourage the toddlers to pretend to hold and rock the babies to sleep. Sing simple lullabies to the dolls with the children.

4. Use the dolls to help the toddlers identify different parts of the body, such as eyes, mouth, arm, etc.

5. Provide additional props for older toddlers to pretend to take care of the dolls. Supply the "toddler nursery" with some of the following: bottles, a baby spoon, a wooden or plastic bowl, baby toys such as rattles, an empty wipes box, a few diapers (cut to dolly size if possible), an empty box of baby cereal, etc.

6. Encourage the toddlers to take care of the babies. Talk with the children about how to keep the babies happy and healthy.

To do again

Make a collage of pictures of babies from magazines.

Skills encouraged

social-emotional
imaginative play

Language to use with toddlers

baby doll
tiny
gentle
names of the parts of the
  body
feed
diaper
cry
sleep
rock

Materials

pictures or books about
  babies
dolls
small blankets
doll bed
bottles
baby spoon
bowl
diaper
baby toys

Bathing Beauties

Bathing babies relaxes toddlers just as if they were taking their nightly bath. It is also a perfect opportunity to talk about health care and identify parts of the body with the toddlers.

Skills encouraged

social-emotional
fine motor
sensory exploration

Language to use with toddlers

bath time
scrub
wash
washcloth
soap
hair
face
eyes
hands
dry
towel

Materials

baby bathtub or basin
mild soap
washcloths
small towels
washable dolls
shower curtain or old bath
  towel

To do

1. Fill the sensory table or baby bathtub with a small amount of soapy water. Place a shower curtain or old bath towel underneath to catch any spills.

2. Place dolls and washcloths in the tub.

3. Encourage the toddler to give the baby dolls a bath. Remind him to avoid getting any soap in the babies' eyes while washing their hair!

4. Talk with the toddler about the different parts of the baby's body. Encourage him to identify various parts, such as eyes, mouth, hands, etc. Emphasize the importance of taking a bath and washing hands as the toddler bathes the dolls.

5. Sing the following song to the tune of "Here We Go 'Round the Mulberry Bush" using the name of the child.

   This is the way Katie washes the baby, washes the baby, washes the baby,
   This is the way Katie washes the baby, to get her nice and clean.

6. Let the toddler dry the doll with a towel when the bath is finished. Sing the song again, changing the words to "drying the baby."

Fancy Necklaces

The process of stringing beads allows older toddlers to exercise their fine motor skills. The children also enjoy making necklaces for their teacher and friends to wear.

To do

1. Collect a variety of circular objects for stringing that pass the choke test, such as large macrame beads, spools, plastic rings or paper towel tubes cut into one inch rings.

2. Cut thick yarn, string or leather pieces into 15-20 inch lengths for stringing. Tape both ends to make a point to help with the threading. Long shoelaces can also be used.

3. Knot a large bead or object at the end of the string to be an anchor.

4. Show the toddlers how to thread the items on the string. Talk with them about the colors and types of objects.

5. Encourage the older toddlers to make fancy necklaces for each other.

To do again

Let toddlers who were successful and enjoyed stringing the large items try threading smaller objects with close supervision.

Teaching hints

Expect that some toddlers may get easily frustrated with the process of threading, while other toddlers enjoy this activity tremendously. At first, the toddlers may enjoy taking the off pieces more than threading them on, so give them already-strung necklaces to undo.

Skills encouraged

fine motor

Language to use with toddlers

string
bead
pull
end
inside
hole
another
necklace
wear
gorgeous
beautiful
names of colors
thread

Materials

large macrame beads
objects for stringing
shoelaces
thick yarn, string, leather
  pieces or shoelaces
macrame string

Blankety-Blank Fun!

Blankets can be used to explore a variety of textures, colors and sizes as well as promoting simple interaction among toddlers.

Skills encouraged

sensory exploration
imaginative play
social skills

Language to use with toddlers

blanket
quilt
warm
cover up
bed
special
small
large
colors
feel

Materials

variety of infant receiving
  blankets or baby quilts,
  other quilts, afghans and
  blankets
dolls
stuffed animals

To do

1. Show the toddlers different types of receiving blankets, quilts, afghans, large blankets, etc.

2. Talk to the children about the colors, designs, materials, uses, etc. of the blankets. Compare the large and small sizes of the regular and baby blankets.

3. Have the children lay down and cover them all together with a large blanket. Sing a lullaby with them.

4. With younger toddlers, play peek-a-boo games with the blankets.

5. Add a few receiving blankets or baby quilts to the home living area for the toddlers to use with the dolls and stuffed animals to help "keep them warm."

6. Encourage older toddlers to pretend to cover each other. Pretend to go to sleep. Sing lullabies with the children.

7. Use receiving blankets like scarves for dancing.

To do again

Have a picnic snack on a large blanket or quilt. If it is too cold to have a picnic outside, have the blanket picnic indoors!

Old Hat, New Hat

Toddlers love hats! Provide a wide variety for simple dress-up activities.

To do

1. Collect a variety of hats, such as baseball caps, cowboy hats, dressy hats, knit hats, hard hats just to name a few. Send a note home to parents to send in their old hats and caps. Washable hats and caps work best.

2. Encourage the toddlers to try on the different hats and look at themselves in the mirror.

3. Talk to the children about the color, fabric and type of hat they may be wearing.

4. Let the children use old cameras to pretend to take pictures of each other (see the "Say Cheese" page 30).

5. Have hats available for outdoor play as well.

6. Have a "Silly Hat Day" or a parade of hats.

To do again

Read *Old Hat, New Hat* by Jan and Stan Berenstain.

Teaching Hints

Try to use adjectives other than just "pretty" for the girls and "handsome" for the boys to avoid sexism when talking to the children. A boy who puts on a frilly pink hat can be "elegant" or "gorgeous" while a girl in a baseball cap can be "athletic" or "strong." Be creative with your descriptions.

Skills encouraged

imaginative play
sensory exploration

Language to use with toddlers

hat
color
design
fabric
head
on
off
handsome
beautiful
elegant
camera

Materials

variety of hats
mirror
old camera

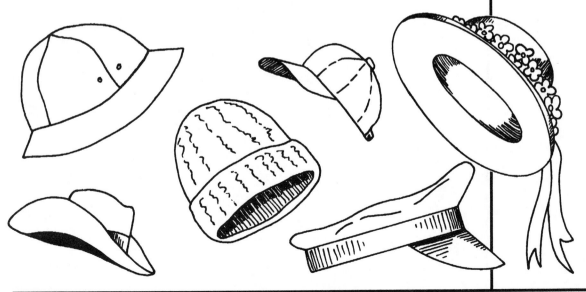

Toddler Accessories

Give new life to old accessories while providing materials for toddlers to explore and use for imaginative play. Purses and tote bags also offer the possibility of a dump-and-fill activity, which is always a toddler favorite.

Skills encouraged

imaginative play
fine motor

Language to use with the children

purse
backpack
tote bag
open
close
full
empty
wallet
billfold
picture
money
scarf
bandanna
necktie
handsome
lovely
athletic
strong

Materials

purses
billfolds
wallets
scarves
bandannas
tote bags
backpacks
neckties
mirror
old cameras

To do

1. Collect a variety of soft purses, tote bags, backpacks, wallets, billfolds, etc. for the toddlers to use. Send a note home to parents for donations to help enlarge your accessories collection.

2. Place the accessories out in the room and let the toddlers play on their own with the purses, wallets and bags. Older toddlers may pretend to go shopping, while younger toddlers will prefer to play at filling and emptying the purses or exploring the closures.

3. Provide rectangular pieces of green paper for money and pictures for the wallets if desired for the older toddlers.

4. Add other accessories, such as scarves, bandannas, neckties, etc. for older toddlers to complete their wardrobe.

5. Encourage the toddlers to look at themselves in a mirror. Talk to the toddlers about the items, their use, the colors and textures. Try to avoid sexist labels when describing how they look (see the teaching hints of Old Hat, New Hat, page 35).

6. Give them old cameras so they may pretend to take pictures of each other going to the "party," "work," "bank" or wherever the todlers decide!

Teaching hints

Look for missing toys and puzzle pieces in the purses. Toddlers have a tendency to fill their bags with small and unusual items.

Dress-Up Time

1½⁺

Hats and purses provide simple fashion for younger toddlers while older toddlers enjoy the challenge of more "grown-up" clothing for their imaginative play.

To do

1. Collect a variety of old clothing that is easy for toddlers to take on and off with little or no assistance. Button-up or sweater vests work well for toddlers. If shoes are included, use only flat shoes and slippers that toddlers can slip on over their own shoes. Send notes home to parents to help build up your collection of toddler dress-up clothing.

2. Simple dresses can be made from skirts with an elastic waist. Cut arm holes in the side of the skirt so that the waist then becomes the neckline. Shorten the length of the skirt if needed. Show the toddlers how to slip the dress on and off by themselves.

3. Provide a mirror for the toddlers to look at themselves. Encourage the toddlers to take pretend pictures with an old camera.

4. Add other accessories with the clothing, such as purses, wallets, tote bags and hats.

5. Provide proper storage for the clothing, such as a wall rack or large basket, so the toddlers may put their clothing away when they are finished.

6. Talk with the toddlers about what they are wearing and where they are pretending to go. Be creative with your ideas to help spur their imagination.

7. Change the dress-up clothing periodically, and keep it clean and in good repair.

Teaching hints

Use the dress-up clothing to promote a broader view of sex role identity early with the toddlers. Encourage the boys to dress up for a party or shopping and the girls to get ready for work or sport activities.

Skills encouraged

imaginative play
social skills
fine motor

Language to use with toddlers

vest
dress
hat
shoes
slippers
names of colors
fabric
handsome
beautiful

Materials

old button-up or sweater vests
old skirts with elastic waistbands
scissors
slippers
flat shoes
mirror
old cameras
purses, tote bags, hats

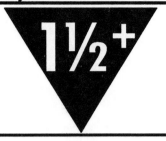

1½⁺

More Please!

Toddlers practice interacting with their peers as they pretend to make something to eat or drink for their friends. Teachers can model good manners, such as saying "please" and "thank you" while pretending to eat with the toddlers.

Skills encouraged

social interaction
imaginative play

Language to use with toddlers

juice
milk
cup
pour
drink
please
thank you
delicious

Materials

plastic cups
empty carton or can of
  juice
empty carton of milk
wooden or plastic dishes
plastic fruits or vegetables
empty food packages

To do

1. Put out plastic cups, empty containers of juice and empty cartons of milk with which the toddlers can pretend.

2. Encourage the toddlers to pour juice or milk into the cups to give to their friends and you.

3. Model the use of "thank you" when given the cup.

4. Pretend to taste the drink and then ask for more, emphasizing the "more, please."

5. Provide wooden or plastic dishes and plastic fruits and vegetables for older toddlers. Empty packages of food can also be used.

6. Encourage the toddlers to make meals for their friends.

7. Talk with the children about what they are making and/or eating. Remind them to say "please" and "thank you."

Teaching hints

The teacher will need to model the social interaction and language of the process with young toddlers in the early stages. Use the offering of pretend juice and food as a way to encourage toddlers to interact with each other, especially when there is a new child in the class.

For Toddlers Anytime:
Transitions, Routines and Playtime

Everyday activities to incorporate into the daily schedule, with any theme, promoting development in:
- ◆ *Social-emotional skills*
- ◆ *Language abilities*
- ◆ *Cognitive skills*
- ◆ *Fine motor skills*
- ◆ *Gross motor skills*

I Am Terrific

Singing about individual special qualities promotes each child's sense of self-worth.

Skills encouraged

social-emotional
language

Language to use with toddlers

terrific
names
special
growing
friend
song
listen
clap
rhythm

Materials

none needed

To do

1. Sing the following to the tune of "London Bridge."

    I am terrific, yes I am.
    Yes I am. Yes I am.
    I am terrific, yes I am.
    I am terrific. (point to self)

2. Use names of the children and their positive attributes. For example:

    Greg is growing, yes he is.
    Yes he is, yes he is.
    Greg is growing, yes he is.
    He is really growing.

3. Clap to the song or tap the rhythm on the individual child's leg.

4. Use other adjectives with the verse, such as "our friend," "extraordinary," "special," "turning two," etc.

5. Sing the verse to the children during their play and transitions. Toileting and diaper times offer wonderful opportunities to give a child individual attention.

To do again

Hold up a picture of the child while singing the verse. Have the toddlers tell you the name before beginning the verse.

Teaching hints

To help maintain a positive attitude with children displaying difficult behaviors or passing through a "stage," sing the song to them to remind yourself that the child is still worthwhile even though the behavior may bother you.

Personalizing Mary's Red Dress

The traditional song, "Mary Wore Her Red Dress," is a terrific, very adaptable song to use anytime during the day to boost awareness of individual identity.

To do

1. Sing "Mary Wore her Red Dress" to the tune of the traditional song. Use a sing-song or chanting rhythm if not familiar with the tune:

    Mary wore her red dress, red dress, red dress.
    Mary wore her red dress all day long.

2. Change the words of the song to identify what the children are wearing by the type, newness or color of the clothing:

    Kori wore her new overalls, new overalls, new overalls.
    Kori wore her new overalls all day long.

3. Let the individual children tell you what article of clothing they want you to sing about. Shoes are usually a popular item!

4. Sing the song with the toddlers as they are playing dress-up with hats, purses, etc.

5. Change the words to use the song during play activities, routines and transitions. Use the song to sing about a child's special qualities:

    Kym has blue eyes, blue eyes, blue eyes.
    Kym has blue eyes to make her special.

    Sing about the children's activities:

    Brenda likes to dance, to dance, to dance.
    Brenda likes to dance with the music.

    Sing about past, present or future events:

    We will go outside, outside, outside.
    We will go outside as soon as we finish snack.

To do again

Read a book version of the song to the children such as the one adapted and illustrated by Merle Peek.

Teaching hints

Adapt the song to use anytime during the toddlers' day. It is also a good song to sing with new children, as it helps everyone become familiar with each other's names.

Skills encouraged

language

Language to use with toddlers

song
names of the children
shirt
shoes
pants
dress
colors
wore
new

Materials

none needed

1+

Sharing Together

A song about sharing helps toddlers wait their turn when duplication of a popular item is not possible.

Skills encouraged

social interaction
language skills

Language to use with toddlers

toy
share
my turn
your turn
together
share
names of the children

Materials

none needed

To do

1. When two toddlers are arguing over the same toy, step in and explain to them that "it seems like you both want the rocking horse, but there is only one, so we will need to share." Help the toddlers take turns with the toy.

2. Chant the following verse to help emphasize the turn-taking process:

   I take my turn.
   You take your turn.
   Together we share,
   Share, share, share.

3. Repeat the verse as needed. Use individual names in the place of "I" and "you" in the chant.

Teaching hints

As much as possible, try to have two or more of the same or closely similar toys available for the toddlers, as sharing is difficult for this age group.

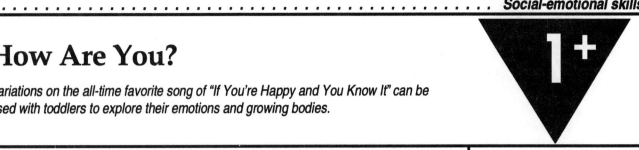

How Are You?

Variations on the all-time favorite song of "If You're Happy and You Know It" can be used with toddlers to explore their emotions and growing bodies.

To do

1. Sing "If You're Happy and You Know It" with the toddlers:

   > *If you're happy and you know it, clap your hands. (clap, clap)*
   > *If you're happy and you know it, clap your hands. (clap, clap)*
   > *If you're happy and you know then your face will surely show it. (point to face)*
   > *If you're happy and you know it, clap your hands. (clap, clap)*

2. Substitute the following emotions and related actions:

   > *silly—shake your head*
   > *angry—stamp your feet*
   > *sad—say boo hoo (rub eyes)*
   > *hungry—rub your tummy*
   > *sleepy—close your eyes*
   > *excited—yell hooray (raise arms overhead)*
   > *scared—hide your eyes*

3. Look at pictures of children displaying different emotions with older toddlers. Talk about what the child in the picture is feeling. Read *Quick as a Cricket* by Audrey Wood, which addresses teh many emotions of a toddler.

To do again

Use the song to identify parts of the body with the children. For example:

> *If you have a nose and you know it, touch it now. (touch nose)*
> *If you have a nose and you know it, touch it now. (touch nose)*
> *If you have a nose and you know it, then it should be on your face.*
> *If you have a nose and you know it, touch it now. (touch nose)*

Change the words to other parts of the body. For a final verse, sing:

> *If you're growing and you know it, stretch up high. (stretch arms up)*
> *If you're growing and you know it, stretch up high. (stretch arms up)*
> *If you're growing and you know it, then you're getting bigger all the time.*
> *If you're growing and you know it, stretch up high. (stretch arms up)*

Teaching hints

This song teaches toddlers to label emotions and to show their feelings.

Skills encouraged

language
fine motor
gross motor
social-emotional skills

Language to use with toddlers

happy
clap
silly
angry
sad
hungry
sleepy
excited
scared
animals
actions
names of parts of the body
growing
stretch
point
touch

Materials

pictures of children
  displaying emotions

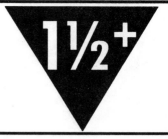

We All Help

Toddlers can help pick up their toys, and it is important to have their contributions be an expected part of the routine. Singing songs about cleaning up encourages toddlers to participate in picking up the toys.

Skills encouraged

social
language

Language to use with toddlers

clean up
help
toys
thank you
helper
on the shelf
there

Materials

none needed

To do

1. Sing the following song with the children at clean-up time.

To the tune of "Mary Had a Little Lamb":

> *We all help clean up the toys, clean up the toys, clean up the toys.*
> *We all help clean up the toys,*
> *We all help today.*

2. Change the words of the chant to refer to specific children and/or toys.

> *RosieAnn picks up the crayons, up the crayons, up the crayons.*
> *RosieAnn picks up the crayons,*
> *She knows how to help.*

3. Repeat the verse throughout the cleaning-up process to provide continuous direction and encouragement.

To do again

Chant another simple verse for variety over the year, such as:

> *Clean up, clean up, pick up the toys and clean up.*
> *Thank you, thank you, thank you for helping today.*

Or, use the children's names:

> *Shelly and Monica pick up your blocks and put them away*
> *Thank you, thank you, thank you for helping today.*

Teaching hints

Using the children's own names and mentioning specific toys can encourage those who are not helping to do so. It also provides recognition to those who are helping.

Lots of Chanting

For any classroom of toddlers, chants are a must to promote language development. They are easy to make up, can be said anytime and tailored to each situation with just a little bit of imagination.

To do

1. Chant throughout the day as the toddlers play and during transitions to focus the children's attention.

2. Make up verses about what a child may be playing with, what you may be doing, or just about anything at the time. For example, when preparing for snack:

   > *Stirring, stirring,*
   > *I am stirring the apple juice.*
   > *'Round and around, 'round and around,*
   > *That is how I stir it.*

   When playing with puzzles:

   > *Puzzles, puzzles,*
   > *We can do the puzzles.*
   > *One piece here and one piece there.*
   > *That's how I put them back together.*

   When drawing:

   > *Up and down,*
   > *And all around.*
   > *That's how (Ricky)*
   > *Draws on the paper.*

3. Use chants to give reminders and guide behavior in positive ways. The verse can be used generally with "Let's"/"We" or individually with specific children's names. Rather than constantly telling a child to sit in their chair at mealtimes or to walk, say the following to encourage sitting:

   > *Sit down and take a seat,*
   > *Sit down so you don't fall.*
   > *Sit down, sit down.*

   To remind children about walking:

   > *Walking, walking,*
   > *Let's walk to the playground.*
   > *Thank you, thank you,*
   > *For remembering to walk.*

4. Use your imagination and use chants throughout the day!

Teaching hints

Toddlers respond with interest to chants. They also help teachers stay calm.

Skills encouraged

language

Language to use with toddlers

chant
words
say with me
beat
clap
let's
listen

Materials

none needed

Lunch Time, Munch Time

Transitions to mealtimes can be the most difficult transitions for toddlers. The following chant provides an easy way to divert their attention away from their hunger pains.

Skills encouraged

language

Language to use with toddlers

lunch time
best
daytime
hungry
eat
names of different foods
like
snack time

Materials

none needed

To do

1. Chant the following with the toddlers:

   Lunch time, munch time,
   Best time of the daytime.

2. Have the toddlers clap or pat their stomachs to the beat of the chant.

3. Add more verses in relation to what the children will be eating for lunch:

   Lunch time, munch time,
   Best time of the daytime.
   Green beans, green beans,
   We'll be having green beans.
   Applesauce, applesauce,
   We like our applesauce.

4. If the children bring their own lunches, then chant about what each child has and use the child's name in the chant:

   Strawberries, strawberries,
   Armandito loves his strawberries.

5. Use the chant at snack time too with just a few changes:

   Snack time, snack time,
   Best time of the daytime.

Teaching hints

Send the words home to the parents for them to use at dinner time.
For example:

   Dinner, dinner
   What a winner
   Catfish, Catfish
   That's what is for dinner.

Toddler Story Time

Reading simple stories to toddlers and having books available for them to look through on their own is the first step in introducing young children to the world of books and the best preparation for later reading.

To do

1. Set aside a quiet, snuggly area in the room for books. Put down a small rug or bath mat with pillows to help make the area comfortable.

2. Add durable books and magazines to the area for the children to look at on their own. Sturdy cardboard books are the best for younger toddlers. More expensive books that might tear should be kept for the teacher to read to the children.

3. Change the books periodically to maintain interest. Use the local library as a resource. The best books for toddlers have bold illustrations and short text. Toddlers especially enjoy books with real pictures of children and animals. See the appendix for a list of books enjoyed by toddlers.

4. Let the children go to the book area as one of their choices of activities at any time during the day.

5. Encourage the toddlers to look at books during transitions, such as before and after nap.

6. Read books to the toddlers in small groups. Start reading a book to a few toddlers and often more children will come over to hear the story.

7. Take books outside to read and look at on a blanket in a shady area.

Teaching hints

It is best to read books to toddlers in small groups rather than the entire group. Let the toddlers also have the choice of joining in or not. Some may prefer to listen to the book from a distance as they play.

Skills encouraged

language
pre-reading/emergent
  literacy

Language to use with toddlers

book
special friend
take care
pages
cover
story
pictures
read
look at
lap
enjoy

Materials

books
pillows
rug or bath mat
magazines

Toddler Books

Making books for toddlers enables the teacher to tailor them to a specific theme or child's need. Teacher-made books are less expensive and quite durable.

Skills encouraged

language
pre-reading/emergent
  literacy

Language to use with toddlers

book
pictures
look at
read
open
close
see
colors

Materials

magazines
stickers
posterboard
glue
scissors
hole punch
yarn
book rings
clear contact paper

To do

1. Collect pictures from magazines, catalogues and stickers of a variety of objects related to a theme. Books can be made throughout the year to use with any topic, such as families, children, babies, toys, foods, fruits, cars and trucks, pets, wild animals, colors, shapes, etc. There is no limit to the possibilities.

2. Cut posterboard into squares of at least six inches by six inches.

3. Glue pictures on both sides of the squares. Leave one side of two squares blank to serve as a front and back cover.

4. Write the name or a simple sentence about each item underneath the picture. Write a title on the front cover.

5. Laminate or cover with clear contact paper each posterboard square with pictures.

6. Assemble the pictures sequentially into a book.

7. Punch holes on the left margin. Thread yarn through the holes or use book rings. Put the book out in the snuggly area for the toddlers to look through and enjoy. Read the book with the children by having them identify some of the pictures.

To do again

Make a "People Book" of pictures of adults and children from different cultures involved in everyday activities. Include pictures of differently-abled children, senior citizens, men in caregiving roles, women in non-traditional roles, etc.

Teaching hints

Try to make a book each month related to one of the themes. This will build up your supply of books. You could work on the books during playtime and allow the children to help when possible. Also, save any potentially useful pictures. This helps when making a specific book, rather than having to search for all the pictures at once.

Magazine Collages

1½⁺

Looking at pictures of real objects fascinates toddlers. While using pictures from magazines does not constitute a true creative art experience, the opportunity for language interactions as the toddlers glue pictures related to a theme is immense.

To do

1. Collect simple pictures related to a specific theme from magazines.

2. Place the pictures in a small basket for the toddlers to look through. Talk with the toddlers about the items, encouraging older toddlers to identify the object by name or use.

3. Let a toddler pick out some of her favorite pictures to make a collage on a piece of paper.

4. Have the child choose her background paper. Show the child how to spread glue thinned with water over the paper using a sponge or wide paintbrush. Or use the sticky side of contact paper as the adhesive (see Sticky Side Up, page 61, in this chapter).

To do again

Have a group of toddlers glue pictures on a large sheet of paper for a class mural. Display the mural in the room.

Skills encouraged

fine motor
language

Language to use with toddlers

picture
color
names of the pictured
   objects
glue
What is this?

Materials

magazine pictures
basket
construction paper
glue
sponge or wide paintbrush
contact paper

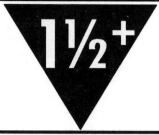

Language Play

Playing with language by saying the "wrong" word, the opposite word or a rhyming word encourages toddlers to produce language on their own without questioning or asking them to "perform."

Skills encouraged

language

Language to use with toddlers

opposite
Oops!
You're so right!
humor
funny
rhyme
same sounds

Materials

none needed

To do

1. While playing with toddlers or during transitions, say the opposite or incorrect item in a playful way in order to encourage the child to say the word. For example, when handing the child a banana, say "Here is your apple."

2. Wait for the child's response. Most often, toddlers will proudly correct you.

3. Tell the child, "You are so right, it is an apple!"

To do again

Play rhyming games with language, such as "oodles of noodles," "very berry strawberry," "boo hoo shoe," etc. Also make rhymes with the children's names.

Teaching hints

Incorporate incorrect words or actions in a humorous way to get beyond the "battles over independence" with toddlers. For example, when a child refuses to put on her shoes, pretend to put them on your feet or her ear. Usually she will show you exactly where her shoes should be!

Loud and Soft

Toddlers become aware of differences in loud and soft when they experiment with singing songs at different volumes.

To do

1. Sing or chant a familiar song or nursery rhyme with the toddlers in a whisper-type voice. Talk to the children about how you are singing softly.

2. Repeat the song or rhyme, each time singing or saying it in a little louder verse. Tell the children you are singing loudly at the end.

Teaching hints

Soft voices grab toddlers' attention. During a chaotic transition, start singing a chant or song in a quiet voice to redirect the toddlers' random behavior. Try talking to a crying or frustrated toddler in a whisper. Sometimes this will divert their attention and change the mood.

Skills encouraged

language

Language to use with toddlers

song
sing
loudly
whisper
yell
listen
hear

Materials

none needed

Slowly and Quickly

Singing familiar songs and doing actions slowly and quickly helps toddlers gain an understanding of tempo in music.

Skills encouraged

language
gross motor

Language to use with toddlers

slowly
fast
quickly
song
actions
clap
roll
rub
pound

Materials

none needed

To do

1. Sing familiar songs or nursery rhymes at a very slow tempo. Sing at a normal speed and then a fast tempo.

2. Say the following movement chant and do the actions as the words indicate. Emphasize the words slowly and quickly in the verse.

   Clap, clap, clap your hands, slooooo-wly just like this.
   Clap, clap, clap your hands, quick, quick, quickly just like this.
   Roll, roll, roll your hands, slooooo-wly just like this.
   Roll, roll, roll your hands, quick, quick, quickly just like this.
   Stamp, stamp, stamp your feet, slooo-wly just like this.
   Stamp, stamp, stamp your feet, quick, quick, quickly just like this.

3. Add other actions, such as "rub your hands," "pound your hands," "nod your head," "blink your eyes," "shake your hands," "wiggle your hands" or "shrug your shoulders."

Teaching hints

Toddlers enjoy the "fast" actions, especially after the anticipation built up by the slow section. This activity works well during unexpected "waiting" times.

Where Oh Where?

Looking for hidden toys and objects can, with little preparation, be turned into a game for toddlers.

To do

1. Encourage the children to look for certain toys, stuffed animals or other items by singing a variation of the "Where Is Thumbkin?" song. With younger toddlers, make sure the items are clearly visible.

    > *Where is the bear puppet? Where is the bear puppet?*
    > *Can you find it? Can you find it?*
    > *Over by the books, on the floor.*
    > *Pick it up. Thank you very much.*

2. Ask older toddlers to look for objects or pictures related to a specific color or themes. Place the items around the room before the children arrive. Sing the verse, asking them to hunt for the item(s).

3. Use the verse to encourage children to put away certain items, especially their personal items in their bag or cubby area.

4. Use the song for learning each others' names:

    > *Where is Ray Alan? Where is Ray Alan?*
    > *There he is, right over there. (touch child on the shoe or shoulder)*
    > *How are you today Ray, very well we hope so.*
    > *Let's say hi, he is our friend.*

5. Use this hunting song when something is "lost" in the room. Toddlers will often find that missing shoe or piece to the puzzle much sooner than the teacher!

Teaching hints

Toddlers' comprehension of language precedes their production in that they will be able to point to the object requested before saying the name of the item. Use the "where is" technique with less verbal children to allow them to demonstrate what they know without language interfering.

Skills encouraged

language
object permanence

Language to use with toddlers

where
lost
Can you find...?
see
bring
over there

Materials

toys
stuffed animals

Shh or Not!

Toddlers experiment with the presence and absence of sound when they explore empty and filled shakers.

Skills encouraged

auditory discrimination
sorting

Language to use with toddlers

shaker
filled
noise
hear
listen
ear
music
empty
silent
Shh!
loud
sort
box
sound

Materials

four to six shakers
two baskets or boxes

To do

1. Choose two or three shakers that are filled with beans or seeds and the same number of empty shakers (see Shaker Maker, page 55).

2. Cover the shakers with contact paper so the toddlers cannot see inside.

3. Let the toddler explore the shakers. Emphasize the words of "shh!" or "silent" with the empty shakers and "music" or "sound" with the filled shakers.

4. Encourage the older toddlers to sort the "shh/silent" shakers into one box and the musical shakers in another box.

To do again

Experiment with "loud" shakers filled with heavier items such as rocks or nuts and "soft" shakers filled with lighter materials such as flour or salt. Sing a song loudly with the loud shakers and a quiet song with the soft shakers. Sort the two types of shakers into separate boxes.

Teaching hints

When reminding toddlers to use an "inside" or quieter voice, use the loud and soft shakers to illustrate the noise levels.

Shaker Maker

Toddlers have an intense desire to make noise and enjoy exploring objects that make a sound. Homemade shakers are an inexpensive, easily-made action-reaction toy that the toddlers will use again and again.

To do

1. Collect an assortment of four to six non-breakable containers, such as plastic spice jars, small plastic peanut butter jars, 16-ounce soda or beverage bottles or even small nut or coffee containers with a lid.

2. Fill each container with a different dry material.

3. Secure the lids with super glue or a hot glue gun.

4. Leave one container empty for the concept of "silence" or "quiet" and to add an element of comparison.

5. Cover with contact paper if desired. If the container is clear, consider leaving it uncovered so the toddlers can see what is making the sounds.

6. Place the shakers in a basket or shoe box on a low shelf. If small plastic soda bottles are used, cover a cardboard six-pack holder with contact paper to make a carrier for the shakers.

7. Let the toddlers explore the shakers on their own. Some children will use the shakers as musical instruments while others may use them for pretend in their play as a "baby bottle" or for cooking. The toddlers will certainly come up with their own unique ideas.

To do again

Let older toddlers make their own shakers. Have a plastic container for each child and two to three fillings for each child to choose from to fill his shaker. Have him use a spoon or his fingers to fill the container. Keep in mind that even a small amount will make a noise. The teacher will have to secure the lid with permanent glue. The toddlers can decorate the outside of the shaker with markers and stickers if desired.

Skills encouraged

fine motor
sensory exploration

Language to use with toddlers

shaker
inside
shake
noise
music
rice
beans
flour
rocks
loud
soft
silence
empty

Materials

plastic containers with lids
dry material, for example,
  beans, rice, flour, rocks,
  nuts, bolts, spools, etc.
super glue or hot glue gun
contact paper
basket or shoe box

Shake Shake Shake

Using shakers with chants and musical activities helps toddlers feel a rhythm.

Skills encouraged

creative expression
fine motor

Language to use with toddlers

shake
shakers
song
chant
rhythm
percussion instruments
tambourine
bells
maracas

Materials

shakers
recorded music
percussion instruments

To do

1. Use the shakers with the following chant, emphasizing the beat:

   Shake, shake, shake the shaker.
   Shake it high and shake it low.
   Shake it where you want it to go.
   Shake, shake, shake the shaker.
   Shake it fast and shake it slow.
   Shake it just how you like it to go.

2. Play music with a definite rhythm to use with the shakers.

3. Show the older toddlers different types of percussion instruments that are played by shaking, such as bells, tambourines, maracas. Let them explore the "shaking" percussion instruments (see Ring the Bells, page 289 and Easy Tambourines, page 291).

To do again

Use the shakers in a parade with marching music (see Let's Have a Parade, page 292).

Teaching hints

Toddlers have their own tempo, so do not expect them to follow the rhythm exactly. However, some children will be surprisingly close to the rhythm of the music.

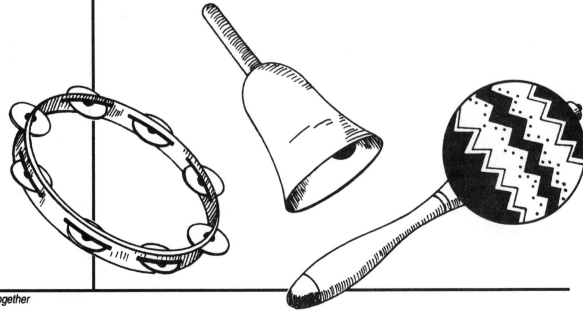

M.I.M.s (Most Important Marks)

*Scribbling is the precursor to writing, just as babbling is to talking. A better term for scribbling would be M.I.M.s, for these are the **Most Important Marks** a toddler can make.*

To do

1. Provide blank sheets of paper and crayons or non-permanent markers for the toddlers to use on a regular basis. Try to offer drawing as a choice at least a few times a week, if not daily.

2. Talk to the toddler about the colors and types of strokes ("up and down," "around and around") she is using as she draws.

3. Remind the toddler to use one marker at a time and to put the cap back on after she finishes. Taking off and putting on the top of the marker is a motor skill in itself and may interest some toddlers more than coloring.

To do again

Encourage older toddlers to write "notes" to their parents or friends. Fold paper in half for the child to make a card (see Occasional Greetings, page 276).

Teaching hints

Plain paper is best. Coloring book pages and ditto sheets are not appropriate, as the picture on the paper has no meaning for the toddlers' drawing. The thick, washable markers work more easily for toddlers than crayons since the markers require less pressure to leave a mark on the paper. Additionally, markers seem to be more "treasured" as many parents tend to let children use crayons rather than markers at home. However, crayons allow the child to make light or dark lines by varying the pressure, while markers give a uniform mark.

Skills encouraged

fine motor
pre-writing/emergent
 literacy
creative expression

Language to use with toddlers

most important marks
write
draw
circles
lines
up and down
round and round
paper
markers
cap
pen
pencil

Materials

paper
crayons
markers

M.I.M. Variations

M.I.M.s (Most Important Marks) are the most important art activities to provide for toddlers. A wide variety of scribbling activities can be developed with different papers and media.

Skills encouraged

fine motor
creative expression
pre-writing/emergent
  literacy

Language to use with toddlers

write
draw
paper
large
small
envelopes
shapes
pens
pencils
markers
chalk
crayons
names of colors

Materials

different items to draw on
different writing media

To do

1. Use a variety of paper and objects for the toddlers' most important marks. The following are a few suggestions: large sheets of paper at an easel, small sheets of paper, paper cut into shapes, discarded computer paper, wallpaper samples, note pads, pieces of cardboard, boxes or sandpaper.

2. Vary the drawing media as well, such as pens, pencils, colored pencils, chalk, markers or crayons.

To do again

Draw with all the different media in the same color to see the differing shades made by each.

Teaching hints

Different sizes of paper encourage different motor skills. The smaller pieces of paper promote finer movements of the hand and wrist while large pieces of paper encourage whole arm action from the shoulder.

Toddler Graffiti

Large sheets of paper on the wall or floor for a mural promote whole arm movements and encourage toddlers to work together.

To do

1. Tape a large sheet of paper to the floor or wall with wide masking tape to provide a visual border. Colored masking tape works best.

2. Provide crayons and/or markers and allow the children to draw together on the large paper.

3. Remind the toddlers to draw only on the paper and not outside the borders, but be prepared for their marks to wander. (Use crayons or markers that will wash off.)

To do again

Place the paper outdoors on the sidewalk or on the side of the building for drawing a mural during outside time. The texture of the concrete will have an interesting effect. Or use sidewalk chalk with older toddlers.

Skills encouraged

fine motor
social interaction
pre-writing/emergent
  literacy

Language to use with toddlers

mural
draw
markers
crayons
everybody
draw together
on the paper
border

Materials

large sheets of paper
masking tape
markers
crayons

Watch Me Grow!

*Many parents do not recognize the importance of scribbling for later writing efforts. Teachers can help parents appreciate the value of M.I.M.s by prominently displaying each toddler's **M**ost **I**mportant **M**arks and collecting samples over the year.*

Skills encouraged

fine motor
creative expression
pre-writing/emergent
literacy

Language to use with toddlers

grown
changes
smaller
bigger
marks
lines
circles
save
special

Materials

paper
crayons
markers
construction paper
tape or stapler
posterboard
folder
yarn or book rings

To do

1. Let the toddlers draw regularly with markers and/or crayons throughout the year.

2. Display the drawings in the room and talk with parents about the importance of scribbling for toddlers.

3. Every month, save a sample of each child's M.I.M.s. Make a folder for each child from construction paper or posterboard folded in half. Seal the two sides with thick tape or staples, leaving the top edge open. Mount the drawings on construction paper if desired. Put the samples together in the folder. Or fasten the papers together like a book, in a chronological sequence, with yarn or book rings.

4. Show the M.I.M. collection to each toddler and his parents. Emphasize the changes in his marks and his use of space that have occurred over the months. Send the collection home.

To do again

Save other samples of the toddlers' growth, such as photos, hand tracings or prints, weight and height, paintings, experiences, sayings, etc. to add to the folder.

Sticky Side Up

Gluing is sometimes difficult for younger toddlers as it requires a sequence of steps. The sticky side of contact paper can be used instead of glue to make collages with the youngest toddlers.

To do

1. Cut a piece of contact paper approximately the same size as a piece of construction paper or cardboard. The contact paper can be patterned or clear.

2. Staple the contact paper to the construction paper or cardboard so that the sticky side is up when the backing is peeled off.

3. Collect items that pass the choke test to use for the collage, such as scraps of construction paper, shapes cut out of gift wrap or construction paper, ribbon, yarn, fabric scraps, cotton balls, jar tops, etc.

4. Let the toddler choose what items he would like to use for his collage.

5. Peel off the back of the contact paper. Show the toddler how the collage materials will stay on the sticky side of the paper. Encourage the toddler to place the collage materials he has chosen on the sticky side of the paper.

Teaching hints

Consider using the contact paper "sticky side up" idea in place of gluing with other collage activities to enable the toddlers to work more independently.

Skills encouraged

fine motor
creative expression

Language to use with toddlers

contact paper
sticky side
stick
leave
collage
design
paper
pieces

Materials

contact paper
construction paper or
  cardboard
stapler
collage items

Wet and Wonderful

Toddlers love water. Adding simple objects to even the smallest amount of water will interest children.

Skills encouraged

sensory exploration
fine motor

Language to use with toddlers

water
scent
smell
color
pour
full
empty
cups
scoops

Materials

sensory or water table
dish tub or baby bathtub
plastic measuring cups
  and spoons
small plastic containers
water
smocks
newspaper or tablecloth

To do

1. Add water to a water play table or sensory table. A dish tub or baby bathtub also works well. Place it on the floor on top of newspaper or a tablecloth to catch any spills.

2. Add plastic containers, plastic measuring cups, spoons, and other plastic toys to the water.

3. Put on smocks and let small groups of toddlers enjoy the wet and wonderful nature of water. Talk with the children about the feel of the water, pouring and other actions with the water, etc..

To do again

Provide frequent opportunities for water play on the playground. As there is less concern with spills, the toddlers have more freedom in exploring the water.

Teaching hints

Remind toddlers "to keep the water in the tub" and that it is "for playing with, not drinking." Large amounts of water are not needed. Add only as much water as you are willing to mop up!

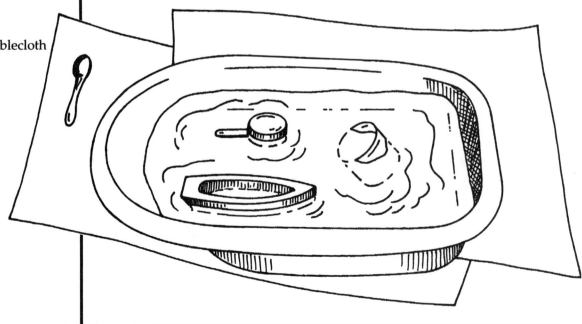

Pinch, Poke, Pull and Press

1½⁺

Toddlers strengthen their fine motor skills as they pinch, poke, pull and press playdough. Homemade playdough can be made inexpensively with a few simple ingredients.

To do

1. Make fresh playdough from the following recipe. A small group of older toddlers can help make the dough if desired, especially with the kneading step.

   Homemade playdough recipe:

   > *1 cup flour*
   > *1 tablespoon oil*
   > *1 cup of water*
   > *1/2 cup salt*
   > *2 teaspoons cream of tartar*
   > *food coloring*

   Combine all ingredients in a saucepan or electric skillet. Cook over medium heat. Stir continually. Mixture will form a ball. Put oil on hands and knead the dough until smooth. Store in a closed container.

2. Provide playdough as a frequent choice for toddlers. Remind the toddlers that the playdough is not for eating.

3. Encourage them to pinch, poke, pull apart and press down the dough. Chant about what they are doing with the dough. For example:

   > *Press, press, press the playdough,*
   > *Press the playdough flat.*

4. Provide plastic knives, cookie cutters, hammers, etc. to use with the playdough. Older toddlers can also use blunt scissors with the dough to practice cutting.

5. Talk with the toddlers about the designs and "pretend objects" (i.e., tacos, cookies, etc.) made with the playdough, the colors and textures of the playdough, what they are doing with their hands, etc.

6. Use the playdough to help toddlers calm down and relax. It is also a peaceful activity for teachers!

Teaching hints

Toddlers who tend to pinch other children or tear books can be redirected to use playdough as a way to practice their fine motor skills in a more appropriate way. Tell them that they can pinch or tear the playdough all they want but not their friends/books.

Skills encouraged

fine motor
sensory exploration
pre-cutting

Language to use with toddlers

playdough
feel
squeeze
pinch
poke
fingers
pull apart
press down
smash
cut
cookie cutter
shapes
soft
warm

Materials

salt
flour
oil
cream of tartar
food coloring
electric skillet
pan
covered container
plastic knives
cookie cutters
small hammers

One Last Time

As playdough dries out, it can be used in new ways one last time before throwing it away.

Skills encouraged

fine motor
sensory exploration

Language to use with toddlers

playdough
feel
textures
bumpy
sand
rice
eggshells
birdseed
outside
too old

Materials

old playdough
dry sensory materials,
  such as birdseed, sand
plastic knives
cookie cutters
hammers
dish tub or sensory table

To do

1. Put playdough that has started to dry out in a dish tub or sensory table with any of the dry sensory materials.

2. Talk with the toddlers about how the dry material sticks to the playdough and makes it feel bumpy.

3. Encourage the toddlers to pinch and tear the playdough into tiny pieces.

4. Use plastic knives, cookie cutters, hammers, etc. with the newly textured dough.

5. Throw away the old dough when finished.

To do again

Add the dough to a small dish tub with about one inch of water. Talk with the toddlers about the changes that occur in the texture of the dough with the liquid. You could also take the playdough outside on the playground to use "one last time" at a small table. Throw the dough away when finished.

Hand Prints

Toddlers enjoy fingerpainting and making hand prints once they get acquainted with the new feeling of the fingerpaint.

To do

1. Put a spoonful or two of fingerpaint on fingerpaint paper.

2. Encourage the toddler to smear the fingerpaint "around and around" and "up and down" with his hands.

3. Talk with the child about the smoothness and color of the fingerpaint.

4. Encourage him to make hand prints and/or fingerprints with the fingerpaint. After a few practice tries, ask him to make hand prints or fingerprints on an extra sheet of construction paper to display in the room.

5. Let older toddlers paint with two different colors of fingerpaint. Talk about the new shades or colors that are created.

To do again

Chill or slightly warm the fingerpaint for variety. For older toddlers, add sand, crushed egg shells, etc. to the fingerpaint for different textures.

Teaching hints

Join in fingerpainting with your own hands to help any toddler hesitant about putting his hands in the paint. Hold his hands in your hands if he will let you. Show excitement over the smooth texture to encourage the child to feel the paint. If a child refuses to fingerpaint, be patient, it may turn out to be one of his favorite activities in time.

Skills encouraged

sensory exploration
fine motor

Language to use with toddlers

fingerpaint
smooth
feel
smear
round and around
up and down
hand prints
color

Materials

fingerpaint
fingerpaint paper
construction paper

Magic Prints

Making prints on paper after toddlers have fingerpainted on a tray makes for easier clean up and uses less paint than painting on individual pieces of paper.

Skills encouraged

sensory exploration
fine motor

Language to use with toddlers

fingerpaint
magic print
surprise
see
tray
around and around
up and down

Materials

fingerpaint
flat tray
construction paper

To do

1. Place one or two spoonfuls of fingerpaint on a flat tray. Older toddlers can use two different colors for mixing new shades.

2. Let the toddler fingerpaint on the flat tray. Talk with her about the movements she is making and the feeling of the paint.

3. When she is finished, place a piece of construction paper over the paint and rub on top of the paper to make a print.

4. Lift the paper to see the "magic print" created. Show surprise as the child helps you lift the paper.

5. The next child can fingerpaint on the same tray. Add more paint as needed.

To do again

Make magic prints on paper cut into large shapes, such as circles or hearts.

Tearing Challenge

Tearing paper presents a fine motor challenge for toddlers. The ability to tear paper is also a pre-cutting skill.

To do

1. Provide scrap pieces of paper, thick gift wrap, wallpaper samples, newspaper, etc. for the toddlers to practice tearing.

2. Show the toddlers how to tear the paper by holding the edge with their fingers and pulling in different directions. Encourage them to tear rather than crumple the paper.

3. Talk with the toddlers about the process, that it is difficult to do and that only scrap paper should be torn.

4. As the toddlers become more skillful with the tearing process, encourage them to tear smaller and smaller pieces of paper.

5. Let the toddlers also practice tearing dry leaves that they find while on the playground.

To do again

Save the pieces of torn paper for the toddlers to glue on a collage another day.

Teaching hints

If toddlers tear pages in a book tell them, "Books are for reading, not tearing. Here is some scrap paper that you can tear if you want." Have them help you repair the book.

Skills encouraged

fine motor
pre-cutting

Language to use with toddlers

tear
paper
pieces
pull apart
fingers
difficult
practice
crumple
leaves

Materials

scrap pieces of paper
dry leaves
glue

Crawling Craze

Even after toddlers start to walk, crawling is still important for their continued development. Crawling can be introduced in a multitude of fun ways.

Skills encouraged

gross motor
creative movement

Language to use with toddlers

crawling
hands and knees
on all fours
on the floor
follow
sideways
backwards
fast
slow

Materials

recorded music

To do

1. Get on your hands and knees and crawl with the toddlers in the following ways:

   crawl like you did when you were a baby
   crawl slowly
   crawl quickly
   crawl under a table
   crawl sideways
   crawl backwards
   spin in a circle on your hands and knees
   crawl with legs straight

2. Put on music and dance by crawling!

3. Crawl quickly or slowly like different animals. Chant the following while crawling:

   Crawl like a turtle, crawl like a turtle,
   Crawl as slowly as you can.
   Crawl like a mouse, crawl like a mouse,
   Crawl as quickly as you can.

To do again

Do the above activities, except walk on your knees instead of crawling.

Teaching hints

If toddlers continually run in the classroom, make sure the room arrangement is not too open as wide spaces invite running. Toddlers who tend to run a lot inside can be encouraged to redirect their desire to move fast into crawling as quickly as they can or "running" only on their knees. Most toddlers will not be able to go very fast, but they will put a lot of energy into crawling as quickly as they can!

Dance the Day Away

Toddlers love to move. Dancing provides an outlet to express this need in a creative and purposeful way.

To do

1. Play a variety of instrumental music that has a definite dancing rhythm such as a waltz, polka samba or other music.

2. Follow the toddlers' lead as you notice individual children moving to the music. Dance with the toddlers and more children will join in the fun.

3. While they will typically follow your lead, encourage the children to dance in their own way. Copy some of their actions.

4. Dance with scarves. Move them side to side, up high, down low, throw them up in the air and watch them float to the ground.

5. Tie a variety of ribbons to a canning ring or embroidery hoop to use like scarves while dancing.

To do again

Have toddlers hold hands and dance with a partner. Try to match less active toddlers with more physical children to provide a balance.

Teaching hints

When doing circle type dances with older toddlers, such as "Ring Around the Rosie" have the children dance together in pairs or threesomes rather than trying to make a large circle of toddlers that inevitably moves like an amoeba!

Skills encouraged

gross motor
creative movement
social interaction

Language to use with toddlers

dance
move
music
rhythm
sway
side to side
twist
bend

Materials

recorded music
scarves
ribbons
canning ring
embroidery hoop

Come On Everybody

A simple chant encourages toddlers to expend their high levels of energy in appropriate ways. Like other chants, it can easily be tailored to the needs of a specific situation.

Skills encouraged

gross motor
fine motor
language

Language to use with toddlers

everybody
do this
like me
follow
copy
actions
clap
stamp
march
jump
names of parts of the body

To do

1. Have the toddlers copy you as you chant the following:

   Come on everybody,
   Do this, do this, do this.
   Come on everybody,
   Do this just like me! (clap hands)

2. Repeat with any of the following possibilities. While sitting, these include, "pound the floor," "move your arms up and down," "move your head from side to side," "move your head up and down," "hug your body," "roll your hands," "rub your hands," "shrug your shoulders," "wiggle your fingers" and "rock from side to side."

3. While standing these include "sway from side to side," "bend up and down at knees," "move up and down on your tiptoes," "twist at your waist," "bend at your waist," "touch your toes" and "wiggle your body."

4. For overall motion, try jumping, crawling, walking on knees, spinning, marching, walking on tiptoes and dancing. Think of new ways to move around the room.

5. For older toddlers, let them suggest ways to move with the chant. Use the child's name in place of "me" in the verse.

6. End with a quiet activity, such as pretending to "sleep" or "rest" to bring down the children's energy level and refocus the group.

Teaching hints

Use this chant when toddlers start to display random, silly behavior as they are showing a need to release their built-up energy. The chant is also a great motor skills activity for a rainy day.

Oh Do, Oh Do

A simple chant with endless possibilities for actions works wonders during transitions, for release of built-up physical energy or anytime of the day.

To do

1. Sing the following chant in a sing-song fashion:

   Sing with me, oh do oh do oh.
   Sing with me, oh do oh do oh.
   Sing with me, oh do oh do oh.
   Oh do, oh do, oh do, Oh!

2. Change the "sing" in the verse to other hand and head movements such as:

   Clap with me...
   Sway with me...
   Nod with me...
   Blink with me...
   Wiggle with me...
   Rub with me...
   Pound with me...
   Wave with me...

3. For more gross motor activity, substitute actions involving the whole body, such as:

   Dance with me...
   Jump with me...
   Spin with me...
   Crawl with me...
   Stamp with me...
   March with me...
   Stretch with me...
   Walk on your tiptoes with me...

4. Have older toddlers tell or show you the actions they want to do. Change the "me" in the chant to the child's name.

5. End the movement activity with the following to refocus the toddlers' energy:

   Hug with me, oh do oh do oh. (hug own body)
   Hug with me, oh do oh do oh.
   Hug with me, oh do oh do oh.
   Oh do oh do oh.

Teaching hints

When asking a toddler to suggest activities, let him show you what he wants to do if he does not seem to have the language ability to express the action. If the child seems hesitant to come up with an idea, watch his body language and pick up on the subtle movements he does (i.e., shrugging shoulders, shaking a foot, smiling, etc.). Provide a word for the action and use it in the chant rather than leaving the toddlers on the spot to produce an idea in words.

Skills encouraged

gross motor
fine motor
language

Language to use with toddlers

copy
actions
with me
do
follow
move
sing
clap
jump
stretch
crawl

Materials

none needed

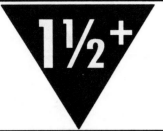

Animal Antics

Toddlers practice a wide variety of whole body movements as they move like different animals.

Skills encouraged

gross motor
creative movement
language

Language to use with toddlers

animals
movements
actions
move like this
pretend
body
jump
up and down
crawl
toes
trunk
fast
slow

Materials

animal pictures

To do

1. Look at pictures of different animals and then move like the animals.

2. Change the words to the familiar "If You're Happy and You Know It" song like the following example:

    If you want to be a monkey, jump up and down.
    If you want to be a monkey, jump up and down.
    If you want to be a monkey, then your actions will really show it.
    If you want to be a monkey, jump up and down.

3. Substitute other animals and their actions, such as:

    bird—flap your wings
    elephant—swing your trunk
       (move arm like trunk)
    mouse—crawl really fast
    little chick—tippy tippy toe
    crab—crawl like this (with
       straight legs)
    flamingo—stand on one leg

4. Use your imagination and let older toddlers suggest other animals.

5. End the activity with a sleeping or quiet animal, such as a snail, turtle or koala bear to help calm down the group.

To do again

Read the toddler favorite, *Brown Bear, Brown Bear* by Bill Martin. Pretend to be the animals in the book.

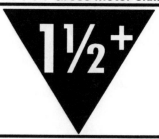

All Creatures Great and Small

Children are fascinated by animals. Pretending to move like different animals allows toddlers a fun way to use their physical energy and learn more about all creatures, great and small.

To do

1. Look at pictures and talk about a specific animal. Have a stuffed animal or puppet of the animal if possible.

2. Move like the animal. Crawl, jump or move like the animal.

3. Pretend to be the animal looking for food or some place to rest. Make noises like the animal.

4. Tell a story about the animal with actions for the toddlers to do with you. For example, with kittens:

   Sleep all curled up like a kitten. Stretch one leg and then the other as you awaken. "Meow." Arch your back, stretch your head up high. "Meow." Crawl slowly while you look for some milk. "Meow." Pretend to drink the milk. "Oh, there goes a mouse." Crawl quickly to catch it. "Shucks, it got away. Let's lay back down and sleep some more."

5. Pretend to be any one of nature's creatures. Use your creative side and relate the animal to a theme, season of the year, and/or special interest of the children. It is possible to be almost anything with a little imagination!

To do again

Read *1, 2, 3 to the Zoo* by Eric Carle. Pretend to be the different zoo animals pictured in the book. Lions, bears and monkeys will be very popular with the toddlers.

Teaching hints

Always join in with the children to promote their participation in the creative movement.

Skills encouraged

gross motor
creative movement

Language to use with toddlers

animals
move like
pretend to be
follow
crawl
jump
noise
eat
food
sleep

Materials

animal pictures
stuffed animals

Toddler-Cise

Moving isolated parts of their bodies helps toddlers become aware of their body and develop a steady beat.

Skills encouraged

gross motor

Language to use with toddlers

rhythm
move
body
follow
up and down
side to side
favorite side
other side
exercise

Materials

music
towels and headbands,
  optional

To do

1. Play instrumental music with a definite rhythm.

2. Encourage the toddlers to follow you as you move to the beat in the following ways:

   > *one arm up and down*
   > *the other arm up and down*
   > *bend up and down at the knees without jumping*
   > *sway side to side*
   > *move head up and down*
   > *pat thighs, stomach or head*
   > *nod*

3. Think of other ways to move parts of the body in isolated ways.

To do again

Many toddlers see a parent exercising, so have an "exercise time" with those who are interested. Use towels as mats, wear headbands and take deep breaths after each section of movements. Have a sip of water after exercising to cool down, just like mommy or daddy.

Teaching hints

Don't expect perfection, as toddlers will and need to do their own thing. When referring to a particular side of the body, say "your favorite side/hand/leg" and then "the other side/hand/leg" rather than left or right.

Up and Down

Squatting up and down helps toddlers develop their leg muscles and refine their jumping skills.

To do

1. Have the toddlers stand and do the actions with the following traditional rhyme:

   The grand ole' Duke of York, (pat hands on thigh to the rhythm)
   He had ten thousand men, (hold up all 10 fingers)
   He marched them up the hill (stretch up high on tiptoes with hands over head)
   And he marched them down again. (squat down and touch ground with hands)
   And when you're up, you're up, (stretch high again)
   And when you're down, you're down, (squat down)
   And when you're only in between (hands on waist)
   You're neither up (stretch high again)
   Nor down! (squat down)

2. Repeat as the toddlers show interest.

3. Start the rhyme slowly and say it faster with each repetition, as the toddlers become familiar with the words. Then slow it down again.

To do again

The actions to the rhyme can also be done sitting down by just moving the arms up and down.

Skills encouraged

gross motor

Language to use with toddlers

up and down
stay in one place
march
stretch up
squat down
in between

Materials

none needed

For Toddlers in Fall: September, October, and November

Filled with changes in the outdoor environment and the annual harvest, fall offers an ideal setting for toddlers to explore nature with the following themes:

◆ *Apples*
◆ *Pumpkins and Jack-o'-Lanterns*
◆ *Corn and Vegetables*
◆ *Farming and Planting*
◆ *Rocks, Stones and Treasures*
◆ *Squirrels*
◆ *Pockets*
◆ *Fall Colors of Red, Yellow and Orange*

Way Up High

A simple chant about apples introduces toddlers to this fruit and teaches them that it comes from trees rather than just the grocery store.

Skills encouraged

language

Language to use with toddlers

up high
stretch
tree
green leaves
apples
red
green
yellow
taste
good
delicious

Materials

red, green and yellow
  apples
felt
scissors
felt board

To do

1. Show the toddlers red, green and yellow apples. Taste some of the apples.

2. Chant the following traditional verse with the toddlers:

    > *Way up high in the apple tree, (reach up high, arms extended over head)*
    > *Two red apples smiled at me. (with arms extended over head, form hands*
    >   *into two fists)*
    > *I shook the tree as hard as I could, (pretend to shake tree)*
    > *Down came the apples, (touch ground)*
    > *Mmm they were good. (rub stomach)*

3. With older toddlers, repeat the rhyme with other descriptions of apples, such as green, yellow, big, shiny, etc. Show the children an apple of the type referred to in the verse before saying the chant.

4. Cut shapes of a tree and two apples out of felt and use on a flannel or felt board as you say the rhyme.

To do again

Change "apples" to other types of tree-bearing fruit in the rhyme, such as pears, cherries or oranges. Show the children some examples of the fruit and taste some pieces before saying the rhyme. Make and use felt pieces for the new rhymes.

Shiny Apples

Heighten toddlers' awareness that apples are harvested in the fall by having them wash and shine the fruit.

To do

1. Put a small amount of water into a dish pan. Add vegetable brushes and/or cloths to the water.

2. Put in two to three apples.

3. Encourage the toddlers to wash the apples to make them shiny.

4. Let the children dry and polish the apples with a dry cloth when finished with the washing.

To do again

Provide sturdy fall vegetables for the toddlers to wash and polish, such as winter squash, turnips, ornamental gourds, pumpkins, etc.

Skills encouraged

sensory exploration
fine motor

Language to use with toddlers

apples
red
shiny
wash
polish
vegetables
fruit
skin
stem

Materials

dish pan
vegetable brushes or
  washcloths
apples

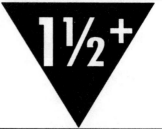

Apple Dance

As toddlers pretend to be and move like apples, they learn specific details about the properties and products of the fruit.

Skills encouraged

gross motor
creative movement

Language to use with toddlers

apple
stem
hanging in the tree
spin
drop
down to the ground
rock
stirred
applesauce

Materials

apples
applesauce
bowls and spoons

To do

1. Show the children an apple. Talk with them about the stem, skin, shape, color, etc.

2. Encourage the children to pretend to be apples with a few verses of the following:

   To the tune of "Here We Go 'Round the Mulberry Bush"

   > *This is the way the apples hang,*
   > *The apples hang, the apples hang.*
   > *This is the way the apples hang,*
   > *Up high in the tree. (sit or stand up straight with arms stretched high over head, hands forming fists)*
   >
   > *This is the way the apples drop,*
   > *The apples drop, the apples drop.*
   > *This is the way the apples drop,*
   > *Down to the ground. (jump down and hit the floor with fists)*
   >
   > *This is the way the apples spin*
   > *The apples spin, the apples spin.*
   > *This is the way the apples spin,*
   > *Around on their stem. (roll hands or spin entire body)*
   >
   > *This is the way the apples rock,*
   > *The apples rock, the apples rock.*
   > *This is the way the apples rock,*
   > *Back and forth in the basket. (rock from side to side while sitting or standing)*
   >
   > *This is the way the apples are stirred,*
   > *The apples are stirred, the apples are stirred.*
   > *This is the way the apples are stirred,*
   > *When making applesauce. (make stirring motion with hands)*

3. Provide applesauce for the toddlers to taste. You could also make it with them.

To do again

Use the "Mulberry Bush" tune to make up other verses about apples or other fruits, such as pears, oranges or pumpkins. Show the toddlers the fruit or vegetable they will pretend to be and taste one of its products.

Apple of My Eye

Toddlers experience the colors of red, yellow and green by exploring the properties of apples.

To do

1. Gather red, yellow and green apples in a basket. Explore the apples with the children.

2. Taste apples for snack. Talk about how each kind tastes. Show the seeds, skin, stem and core of the apple to the toddlers.

3. Provide red, yellow and green markers, crayons or paints for the toddlers to use. encourage them to draw or apint on large oval and/or rectangular pieces of brown or tan paper to represent a "basket" at the easel, table top or floor. Place the basket of real apples nearby.

4. For an additional activity, obtain apple-shaped cookie cutters or craft sponges. Or, cut apple shapes out of a thin sponge or meat trays. Some craft stores have small pieces of wood or plastic pieces shaped like apples. Use a hot glue gun to attach the flat pieces to a small piece of wood or spray can top as a handle.

5. Pour red, yellow and green paint in three separate flat containers.

6. Let the toddlers print with the apple-shaped objects on brown or tan paper, chanting "paint-paper, we're printing apples," during the process. Talk with the toddlers about the different colors of apples.

To do again

For a special activity, cut out a large basket shape from tan or brown paper. Also cut out apple shapes of different sizes from red, green and yellow paper and attach to the "basket." Let each toddler pick out his "favorite apple." Attach an individual photo of the child on the apple (have the parent send one from home if needed). Place the basket and apples on the wall or bulletin board for all to enjoy. Add "You're the Apple of My Eye" saying to the display of pictures. Look at the picutres with the toddlers, emphasizing the special qualities of each child.

Skills encouraged

fine motor
self-esteem

Language to use with toddlers

apples
red
yellow
green
sweet
tart
MMM!
basket
paint
apple-shape
picture

Materials

apples
basket
paint
paper
crayons
markers
craft sponges
apple-shaped cookie cutters, sponges or craft items
small pieces of wood or spray can top
glue
optional, hot glue gun
flat containers
pictures of the children

All Kinds of Pumpkins!

Pumpkins signal the arrival of fall and Halloween. Toddlers can be introduced to this annual event by exploring all the sizes and shapes of pumpkins.

Skills encouraged

sensory exploration
gross motor
fine motor

Language to use with toddlers

orange
pumpkin
stem
smooth
bumpy
round
big and heavy
medium
little and light
baking
pie
bread
seeds
jack-o'-lantern

Materials

different sizes of
 pumpkins

To do

1. Obtain several different sizes of pumpkins from small ornamental pumpkins to larger pumpkins for a definite size comparison.

2. Talk with the toddlers about the color, texture, parts and uses of the pumpkin.

3. Emphasize size differences with the following, sung to the tune of "Are You Sleeping?"

   > *Big pumpkins, little pumpkins,*
   > *Big pumpkins, little pumpkins,*
   > *See them here, see them here,*
   > *They can be big,*
   > *Or they can be little,*
   > *Just like these, just like these. (touch big and little pumpkins)*

4. Leave the pumpkins out for the toddlers to explore on their own. Toddlers will enjoy carrying around the smaller pumpkins and trying to pick up the heavier ones.

Peter, Peter

A traditional nursery rhyme highlights the pretend nature of pumpkins and Halloween.

To do

1. Say the traditional nursery rhyme of "Peter, Peter Pumpkin Eater" with the toddlers. Tap your hands on a large pumpkin to the beat of the chant.

   Peter, Peter, pumpkin eater,
   Had a wife and couldn't keep her.
   He put her in a pumpkin shell,
   And there he kept her very well.

2. Substitute the children's names for "Peter." Change "wife" to "friend."

3. Change the last two lines of the poem.

   He put her in a pumpkin shell,
   Joined her there and all was well.

To do again

Cut out flannel board pieces for the rhyme to add a visual stimulus.

Skills encouraged

language

Language to use with toddlers

rhyme
pumpkin
shell
Peter
name
wife
well
friends

Materials

none needed

Just Like That

Toddlers become familiar with Halloween traditions with a simple rhyme about a pumpkin turning into a jack-o'-lantern.

Skills encouraged

language

Language to use with toddlers

pumpkin
orange
huge
little
fat
jack-o'-lantern
face
smile

Materials

large pumpkin
small pumpkin
black marker

To do

1. Show the toddlers a large pumpkin that has a face carved out or drawn with a permanent marker on one side.

2. Use the pumpkin with the following chant:

   Pumpkin orange and very fat, (show plain side of the pumpkin)
   Make it a jack-o'-lantern,
   Just like that! (show side of pumpkin with face)

3. Show the toddlers a smaller pumpkin. Change the words in the following ways to use with the small jack-o'-lantern:

   Pumpkin small and not so fat,
   Make it a little jack-o'-lantern,
   Just like that!

To do again

Cut small and large pumpkin shapes out of orange felt. Make eyes, nose and mouth out of black felt to put on the pumpkin. Use the felt pieces at the flannel board while saying the chant.

Pumpkin Wash

Helping clean pumpkins for display, even if there isn't any dirt or mud, is a satisfying activity for toddlers.

To do

1. Cover an area of the floor with old bath towels or an old vinyl tablecloth. Fill a dish tub with a small amount of warm soapy water and place it on the towel. Add small cloths, sponges, and/or scrub brushes.

2. Provide various sizes of pumpkins for the toddlers to wash, preferably ones that have some mud or dirt on them.

3. Encourage the toddlers to wash the pumpkins. You may need to begin by doing it yourself.

4. When finished, let the toddlers dry the pumpkins with a cloth.

Teaching hints

If the toddlers have previously been allowed to carry the pumpkins around on their own, remind them that the pumpkins have to stay in the water when they are being cleaned, as wet pumpkins tend to be very slippery.

Skills encouraged

sensory exploration
fine motor

Language to use with toddlers

pumpkin
orange
mud
dirty
shiny
clean
sponge
cloth
water
soap

Materials

pumpkins
old bath towel or
   tablecloth
small cloths, sponges,
   scrub brushes
dish tub

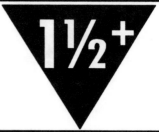

Pumpkin Roll

Toddlers experiment with the weight and shape of pumpkins when they use them for rolling.

Skills encouraged

gross motor

Language to use with toddlers

pumpkin
orange
roll
wobbly
ball
smooth
roll it back
gentle
heavy
light
easy
hard
bigger
smaller

Materials

large pumpkin
small pumpkin

To do

1. Have a toddler sit facing you.

2. Carefully roll a large pumpkin to the toddler.

3. Encourage her to gently roll it back to you.

4. Do the same with a smaller pumpkin.

5. Talk with her about the different sizes and weights of the two pumpkins. Point out how the larger, heavier pumpkin is harder to roll while the smaller, lighter pumpkin is easier to roll.

6. Allow older toddlers to roll pumpkins back and forth to each other.

To do again

Roll a ball with the toddler and then a large pumpkin. Discuss the differences between the two objects, how the ball rolls smoothly while the pumpkin rolls wobbly.

Just Like a Pumpkin

After working and playing with jack-o'-lanterns, have the toddlers pretend to be pumpkins.

To do

1. Pretend to be pumpkins or jack-o'-lanterns while acting out the following chant:

   > *Sit like a pumpkin, sit like a pumpkin, sit like a pumpkin,*
   > *Just like this. (sit with legs crossed and arms forming circle in front)*

   > *Roll like a pumpkin, roll like a pumpkin, roll like a pumpkin,*
   > *Just like this. (roll hands)*

   > *Rock like a pumpkin, rock like a pumpkin, rock like a pumpkin,*
   > *Just like this. (stand or sit and rock side to side)*

   > *Grin like a jack-o'-lantern, grin like a jack-o'-lantern, grin like a jack-o'-lantern,*
   > *Just like this. (smile and point to cheeks)*

   > *Wink like a jack-o'-lantern, wink like a jack-o'-lantern, wink like a jack-o'-lantern,*
   > *Just like this. (wink)*

2. Add in other actions for the jack-o'-lanterns, such as spin, jump, wobble (walk with legs moving side to side), laugh, watch (move eyes side to side), etc.

3. End the activity with the following to refocus the toddlers' energy:

   > *Sleep like a jack-o'-lantern, sleep like a jack-o'-lantern, sleep like a jack-o'-lantern,*
   > *Just like this. (eyes closed, head down)*

Skills encouraged

creative movement
gross motor
language

Language to use with toddlers

pumpkin
jack-o'-lantern
roll
sit
rock
grin
wink

Materials

none needed

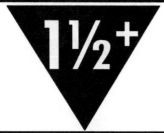

Toddler-o'-Lanterns

Toddlers can create their own jack-o'-lanterns with markers and stickers.

Skills encouraged

fine motor
creative expression

Language to use with toddlers

pumpkin
decorate
jack-o'-lantern
face
smile
grin
nose
smell
eyes
see
ears
hear
markers
stickers

Materials

large pumpkin
several small ornamental
   pumpkins
markers
stickers
knife
spoon

To do

1. Draw a face on a large pumpkin with a permanent marker. Have the children point to their own eyes, nose, mouth, etc. before you draw each feature. Emphasize the importance of each feature, such as "Now the jack-o'-lantern has eyes to see with, and he can see how big you all are!"

2. Or, carve out the facial features on a large pumpkin with the toddlers. This is often more difficult with a group of young toddlers. See teaching hints for suggestions on how to make it work. Let the toddlers explore the pulp and seeds inside the pumpkin.

3. Allow the toddlers to decorate their own jack-o'-lantern with washable markers and stickers either as a group on a large pumpkin or individually on small ornamental pumpkins. Most toddlers will not make facial features on the pumpkin, but they do enjoy decorating their own jack-o'-lantern in their own way!

To do again

Bake or bring pumpkin bread or cookies for snack.

Teaching hints

When carving a pumpkin with a group of toddlers, many of the children may not have the attention span to sit through the entire process. Pre-carving the facial features without the children present, then inserting the pieces back in and later "pretending" to cut the features out with the children works best for carving jack-o'-lanterns with toddler groups. You can have the children push out the pre-cut features.

All Kinds of Squash

The various kinds of squash and gourds available in fall offer toddlers simple sensory experiences in color, texture and shape.

To do

1. Collect different kinds of squash and gourds in a basket.

2. Show the squash and gourds to the toddlers. Talk with them about the colors, textures, sizes, shapes, etc.

3. Have cooked zucchini and/or yellow squash for the toddlers to taste. Older toddlers can also have raw zucchini to taste with dip.

To do again

Paint pictures with green and yellow paint.

Skills encouraged

sensory exploration

Language to use with toddlers

squash
gourds
pumpkins
zucchini
yellow
green
orange
bumpy
smooth
stripes
smaller
bigger
round
long
stem

Materials

variety of squash and
  gourds
basket
cooked zucchini and/or
  yellow squash
raw zucchini and dip,
  optional

Growing Ways

Variations on a traditional chant introduce toddlers to the needs of plants and people for growth.

Skills encouraged

language

Language to use with toddlers

how
garden
grow
silver bells
cockle shells
sun
rain
water
tender care
flowers
plants
body
nutritious food
play
rest
love

Materials

none needed

To do

1. Say the following traditional nursery rhyme with your toddlers:

   Mary, Mary quite contrary
   How does your garden grow?
   With silver bells and cockle shells
   And pretty maids all in a row.

2. Use the names of the children in the group in place of Mary.

3. Change the verse with older toddlers to emphasize the importance of rain, sun and care of flowers and plants:

   Sharon, Sharon quite contrary
   How does your garden grow?
   With lots of rain and sunshine
   And care of the flowers/plants, just so.

To do again

The verse can also be changed to discuss the needs of their bodies:

   Sharon, Sharon quite contrary
   How does your body grow?
   With good food, play and rest
   And lots of love, that's the best.

Seed Shakers

Seeds inside a closed container make ideal toddler instruments for exploring sounds and to use with chants.

To do

1. Show the toddlers different kinds of seeds, including popcorn and pumpkin seeds. Let toddlers practice their fine motor skills picking up and exploring the seeds. Closely supervise this activity.

2. Gather containers with tight fitting lids, such as 35mm film canisters. Try to have one for each child.

3. Put different seeds into each container. Older toddlers can help with this.

4. For extra security, attach the lids with glue.

5. Encourage the toddlers to shake the seed shakers. Compare the sounds the different seeds make.

6. Use the shakers while marching, singing or keeping rhythm with recorded music.

Skills encouraged

fine motor
sensory exploration

Language to use with toddlers

seeds
small
pumpkin
popcorn
bean
inside
cover
shake
noise
music

Materials

small unbreakable
  containers with lids
seeds
glue

How Corny!

The many familiar foods made from fruits and vegetables allow toddlers to explore texture, color, taste and even nutrition.

Skills encouraged

sensory exploration

Language to use with toddlers

yellow corn
corn on the cob
kernels
corn meal
corn bread
cream of corn
popcorn
corn tortilla

Materials

samples of foods made
from corn

To do

1. Collect samples of some of the following corn products to show the children: fresh corn on the cob, creamed corn, dried corn, corn meal, cornbread or corn muffins, corn chips, popcorn and corn tortillas.

2. Show the children fresh corn on the cob. Talk about the green husk, fibers, yellow kernels, etc. Make fresh corn on the cob to eat for snack or with lunch.

3. Show the toddlers the other items made from corn. Discuss how the foods are all yellow but look, taste and feel different. Emphasize the nutritional qualities of the items.

4. Taste some of the corn products, or have one each day with lunch or snack. Popcorn and corn chips present a choking hazard for children under three so just show these foods to the toddlers.

To do again

Taste and examine apple products, such as applesauce, dried apple, apple juice, apple muffins, etc.

Teaching hints

Be aware of any food sensitivities or allergies the toddlers may have before attempting any tasting activity.

Corn Play

Sand and water are not the only appropriate media for sensory activities. Dry ingredients such as corn meal offer an alternative.

To do

1. Pour corn meal into a dish tub.

2. Add plastic containers, scoops, sifters, etc. to use with the corn meal. If desired, provide a few cobs of small decorative corn or just plain cobs from which the corn has been removed.

3. Let the toddlers explore the corn meal. Encourage them to pour, stir and fill the containers with the corn meal. Talk with the children about the color and texture of the corn meal and about what they are doing.

4. Add a few plastic or wooden farm animals to the corn meal for the toddlers to pretend to feed.

To do again

Use dry oats in the dish tub instead with the same accessories.

Teaching hints

Torn bags of corn meal can often be obtained from the grocery store for free as they can no longer be sold.

Skills encouraged

sensory exploration

Language to use with toddlers

yellow corn meal
ground corn
scoops
grainy
pour
stir
feel
feed
animals
oats

Materials

corn meal
decorative corn
scoops
plastic containers
dish tub
wooden or plastic farm
 animals, optional

Shucks!

The skills used to shuck corn challenge older toddlers' fine motor abilities while the husks and fibers offer a unique sensory exploration.

Skills encouraged

fine motor
sensory exploration

Language to use with toddlers

corn
ornamental corn
dry
colors
kernels
husk
shuck
fibers
peel
silky
pull
wash

Materials

basket
dish tub
decorative corn
corn on the cob
plastic container with lid

To do

1. Put small and large decorative corn in a basket.

2. Let the toddlers explore the corn. Talk to them about the different colors of the kernels.

3. Save any kernels that fall off. Place in a plastic container with a lid to make a shaker.

4. Put several pieces of corn on the cob in a dish tub.

5. Show the toddlers how to shuck the corn. Encourage them to try to shuck some corn too.

6. Talk to the toddlers about the process and the silky texture of the fibers.

7. When all the cobs have been shucked, let some of the toddlers wash the corn at the sink.

8. Cook the corn for a lunch or snack treat. Yummy!

Teaching hints

The teacher may have to finish shucking some of the pieces before washing the corn. Some toddlers will not find the activity at all interesting, while others will be fascinated and work hard at shucking the corn.

Garden Party

Surprisingly, many toddlers enjoy crunchy foods. Have a tasting party with raw vegetables to expose the children to this highly nutritious food.

1½⁺

To do

1. Obtain a wide variety of raw vegetables, such as celery, green pepper, carrots, broccoli, cauliflower, etc.

2. Let older toddlers help wash the vegetables at the sink. Show them how to use a vegetable scrubber.

3. Cut the vegetables into bite-sized pieces. Help older toddlers arrange the vegetables beautifully on a serving plate.

4. Give each toddler a small sampling of the raw vegetables on a plate. Provide a dip if desired. Show the toddler how to dip the vegetables into the dressing. (Carrots can be grated for the toddlers if choking is of concern.)

5. Talk with the children about the different colors, tastes, crunchy textures, etc. Emphasize that nutritious food helps them to grow strong.

To do again

Have a fruit tasting party using the fruits harvested in the fall, such as apples, pears, plums and grapes. Cut grapes in half for children under three.

Teaching hints

Toddlers often have not been exposed to the crunchy texture of raw vegetables, but many children enjoy them, especially when they see their teachers and other children enjoying the new taste treat. Be sure to tell the parents if a child seemed to enjoy some of the raw vegetables.

Skills encouraged

fine motor
sensory exploration

Language to use with toddlers

raw
vegetable
crunchy
taste
green
celery
broccoli
green pepper
orange carrot
break
wash
vegetable scrubber
dip

Materials

raw vegetables
vegetable scrubber
cutting board
knife for the teacher
vegetable dip

2⁺

Corn Roll

Ornamental corn can be used with paint to create interesting designs on paper.

Skills encouraged

gross motor

Language to use with toddlers

ornamental corn
dried
husks
paint
paper
roll
side to side
back and forth
designs

Materials

ornamental corn
paint
flat container
box
paper
scissors

To do

1. Remove the dried husks of a few pieces of ornamental corn.

2. Show the toddler the corn. Talk about the colors, kernels, husks, etc.

3. Mix paint in yellow, brown, red, deep purple, etc. to match the colors of the kernels. Pour the paint into a flat container.

4. Find a large shirt or sweater-sized gift box. Cut paper to fit inside the box.

5. Place one whole cob of corn into a container of paint. Roll the corn around so that all sides are covered with paint.

6. Let the toddler choose what color of paper he would like to use. Place the paper inside the box.

7. Put an ear of corn covered with paint on top of the paper in the box.

8. Have the toddler hold the box in both hands and rock it side to side so that the corn rolls around in the box.

9. Remove corn and add a different colored cob, if desired. Repeat the rolling process.

10. Talk to the toddler about the process, the different colors of paint, the patterns made, etc.

To do again

Give the toddlers the dry husks from the decorative corn to use like a paint-brush with paint.

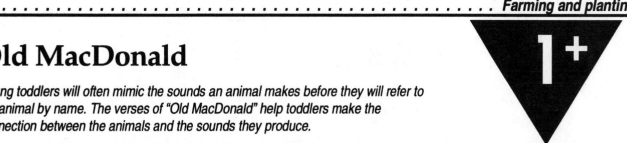

Old MacDonald

Young toddlers will often mimic the sounds an animal makes before they will refer to the animal by name. The verses of "Old MacDonald" help toddlers make the connection between the animals and the sounds they produce.

To do

1. Sing the traditional song, "Old MacDonald," with the toddlers during their play with the farm animals. Talk about the animals with the children.

2. Let an individual child tell you what animals she wants you to sing about. Use the child's full name with the verse of the animal she suggests. For example, "Dari North had a goat...."

3. Find pictures of farm animals from magazines or pattern books.

4. Color the pictures if needed. Cut out the different animals and laminate or cover with clear contact paper. Attach the picture to a craft stick. Make enough for each child to have an animal to hold.

5. Use the farm animal stick puppets while singing the song with the children. Move the puppets to the rhythm of the song.

6. Encourage the older toddlers to stand up during the verse of the animal they are holding.

To do again

Cut farm animal shapes out of felt to use at the flannel board with the song. Allow the older toddlers to use the felt pieces at the flannel board on their own.

Skills encouraged

language

Language to use with toddlers

farm animals
sounds
baa
moo
neigh
quack
cluck
song

Materials

wooden, plastic or stuffed
  farm animals
farm animal pictures
clear contact paper
craft sticks
glue or tape

Baa Baa

Variations on a traditional nursery rhyme can be used to introduce toddlers to sounds, names and even colors.

Skills encouraged

language

Language to use with toddlers

sheep
lamb
wool
shear
baa baa
master
dame

Materials

black, white and gray felt
scissors
posterboard
glue
pictures of lambs and sheep
sheepskin
wool sweater

To do

1. Sing the following traditional nursery rhyme with the toddlers.

   Baa, baa, black sheep, have you any wool?
   Yes sir, yes sir, three bags full.
   One for my master, one for my dame,
   And one for the little one who lives down the lane.

2. Substitute the children's names in place of master, dame and little one. Touch the child's hand or knee when saying their name.

3. Cut sheep out of black, white and gray felt. Glue the shapes on to posterboard to add strength.

4. Use the felt sheep with the verse. Change the color of the sheep in the rhyme and hold up that color of prop. For example, sing the verse as "Baa, baa, white sheep...." and hold up the felt piece for the white sheep.

5. Look at pictures of lambs and sheep. Talk about the animals with the toddlers. Let the toddlers feel pieces of lamb's wool and a wool sweater.

To do again

Make felt pieces for the rest of the rhyme: a master, a dame, three bags of wool and a little boy and/or girl. Do the rhyme as a felt board story. Once they are familiar with the rhyme, let older toddlers use the felt pieces on their own.

To Market, To Market

Nursery rhymes expose toddlers to the rhythm and flow of language. Some verses, such as, "To Market," display a playful side and encourage the children to make up new nonsense rhyming words as well.

To do

1. Say the following traditional nursery rhyme with the toddlers.

   > *To market, to market,*
   > *To buy a fat pig.*
   > *Home again, home again,*
   > *Jiggety jig.*
   > *To market, to market,*
   > *To buy a fat hog.*
   > *Home again, home again,*
   > *Jiggety jog.*

2. Tap the rhythm of the rhyme on your legs or the floor while saying the rhyme.

3. Cut pig and hog (bigger pig) shapes out of different colors of felt or construction paper to use with a flannel board.

4. Use the pieces with the rhyme. Say the rhyme substituting a color for the word "fat." For example, when holding up a purple pig, say:

   > *To market, to market,*
   > *To buy a purple pig.*
   > *Home again, home again,*
   > *Jiggety jig.*

5. Look at pictures of pigs and talk about the characteristics of the animals with the toddlers.

6. Once the older toddlers are familiar with the different colors, play a color game with them. Display all your colored pigs on the felt board. Say the rhyme substituting different-colored pigs and have them choose the pig that is the correct color.

To do again

Look at pictures of other farm animals. Change the verse to include those animals. For example:

   > *To market, to market,*
   > *To buy a huge cow.*
   > *Home again, home again,*
   > *Jiggety jow.*

Skills encouraged

language

Language to use with toddlers

pig
color
big
little
market
hog
rhyme

Materials

felt or construction paper
scissors

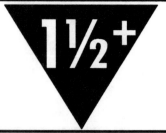

Toddler Farm

Setting up a pretend farm with props provides a way for toddlers to learn about farm animals through play.

Skills encouraged

imaginative play

Language to use with toddlers

farm
animals
cows
calf
pigs
piglets
sheep
lambs
chickens
chicks
young
families
feed
hay
apple
carrot

Materials

wooden, plastic or stuffed
  farm animals
orange felt
red felt
boxes
scissors
yellow construction paper
glue or tape
blocks
bed sheet

To do

1. Gather a variety of farm animals. Send a note home to parents asking to borrow any farm animals they might have for a few weeks.

2. In a corner of the room, lay a bed sheet down on the floor to define an area for the pretend farm. Put the farm animals on the bed sheet for the children to take care of at the "farm."

3. Provide blocks with which older toddlers can build fences and pens for the animals.

4. Cover a few small boxes with yellow construction paper to look like bales of hay. Encourage the toddlers to feed the animals the hay.

5. Cut a few carrot and apple shapes out of felt for the toddlers to use to pretend to feed the horses.

6. While playing on the farm with the children, talk with them about the names of the animals and their young, the products the animals provide, how to care for the animals, etc.

7. Add books about farm animals to the area for the toddlers to look at while they play on the farm. *The Very Busy Spider* by Eric Carle is a must for toddlers.

To do again

Make a barn out of a large box to use with the animals. Paint the barn red. If the box is large enough, let the children get inside.

Animal Show

Toddlers benefit from the enjoyment of playing with water as they pretend to wash farm animals for an animal show.

To do

1. Mix a small amount of mild dish soap with water in a dish tub.

2. Place the farm animals in the tub for the toddlers to clean with sponges, cloths, and/or scrub brushes.

3. Encourage the toddlers to "clean" the animals for the show. Talk with the children about the different animals, the process of cleaning them for the show and how the animals earn ribbons for being the best groomed at the show.

4. Have the children dry the animals when finished.

5. Give the children ribbons for washing the animals if desired.

To do again

Wash other plastic animals related to a topic, such as zoo animals or pets.

Skills encouraged

fine motor
sensory exploration

Language to use with toddlers

farm
cows
horses
pigs
wash
brush
clean
mud
show
ribbons

Materials

plastic farm animals
dish tub
dish soap
sponge
washcloth
scrub brush
ribbons

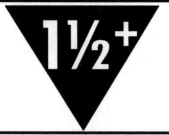

Prance, Waddle and Scamper

Pretending to be different farm animals is an ideal way for toddlers to expend their high energy and practice their developing gross motor skills.

Skills encouraged

gross motor
creative movement

Language to use with toddlers

horse
prance
cow
move
crawl
duck
waddle
chicks
scamper
pig
move
pretend

Materials

pictures of farm animals

To do

1. Look at pictures of farm animals.

2. Encourage the children to pretend to move like different farm animals and sing the following song to the tune of "Here We Go 'Round the Mulberry Bush":

> *This is the way the horses prance,*
> *Horses prance, horses prance.*
> *This is the way the horses prance,*
> *Out of the barn. (lift knees high to make prancing steps)*
>
> *This is the way the huge cows move,*
> *The huge cows move, the huge cows move.*
> *This is the way the huge cows move,*
> *While grazing in the field. (crawl slowly)*
>
> *This is the way the yellow ducks waddle,*
> *Yellow ducks waddle, yellow ducks waddle.*
> *This is the way the yellow ducks waddle,*
> *Down to the pond. (hands on hips to bend arms like wings, toes pointed out*
>   *and waddle when walking)*
>
> *This is the way the little chicks scamper,*
> *Little chicks scamper, little chicks scamper.*
> *This is the way the little chicks scamper,*
> *Behind the mother hen. (take little steps quickly on tiptoes)*

2. End the activity by laying down to refocus the children's attention with the following verse.

> *This is the way the big pig sleeps,*
> *The big pig sleeps, the big pig sleeps.*
> *This is the way the big pig sleeps,*
> *in the mud and hay. (lay down)*

To do again

Substitute other types of animals and actions using the same tune.

Down on the Farm

Adding trucks and farm animals to soil allows toddlers to explore a medium which fascinates them, dirt.

1½+

To do

1. Fill a large dish tub, baby bathtub or sensory table with about one half inch of potting soil. Place a shower curtain or newspaper underneath.

2. Add plastic farm animals, a few large rocks, soil, dump truck, tractor, shovels, etc.

3. Let the toddlers play with the animals and trucks in the soil. Talk with them about the items. Make up pretend stories about life on the farm.

To do again

Use the animals, trucks, shovels, etc. with wet sand.

Teaching hints

This is a perfect activity to take outside, as you'll have little or no clean-up afterwards.

Skills encouraged

fine motor
sensory exploration

Language to use with toddlers

farm
dirt
soil
rocks
animals
cow
pig
horse
mud
tractor
dump truck

Materials

potting soil
shower curtain or
  newspaper
rocks
wooden or plastic farm
  animals
dump truck
tractor
shovel
large dish tub or baby
  bathtub

Planting Fun

Toddlers truly enjoy playing in soil and mud. Using soil for a planting activity permits toddlers to explore this enticing material.

Skills encouraged

sensory exploration
fine motor

Language to use with toddlers

soil
garden
plant
flowers
leaves
seed
water
shovel

Materials

potting soil
dish tub
newspaper
small containers
scoops
shovels
small watering can
flower or vegetable seeds
small cups or bowls

To do

1. Put about an inch of potting soil in a dish tub. Place newspaper under the dish tub.

2. Place small containers, large spoons, scoops and/or shovels in the tub.

3. Let the toddlers explore the soil.

4. Have each child help you plant a seed or seeds in her own cup or bowl. Large seeds (such as sunflowers or beans) work best as they are easier to handle. If you use clear plastic cups, you may be able to watch the plant's roots grow. Use the little watering can to water your seeds. Care for them in the classroom until the plants emerge. Then send them home for transplanting to a garden if desired.

5. After the planting activity is finished, replenish the soil and add a small amount of water for a truly sensational, but messy, activity. This is a perfect activity for outdoors. Toddlers love the mud!

To do again

Fill a small wading pool with potting soil, artificial flowers, shovels, containers, etc. for the children to play with on the playground.

Teaching hints

This is a terrific activity for outdoors as the clean-up is much easier! Natural items from the playground can also be added to the soil in the dish tub or wading pool.

Rock Collections

Toddlers are often fascinated with small objects such as rocks which they enjoy carrying around and examining.

To do

1. Gather an assortment of rocks that are large enough to pass the choke test. If there are rocks around the school grounds, take a walk with the toddlers to collect some. Give each child a small bucket to carry the rocks they find.

2. Put a few of the rocks out on a shelf for the children to explore.

3. Talk to the children about the colors, sizes, textures, etc. Emphasize how the rock is "hard like the floor."

4. Place a few empty containers near the rocks for a dump-and-fill activity. Encourage the toddlers to take the rocks out of a container and put them back in one by one or transfer them to another container.

5. Allow the toddlers to carry the rocks around if they desire. Show them how to put the rocks in their pocket, purse or bucket to carry with them.

To do again

Have the toddlers put a few rocks in containers with lids, such as a coffee can or diaper wipe box. Close the top and encourage them to shake the rocks. What sounds the rocks can make!

Teaching hints

The rocks the children use should pass the choke test. If a toddler tries to throw a rock, tell him firmly, "Rocks will hurt someone if we throw them. You may throw a ball but not rocks." Give him a ball to throw.

Skills encouraged

fine motor
sensory exploration

Language to use with toddlers

rocks
big
little
huge
heavy
hard
smooth
bumpy

Materials

rocks
buckets
containers with lids

Natural Textures

Items from nature provide a simple way to explore colors and textures with toddlers.

Skills encouraged

fine motor
sensory exploration

Language to use with toddlers

acorns
pine cones
leaves
colors
fall
ground
tree
pick up
bucket
feel
hard
dry
crumble
smooth
rough

Materials

leaves
acorns
pine cones
twigs
dish tub
buckets, baskets or paper
  sacks

To do

1. Let the toddlers help you gather leaves that have fallen from the trees. Give each child a small bucket, basket or paper sack.

2. Place the leaves in a dish or sensory tub.

3. Talk with the toddlers about the colors, the textures, sizes, etc. while they feel and explore the leaves.

4. Encourage the toddlers to crumble or tear some of the leaves.

5. Pine cones, small twigs and/or other natural objects can be added to the leaves to extend the activity. Acorns can be included, with supervision, for older toddlers.

6. Talk to the children about the different items, the hard and smooth textures, where they come from, etc.

7. If leaves, acorns and/or pine cones have fallen on the playground or near the classroom, give each toddler a bucket or basket for collecting to help clean up the play area. With acorns, pretend to be squirrels gathering food to store for the winter.

To do again

Take the sensory tub filled with nature items outside for the toddlers to continue to explore. Add more natural objects to the collection. Don't forget what fun raking leaves can be, especially if you have a few child-sized rakes available. And remember what fun it is to play in the piles you make—for jumping in or playing like squirrels nesting.

Teaching hints

The acorns will require close supervision, as they are not large enough to pass the choke test.

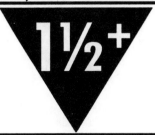

Rock Polishing

Toddlers practice fine motor skills when they clean and polish small rocks and stones.

To do

1. Fill a dish or sensory tub with a small amount of water. Add a little dish soap.

2. In the water place a variety of rocks that pass the choke test and some old toothbrushes. Small scrub brushes or sponges can also be added.

3. Show the toddlers how to scrub the rocks to get them clean. Chant "scrub, scrub, scrub a dub dub" while scrubbing the rocks.

4. Provide a cloth for the toddlers to dry and "polish" the rocks that have been washed.

To do again

Polish a variety of shells in the same manner, especially as a summertime activity. Add pebbles for older toddlers, with close supervision.

Teaching hints

Make sure the rocks pass the choke test if an adult will not be closely supervising the toddlers the entire time.

Skills encouraged

fine motor
sensory exploration

Language to use with toddlers

rocks
smooth
stones
rough
clean
scrub
shiny
brush
dry

Materials

rocks
dish tub
dish soap
old toothbrushes
small scrub brushes
cloths
sponge

M.I.M.'s Preserved in Stone

Rocks provide a three-dimensional background for the toddlers' drawings and preserve their Most Important Marks in stone.

Skills encouraged

fine motor
creative expression

Language to use with toddlers

rock
stone
hard
smooth
draw
paint
colors
lines
heavy
paper weight

Materials

large rocks
markers

To do

1. Collect large, smooth rocks.

2. Let the toddler pick which rock he would like to use.

3. Allow him to use colorful markers to draw on the rock.

4. Talk to him about the lines he is making, the colors, the bumpy surface, etc.

To do again

Paint large rocks with tempera paint and paintbrushes.

Teaching hints

The rocks can be given as paper weight presents to parents or other special people.

Nature Collage

Simple materials for collages can be easily found just outside the door.

To do

1. Collect a variety of fallen leaves and other nature items, such as twigs, rocks, etc. for a collage.

2. If possible, involve the toddlers in collecting some of the items from the playground or on a nature walk prior to the activity. Give each child on the walk a bucket or basket to save the different items collected.

3. Back in the classroom give each child a piece of cardboard.

4. Let her choose from the collection the items she would like to put on her collage.

5. Pour glue into a flat container.

6. Have the child dip the nature item into the glue and then place it on the paper. Heavier objects may require extra glue.

7. Talk to her about the textures, colors, etc. of the nature items she has chosen for her collage.

Teaching hints

This is a wonderful activity to do outside where the items were originally found.

Skills encouraged

fine motor
creative expression

Language to use with toddlers

leaves
colors
twigs
textures
rocks
collect
glue
collage

Materials

leaves and other natural
  items
glue
flat container
cardboard
buckets or baskets

Hard as a Rock

Rocks and cotton balls offer an opportunity to experiment with differences in hard and soft textures.

Skills encouraged

sensory exploration
fine motor
classification

Language to use with toddlers

hard
soft
feel
different
same
together
group
alike
loud
silent

Materials

assorted rocks
cotton balls
bowls
dish tub
plastic containers with lids

To do

1. Place cotton balls and rocks together in a dish or sensory tub. The rocks should be large enough to pass the choke test.

2. Talk to the toddlers about the hard/soft and heavy/light differences between the rocks and cotton.

3. Add plastic containers and cups for the children to use with the items.

4. Provide some containers with lids. Have the toddlers place only cotton in one and only rocks in another. Listen to the difference when you shake them.

5. For a sorting activity, place three to five rocks and three to five cotton balls in a basket. Provide two bowls for the toddlers to sort the "hard rocks" and "soft cotton" into separate containers.

To do again

Sort other hard items, such as shells or nuts with the cotton balls.

Teaching hint

As always, be sure the items the children are using are large enough to pass the choke test or provide only with close supervision.

Splash!

The two toddler favorites of water and rocks combine to make a splash!

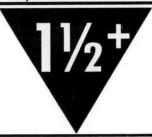

To do

1. Fill a small wading pool with just enough water to cover the bottom. A baby bathtub can also be used. Place the tub or pool outside on the playground.

2. Place rocks around the pool or tub.

3. Encourage the toddlers to drop the rocks into the pool. Say "splash" with excitement when the rock hits the water.

4. Talk to the toddlers about how the bigger rocks make a bigger splash than the smaller rocks.

5. On a warm day, let older toddlers take off their shoes and socks and stand in the water to splash like the rocks.

To do again

After a rain, put on everyone's boots and take a walk to let the toddlers splash rocks in puddles that have formed around the school grounds. The children will want to have fun splashing in the puddles themselves, so be prepared.

Teaching hints

Remind the toddlers to drop the rocks, not throw them.

Skills encouraged

gross motor

Language to use with toddlers

rocks
water
drop
big
small
splash

Materials

rocks
wading pool or baby bathtub

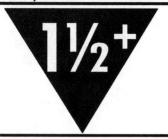

Pebbles and Rocks

Toddlers can explore size differences when they experiment with pebbles and rocks.

Skills encouraged

sensory exploration
fine motor
classification

Language to use with toddlers

small
tiny
pebbles
light
big
large
rocks
stones
heavy
sounds

Materials

dish tub
rocks
pebbles
plastic containers with lids
baskets
bowls

To do

1. Place different sizes of rocks in a dish or sensory tub. Add containers of various sizes. Include some that are too small for the rocks, such as 35mm film canisters.

2. Let the toddlers experiment with putting the rocks into the containers. Talk to the children about rocks that are "too big" and the containers that are "too small."

3. With close supervision, add some pebbles to the containers and rocks.

4. Provide containers with lids so the children can make shakers with different-sized rocks and/or pebbles. Listen to the different sounds made by the rocks and pebbles.

5. Place large and small rocks in a basket. Provide two more baskets, one large and one small, and encourage the toddlers to sort the large/big rocks and the small/tiny stones into the separate baskets.

Teaching hints

Make sure the rocks placed out for the toddlers to explore on their own are large enough to pass the choke test. When closer supervision is possible, the toddlers enjoy exploring the smaller rocks and pebbles.

Natural Sorting

The outdoors in fall provides a multitude of items that older toddlers can use for sorting activities.

To do

1. Collect different nature items for the children to sort, such as rocks, leaves, nuts, pine cones, shells, etc.

2. Provide the same number of bowls or containers as the number of different nature items. Begin with two or three different kinds.

3. In each of the containers, place a different item. Glue or tape them down if desired.

4. Encourage the toddlers to sort the items into the separate bowls.

5. Talk with the toddlers about the different items, the shapes, textures, where they are found, etc.

Teaching hints

It is best to start with sorting just two or three different items until the children are familiar with the process. Add more items as individual children are ready. Make sure all of the items pass the choke test.

Skills encouraged

classification
sensory exploration

Language to use with toddlers

rocks
nuts
leaves
pine cones
shells
twigs
separate
match
same
different
sort

Materials

nature items
bowls, baskets or plastic
  containers
glue or tape

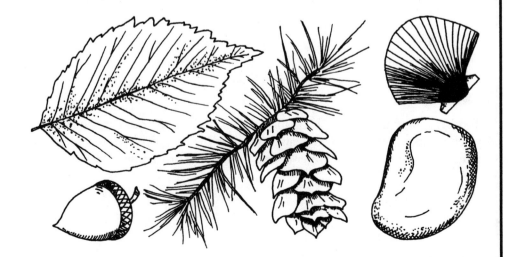

Rock and Roll Surprise

Create a rock and roll painting surprise by dipping stones in paint and shaking them in a closed box.

Skills encouraged

gross motor
fine motor

Language to use with toddlers

surprise
rock
inside
paint
close
lid
shake
roll
paper
color
design
nuts
side to side
up and down

Materials

rocks
box or container with lid
plastic dishes or bowls
paper
paint
nuts

To do

1. Find a sturdy box or container with a lid. Diaper wipe boxes work well. Cut different colors of construction paper to fit on the bottom or around the sides depending on the dimensions of the container. For example, with a diaper wipes box you could put the paper in the bottom; with a large cottage cheese or yogurt tub, you could place a piece of paper around the sides.

2. Mix paint in two or three contrasting colors. White should be one of the options as it mixes well with all colors to make pastels.

3. Pour the paints into plastic dishes or bowls. Put one rock in each color.

4. Let the toddler choose the color of paper she wants to use. Place the paper inside the container.

5. Have the toddler pick the color of paint she wants to use first. Put the rock from that color of paint inside the box.

6. Close the top and encourage the toddler to jiggle the container side to side or up and down. Model the action if necessary. Chant "Shake, shake, shake for a rock and roll surprise" as she shakes the box.

7. Let her shake as long as she wants. When finished, open the lid to look at the "rock and roll surprise."

8. Use a rock from one of the different colors of paint if the toddler wants to repeat the process.

9. Remove the paper from the container when completely finished. Talk about the different lines and colors made by the rolling action of the rock.

To do again

Use nuts or acorns instead of rocks for a "nutty surprise."

Teaching hints

Toddlers enjoy the "magical" quality of the activity even more when the teacher shows enthusiasm and surprise when the lid is opened. Ask older toddlers, "How did that happen?" and explore the process with them.

Natural Sculptures

Nature items make perfect tools to use with playdough and can be made into three-dimensional sculptures as well.

2+

To do

1. Gather various nature items such as rocks, twigs, small sticks, shells, nuts, etc. in a bowl.

2. Give the child a handful of playdough, and let him use the nature items as "tools" for scraping, poking, cutting, etc.

3. Encourage him to press a nature item into the playdough and then remove the object to leave a print or design.

4. Flatten a small handful of the playdough. Have the toddler press down and leave some nature items in the playdough for a "permanent sculpture" when it dries.

To do again

Mix plaster of Paris. Pour a thin amount in a foil tart tin. Let older toddlers place nature items in the plaster when it starts to thicken for another type of "natural sculpture."

Skills encouraged

sensory exploration
fine motor
creative expression

Language to use with toddlers

playdough
plaster of Paris
permanent
leave
sculpture
tools
rocks
twigs
sticks
shells
acorns
nuts
pine cones
pattern

Materials

playdough
nature items
bowl

Squirrel's Visit

Squirrels fascinate toddlers as they scamper up and down trees. A simple verse about the squirrel can help toddlers learn the names of different parts of their body.

Skills encouraged

language

Language to use with toddlers

squirrel
furry
claws
long tail
crawl
knee
toes
nose
touch
tickle
hug
names of parts of the body

Materials

stuffed animal or puppet
  squirrel
picture of a squirrel

To do

1. Show the toddlers a picture of a squirrel. Talk about the animal's bushy tail, furry body, tiny ears, etc. Look for squirrels from the classroom window if possible.

2. Say the following verse with the toddlers.

   A squirrel came to visit me!
   He thought I was a tree!
   First he sat on my knee. (point to knee)
   Then he climbed down to my toes. (crawl fingers down leg to toes)
   Oh no, now he's looking at my nose! (point to nose)

3. Say the verse with individual children using a squirrel stuffed animal or puppet. Have the squirrel pretend to tickle or hug different parts of the child's body. Say, "He's going to tickle your ear now!" as the puppet touches the child's ear.

To do again

Substitute other animals for the squirrel, especially ones for which you have a stuffed animal or puppet.

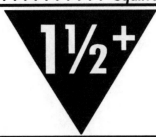

Nutty Fun

Like other small objects, nuts fascinate toddlers and provide them with a fine motor challenge as they explore the different kinds.

To do

1. Place a variety of nuts in a dish tub with small plastic cups and containers. It is best to use nuts that are large enough to pass the choke test, such as pecans, walnuts and Brazil nuts.

2. Let the toddlers explore the nuts. Encourage them to empty and fill the cups with the nuts. Provide lids for some of the containers so the children can make shakers.

3. Tell the toddlers the names of the different nuts. Talk about the smooth or bumpy textures of the various nuts.

4. Provide stuffed or puppet squirrels and/or bears for the toddlers to pretend to feed.

Teaching hints

Children under three should not be given whole shelled nuts to eat as they present a choking hazard. Make fruit bread or muffins with chopped nuts so the toddlers may taste the nuts.

Skills encouraged

sensory exploration
fine motor

Language to use with toddlers

nuts
pecan
walnut
peanut
Brazil nuts
shell
hard
smooth
bumpy
crack

Materials

a variety of nuts: pecans,
   walnuts, Brazil nuts,
   peanuts, etc.
dish tub
plastic cups
plastic containers with lids
stuffed animals
toothbrushes
sponge
washcloth
dish soap

1½⁺ Bushy Tails

Feather dusters can be used in a new way as pretend squirrels' tails and for a painting activity.

Skills encouraged

creative expression

Language to use with toddlers

squirrel's tail
bushy
furry
feather duster
similar
swish
back and forth
paint
paper

Materials

feather dusters
paint
flat containers
butcher paper
tape
newspapers

To do

1. Obtain two to three small, inexpensive feather dusters.

2. Show the dusters to the children. Let them feel the feathers. Talk to them about how they are used for cleaning.

3. Tell them that they are bushy like a squirrel's tail. Gently tickle the toddlers with the "tail."

4. Mix paint to the thickness of yogurt. If the feather dusters are different colors, mix paint to match the colors of the dusters.

5. Pour the paint into a flat container. Put one feather duster in each batch of paint.

6. Put a large sheet of butcher paper on the wall or on the fence. Tape in place. Place newspapers underneath if painting inside.

7. Place the paint with feather dusters under the paper.

8. Let the toddlers paint with the feather dusters. Encourage them to swish the duster back and forth, just like a squirrel's tail.

Teaching hints

This activity works best outside as the clean-up is easier.

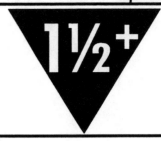

Squirrel-ly Fun

Toddlers get exercise and develop creative movement abilities as they imitate squirrels playing outside.

To do

1. Take a walk outside near some trees to look for squirrels.

2. Have the toddlers feel the bark of the tree. Talk with them about the texture and how the squirrels climb the trees with their sharp claws. Look up in the tree to see if there are any squirrels hiding.

3. Pretend to be squirrels by doing the following actions:
   crawl around on the ground
   pretend to crawl up the tree
   stand up on knees with front paws held in front
   jump while squatting
   curl up on the ground to go to sleep

4. Sit under the tree and have a squirrel-type snack. Show them how the squirrels eat by holding their food in both hands ("paws") and nibbling it with their front teeth. Give each toddler a cracker to eat like a squirrel.

5. Have a few shelled sunflower seeds for the toddlers to taste like the nuts and acorns that squirrels like to eat.

6. Leave some seeds or a cracker out near the tree for the squirrels to find later.

To do again

Read or look at pictures of squirrels in *Squirrels* by Brian Wildsmith.

Skills encouraged

creative movement
gross motor

Language to use with toddlers

squirrel
pretend
move
crawl
scamper
tree
bark
rough
tail
curl up
eat
nibble
cracker
sharp claws
paws
front teeth

Materials

crackers
shelled sunflower seeds

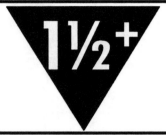

Pocket Day

Toddlers enjoy collecting and hiding small treasures in their pockets. Plan a day to celebrate the fun of pockets.

Skills encouraged

fine motor
sensory exploration

Language to use with toddlers

pocket
clothes
pants
coat
inside
treasures
save

Materials

small objects
small pieces of paper
crayons or markers

To do

1. Over a series of days, emphasize the different types and locations of pockets by pointing out the ones on the toddlers' clothing and on your clothing. Emphasize to the children that pockets can keep their hands warm on cold days or can be used to hold special items.

2. Plan a special pocket day. Send a note home asking parents to dress their child in an outfit with a pocket on "Pocket Day."

3. Talk about each child's pocket. Emphasize the size, location, design, etc. of the pockets.

4. Have each child put her hand in her pocket. Sing the following song to the tune of "If You're Happy and You Know It" with the children.

   Put your hand in your pocket, in your pocket,
   Put your hand in your pocket, in your pocket.
   Put your hand in your pocket, deep down inside it,
   To see what it can hide.

5. Allow the toddlers to hide small objects from the room in their pockets. Show surprise when you find something inside their pockets.

6. Provide small pieces of paper and crayons or markers for the toddlers to draw on. Encourage them to fold up the paper and put it in their pocket to take home.

To do again

Have pita bread with peanut butter, tuna fish or another filling for snack or lunch. Talk about how the bread is like a pocket.

Pocket Treasures

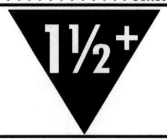

Fall is an ideal season to introduce toddlers to using pockets for for hiding special treasures.

To do

1. Wear an article of clothing with a large pocket or pockets.

2. Find a small stuffed animal or doll that will fit inside the pocket.

3. Place the doll or animal in your pocket to use with the following nursery rhyme variation.

   Stacey, Stacey (your name), our teacher,
   Had a tiny doll and couldn't keep her.
   She put her in her pocket for sure,
   And there she kept her quite secure!

4. Let the toddlers bring you other special items from around the room or nature items from the playground to put in your pocket. Change the words of the chant to refer to the item.

5. With older toddlers, have a basket of "special treasures" such as small toys or rocks that pass the choke test. Allow the toddlers to "hide" one of the treasures inside their pocket.

6. Say the previous rhyme substituting the child's name. Or sing about what is in their pocket to the tune of "Are You Sleeping?"

   Who has a little rock, who has a little rock,
   In their pocket, in their pocket?
   Beth has one, so does Roby,
   In their pockets, in their pockets.

To do again

Take a walk to collect some nature treasures in everyone's pockets. If hands get chilly, suggest the children warm them up by putting them in their pockets too!

Skills encouraged

language
fine motor

Language to use with toddlers

pocket
inside
happy
live
safe

Materials

clothing with a pocket
small stuffed animal

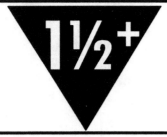

Pocket Patterns

A simple matching game can be made with pocket and handkerchief-shaped pieces.

Skills encouraged

fine motor
matching

Language to use with toddlers

pocket
handkerchief
match
same
inside

Materials

posterboard
fabric, gift wrap or
  wallpaper samples
scissors
glue
clear contact paper
utility blade
double-faced tape
envelope or resealable
  plastic bag

To do

1. Gather two to four different scraps of fabric, gift wrap or wallpaper samples. Make sure each is a distinctly different pattern or color.

2. Cut out a pocket shape from the fabric, gift wrap or wallpaper.

3. Glue the "pockets" on a large sheet of posterboard. Leave the top seams open.

4. Cut rectangles out of the same material to be the matching "handkerchiefs." Be sure that they will fit inside the pockets.

5. Glue the handkerchief pieces to posterboard of the same size to make them more sturdy.

6. Laminate or cover the pockets and handkerchiefs with clear contact paper. Be sure to open the top seam of the pockets with a utility blade.

7. Using double-faced tape, attach an envelope or resealable storage bag to the back side of the game to store the handkerchief pieces.

8. Encourage the toddlers to match the handkerchiefs and pockets by putting the hanky inside the pocket of the same pattern.

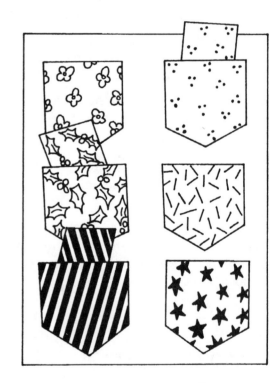

Teaching hints

Vary the game according to the ability of the children. Some may find matching two patterns very challeng-ing while other children will enjoy matching more.

Pocket Dance

2⁺

Dancing with their hands in their pockets encourages toddlers to isolate the movements of the legs and upper body.

To do

1. Put on your favorite music with a definite rhythm for dancing.

2. Have the toddlers put their hands in their pockets. If some do not have pockets, have them put their hands on their hips where "pockets are usually found on pants" or provide aprons with pockets.

3. Tell the children to try to remember to leave their hands in their pockets while dancing with you.

4. Move your upper body side to side, shake your head, bend your knees, tap your toe, etc. to the beat of the music.

Teaching hints

Some toddlers **and** teachers will find it difficult to leave their hands in their pockets as they are so used to involving hand or arm movements or clapping actions with music.

Skills encouraged

gross motor

Language to use with toddlers

pocket
leave
remember
dance
move
legs
upper body
torso
hips

Color Collections

Toddlers enjoy exploring everyday household items—often more than expensive toys. A collection of everyday objects of the same color provides a simple way to examine colors and shades with the toddlers.

Skills encouraged

language
sensory exploration

Language to use with toddlers

color names
lighter
darker
touch
see
find

Materials

basket
variety of toddler-safe
  items in the same color

To do

1. In a basket, collect an assortment of everyday household objects that are the same color such as a plastic cup, plastic container, bowl, washcloth, socks, scarf, toy, etc. Collect anything that is the desired color and large enough to pass the choke test.

2. Let the toddlers explore the objects. Emphasize the color of the item as you name it for the child. Discuss the features and use of the object. Let the child pretend to use the item if suitable.

3. While exploring the objects with the children, sing the following variations to the tune of "Are You Sleeping?"

   Look at this sponge, look at this sponge.
   It is orange, very orange.
   Orange like a pumpkin, orange just like orange juice,
   What else is orange, what else is orange?

   Repeat verse with the other objects.

4. With older toddlers, have the children help you find objects of a certain color from around the room. Turn the search into a game. Show excitement as the toddlers discover toys and objects of the focus color.

Teaching hints

Good colors for fall are red, yellow, orange or brown.

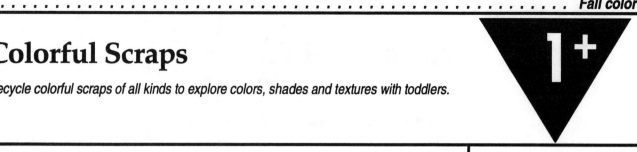

Colorful Scraps

Recycle colorful scraps of all kinds to explore colors, shades and textures with toddlers.

To do

1. Collect fabric scraps, ribbons, bows, yarn, strips or scraps of tissue and construction paper, etc. in the focus color.

2. Place the scraps in a dish tub, large box or sensory tub for the toddlers to explore.

3. Add plastic containers and/or small boxes with lids for the toddlers to stuff the colored scraps into.

4. Encourage the toddlers to leave the scraps in the tub or box.

5. Talk with the children about the textures and different shades of the focus color.

To do again

Provide just paper scraps for toddlers to tear. Allow older toddlers to use blunt scissors with the scraps to practice their cutting skills.

Teaching hints

Avoid using streamers with younger and/or highly oral toddlers since the dye will easily come off if the children put the streamers in their mouth.

Skills encouraged

sensory exploration
fine motor

Language to use with toddlers

color
shade
see
feel
fabric
ribbon
yarn
bows
paper
squish
cut
scissors
tear

Materials

dish tub, box or sensory
 table
fabric scraps
ribbons
bows
paper scraps
yarn
cups
plastic containers
small boxes

A Colorful Picture Says a Thousand Words

Explore color using stickers and pictures from magazines.

Skills encouraged

language
fine motor

Language to use with toddlers

picture
color names
names of objects
look at
book
file

Materials

magazines
stickers
construction paper
posterboard
glue
contact paper
shoe box or basket
hole punch
yarn or metal rings

To do

1. Collect a variety of magazine pictures and stickers that emphasize the focus color.

2. Make a Color Book with some of the pictures and stickers (see Toddler Books, page 48). Place the book in the classroom snuggly area where the toddlers may look through it.

3. Mount some of the larger pictures on single sheets of construction paper. Laminate or cover with clear contact paper.

4. Put some of the laminated pictures on the wall for the toddlers to look at.

5. Place some of the laminated pictures in a shoe box or basket for the toddlers to enjoy in the snuggly area.

6. Gather a small group of toddlers around you and talk about the pictures in the basket.

7. With older toddlers, give each child a different picture. Sing variations of the following verse to the tune of "Are You Sleeping?"

   Who has the blue tractor? Who has the blue tractor?
   Michael has. Michael has.
   Show us the blue tractor. Hold it up high, please.
   It is blue. Yes, it is blue. (Have the child hold up his picture)

To do again

Let the toddlers make a color collage with some of the smaller magazine pictures (see Magazine Collages, page 49). Use the individual collages or a group color mural to decorate the room.

Teaching hints

Catalogues, coupons and Sunday newspaper advertisements are another good source of pictures. Save pictures as some colors are harder to find in pictures than others. If you have a supply handy, then you are already a few steps ahead when you need the pictures.

For Toddlers in Winter: December, January and February

The arrival of cold temperatures and long nights in winter is a perfect time to explore ways to keep warm and healthy with the following themes:

◆ *Cooking Warm Foods*

◆ *Scarves and Mittens*

◆ *Shoes and Socks*

◆ *Stripes, Patterns and Warm clothing*

◆ *Stars and Nighttime*

◆ *Pets and Pet Care*

◆ *Winter Colors of White, Black, Blue and Purple*

Hot Cross Buns

Winter is a time for hot foods. Variations on a traditional nursery rhyme introduce toddlers to different types of nutritious foods that they can eat in cold weather.

Skills encouraged

language

Language to use with toddlers

song
hot food
warm
grow strong
nutritious
winter
buns
penny
one
two
foods

Materials

pictures or flannel board
  pieces of different baked
  goods and foods that are
  eaten warm

To do

1. Show the toddlers pictures of different warm foods such as oatmeal, biscuits, soups, spaghetti, etc. Talk with them about how eating warm foods can help keep them warm in cold weather. Emphasize how nutritious meals will help them grow strong and healthy.

2. Sing the traditional rhyme, "Hot Cross Buns" with the toddlers. Clap to the rhythm.

   > *Hot cross buns, hot cross buns,*
   > *One a penny, two a penny,*
   > *Hot cross buns.*

3. Substitute other warm foods that the toddlers eat. Have older toddlers tell you what to sing about in the verse.

   > *Hot spaghetti, hot spaghetti,*
   > *One a penny, two a penny,*
   > *Hot spaghetti!*

4. Use pictures or flannel boardpieces of different warm foods and baked goods with the verse.

To do again

Cook or bake warm foods such as rolls, soup or spaghetti and allow the children to watch, or help as much as possible. Eat them warm for snack or lunch. Children are often more interested in trying new foods when they have helped with the preparation.

Teaching hints

Use this song with the children at snack or lunch time in relation to the foods they are eating.

Using Common Scents

Toddlers explore the common scents associated with cooking and baking as they smell extracts and spices made into simple "smelling containers."

To do

1. Collect liquid extracts, such as lemon, vanilla and peppermint. Gather spices such as cinnamon, garlic, ground cloves. Remember the pungent scents of coffee and vinegar too!

2. Thoroughly saturate three to five cotton balls with each one of the liquid scents. Liberally sprinkle the powder spices over the cotton balls.

3. Put each cotton ball inside a small plastic container and cover with the lid.

4. Carefully make four or five small holes in the plastic lid with a sharp metal object such as an ice pick.

5. Label the outside of the container with the name of each scent.

6. Repeat the above steps to make other "smelling containers."

7. Encourage the toddlers to smell the spices and extracts. Identify the scent for the child and what type of food it is used to make. For example, "Mmmm cinnamon, Daddy uses that when he fixes your toast." or "Oooh. The vinegar smells strong. My grandma used it when she made pickles."

8. Replace the cotton balls as needed to freshen the scent.

9. For snack or lunch, taste a food made with one of the scents and smell the spice used.

To do again

Make other smelling containers with everyday scents, such as coffee, perfume, aftershave, mouthwash, etc. Talk to the children about their uses.

Teaching hints

For a toddler having a difficult time adjusting to being away from mom or dad, have one of the parents make one of the smelling containers with their usual perfume or aftershave. When the child is upset, have him smell the container. Let the child smell it during the day. Talk to him about it smelling just like the cologne his parent usually wears.

Skills encouraged

sensory exploration

Language to use with toddlers

smell
nose
vinegar
lemon
vanilla
peppermint
coffee
cinnamon
garlic
scent
spice
baking

Materials

small plastic containers with lids, such as film canisters
various spices, extracts and other scents
cotton balls
ice-pick type object (for teacher only)
masking tape
marker

Mmmmm!!

Young toddlers enjoy carrying around small objects, such as spice canisters. The containers also provide a sensory experience from the lingering aroma and a fine motor challenge with the pop up section of the lids.

Skills encouraged

fine motor
sensory exploration
dramatic play

Language to use with toddlers

spice
container
top
lift
open
close
smell
nose
MMM!
delicious
cinnamon
allspice
seasoning
cooking
baking

Materials

empty spice containers

To do

1. Collect metal and plastic spice containers. Ask parents to send in their empty containers. The metal spice containers work best since the lid does not come off. With most spices, the aroma will stay in the container even after it has been washed.

2. Show the toddlers how to open the tops and smell the spice. "Mmmm!" Name the spice and its use for the toddlers as they smell the scent.

3. Encourage the children to use the pretend spices in their baking and cooking play. Show them how to shake the spice over the pan or dish.

More Than Just Juice Can Lids!

Recycle the metal lids from pull-top frozen juice cans into a multitude of new uses for toddlers' explorations.

To do

1. Collect the lids from juice cans opened with a pull tab. The ends of the metal lid will already be smooth. You can send a note home asking parents to help collect them.

2. Let the toddlers add stickers to the lids for decoration if desired.

3. Have the lids in a basket or box for the younger toddlers to just freely explore. See what they do with the lids on their own.

4. Place a few lids in a plastic container or can with a plastic lid, such as a margarine tub or coffee can. Encourage the young toddlers to make music with the lids by shaking the container.

5. Play dump and fill with the toddlers. Encourage them to fill the containers with the lids and then dump them out again.

6. Cut a slit in the plastic top of a container such as a diaper wipe box or shoe box. Drop the lids one by one into the opening. This is a good exercise to develop eye-hand coordination and to introduce shape sorter toys.

7. Encourage older toddlers to use the lids in their imaginative play, such as for "money" in their purses or as "food" to feed the stuffed animals.

To do again

With older toddlers, make a simple matching game with the lids and stickers. Use two to four different designs of stickers. Attach them to the lids and show the children how to match the pairs. Vary the difficulty (i.e., the number of different pairs to be matched) according to the developmental level of individual children.

Teaching hints

The toddlers will often show you new and unusual uses for the lids. Just observe them in their play and follow their lead!

Skills encouraged

fine motor
sensory exploration
eye-hand coordination

Language to use with the children

metal lid
round
circle
stickers
drop inside
shake
feed
cookie
money

Materials

metal lids from cans
opened with a pull tab
stickers
shoe box
plastic container with a lid

Tip Top Actions

Opening and closing, squeezing and pumping the tops of plastic containers allows toddlers to practice their fine motor skills.

Skills encouraged

sensory exploration
fine motor
imaginative play

Language to use with toddlers

package
box top
top
open
close
empty
reuse
pull up
push down
pump

Materials

empty containers
basket

To do

1. Collect plastic containers with different types of tops, such as dish washing soap, syrup bottles, condiments, liquid soap, lotion, contact lens solutions, etc. Be sure all removable parts are large enough to pass the choke test.

2. Place the items in a basket. Encourage even the youngest toddlers to open and close the tops, squeeze the containers to feel the air, pump the spouts, etc. to promote their motor skills.

3. Add the containers to the home living area for the older toddlers to use in their imaginative play.

To do again

Add the plastic containers with tops to the water in a dish tub for older toddlers. Encourage the toddlers to fill the containers with water, replace the tops and then empty out the water by pumping, squeezing, etc. Make sure the tops pass the choke test.

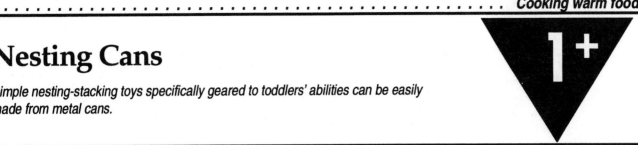

Nesting Cans

Simple nesting-stacking toys specifically geared to toddlers' abilities can be easily made from metal cans.

To do

1. Collect three to five different sizes of metal cans that will fit inside each other in a sequence.

2. Smooth the inside edge of the can with the back of a spoon. Then cover the edge with duct tape for extra precaution.

3. Cover each can with contact paper. The same or different designs can be used.

4. Place the nesting cans out for the toddlers to explore and fit back together. Talk to the children about the different sizes.

To do again

Provide measuring spoons and graduated plastic measuring scoops or cups for the toddlers to nest. Even nesting plastic or metal mixing bowls can be fun.

Teaching hints

Nesting toys often have too many pieces for young children. This can be overwhelming for most children under three. The children dump the items and leave the pieces out of frustration. The teacher is the one who ends up putting the toys back together! Use nesting toys with just two to five items for the toddlers to fit together, depending on the abilities of the child. While it is important to provide a challenge, toddlers need to achieve success on their own.

Skills encouraged

sequencing
fine motor

Language to use with toddlers

cans
put inside
stack
big
medium
small

Materials

different sizes of cans
spoon
duct tape
contact paper

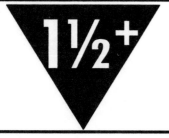

Keeping Warm and Healthy

Study basic health and nutrition with toddlers as they pretend to buy and then cook nutritious, warm foods for their friends in the cold winter months.

Skills encouraged

imaginative play

Language to use with toddlers

groceries
grocery store
food
buy
cart
sack
money
purse
wallet
nutritious
warm
cook
wholesome
names of foods

Materials

empty food containers
plastic vegetables and
fruits
empty bread bags
empty frozen vegetable
  packages
paper
tape
paper sacks
child-size grocery cart
plastic baskets
green paper
wallets
purses

To do

1. Collect a variety of empty food containers from nutritious foods. Parents can be a viable source of these, if needed. Since it is winter, place an emphasis on warm foods, such as soups, oatmeal, noodle dinners, etc.

2. Fill empty bread bags with crumpled paper to make "loaves of bread." Do the same with packages of frozen vegetables. Don't forget to include "fresh" vegetables and fruits, as these are an important part of eating well all year round.

3. Put the groceries out on a shelf with paper sacks for the toddlers to go shopping.

4. Provide child-size grocery carts, too, if possible. Baskets can also be used.

5. Older toddlers may enjoy purses, wallets and green paper cut into the size of money to pretend to buy their items.

6. Talk to the toddlers about the food items they are putting in their bags. Emphasize the nutritional quality of the food and how it helps them grow strong and healthy.

7. Encourage the children to take the items "home" to cook a hot meal for their friends.

To do again

Use magazine pictures of nutritious foods to make a collage or "hot meal book" (see Toddler Books, page 48 or Magazine Collage, page 49). Use the pictures to discuss nutrition with the toddlers and what foods they like to eat.

Teaching hints

With any food related activity, it is best to avoid junk food and emphasize nutritious foods, so that early on children begin to understand how to eat food that is good for them.

Toddlers' House of Pancakes

A warm breakfast is a good start to any day so provide props for toddlers to pretend to make breakfast for their friends on a cold winter morning.

To do

1. Cut circles out of yellow felt the size of small pancakes.

2. Collect the cooking utensils. Make a pretend stove top out of a cardboard box if needed.

3. Add the supplies for making "pancakes" to the home living area.

4. Pretend to make pancakes with the children. Talk about the supplies and the process of cooking. Emphasize how the pancakes are "round like a circle."

5. Have some "juice" or "milk" too with the warm pancakes. Enjoy the "warm breakfast for a cold morning."

6. Have warm pancakes for snack one day!

To do again

Color on yellow construction paper circles, just like the shape of pancakes.

Teaching hints

Pretend cooking with toddlers offers an excellent opportunity to emphasize being cautious around a hot stove and pans.

Skills encouraged

social skills
imaginative play

Language to use with toddlers

warm pancakes
round like a circle
cook
mix
stir
spatula
pan
syrup
delicious
breakfast

Materials

yellow felt
scissors
cardboard box
markers
metal or plastic bowl
wire whisk
pot holders
empty box of pancake mix
empty syrup container
empty juice and milk
  containers
frying pan
spatula
plastic plates
cups

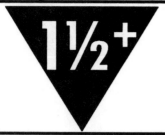

Flour Power

The fine, soft texture of flour makes for a unique sensory experience for toddlers to explore with sifters and cups.

Skills encouraged

sensory exploration
fine motor

Language to use with toddlers

flour
baking
white
fill
pour
sift
scoop
stir
corn meal

Materials

flour
sifters
scoops
plastic measuring cups
dish tub

To do

1. Place flour in a dish or sensory tub. Torn packages of flour, which cannot be sold, can be obtained from grocery stores for free.

2. Put newspapers under the tub for easier clean up.

3. Place plastic containers, measuring cups and scoops in the tub for the toddlers to use with the flour.

4. Strainers and sifters can be added as a fine motor challenge for older toddlers.

5. Encourage the toddlers explore the flour. Show them how to fill and empty the containers, stir the flour, how to use the sifters, etc.

6. Talk about nutritious foods made with flour, such as pancakes and bread.

To do again

Use corn meal in place of the flour.

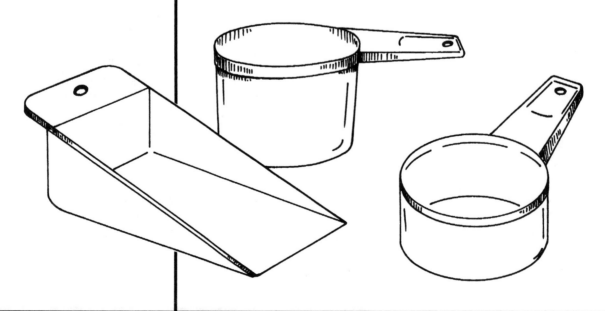

Gadget Designs

1½⁺

Toddlers can paint with a variety of kitchen utensils and gadgets to make unique designs on paper.

To do

1. Collect a variety of kitchen utensils and gadgets that can be used for printing with paint, such as spatulas, wire whisks, mallets, potato masher, forks, etc.

2. Show the utensils to the toddlers and demonstrate how they are used.

3. Let the toddlers explore the different items.

4. Mix a few different colors of paint fairly thickly. Pour the paint into flat containers and add one or two of the gadgets to each color.

5. Have the toddler pick out the color of paper he wants to use for printing.

6. Encourage the child to print with the gadgets. As he works, quietly chant:

   Printing, printing,
   Bobby is printing with the spatula.

To do again

Use the gadgets and utensils with playdough.

Teaching hints

Limit choices for the younger toddlers while older toddlers will benefit from greater variety.

Skills encouraged

fine motor
creative expression

Language to use with toddlers

utensils
gadgets
designs
patterns
prints
spatula
wire whisk
potato masher
kitchen
paint
paper

Materials

kitchen utensils and
  gadgets
paint
paper
flat containers

2⁺

Magic Batter

Cornstarch mixed with water provides a magical sensory experience for toddlers.

Skills encouraged

sensory exploration
fine motor

Language to use with toddlers

hands
feel
squish
squeeze
color
drips
thickens
wash

Materials

dish tub
cornstarch
water
food coloring, optional

To do

1. Pour the box of cornstarch into the dish tub. While stirring, add water in small amounts to the starch until it has the thickness of batter.

2. Add food coloring if desired and continue to stir.

3. Put on smocks and have one or two of the older toddlers explore the mixture with their hands.

4. Talk with the children about how the batter thickens when they squeeze it in their fist but starts dripping when they open their hand.

5. Wash hands afterwards.

Teaching hints

The cornstarch can be messy, but the magical quality of the thickening and then dripping fascinates the children. This magic dough can also be very relaxing for the teacher on a challenging day!

Feeling the Temp

Playing with warm and cool playdough allows toddlers to explore temperatures—hands on.

To do

1. Make a large batch of playdough with the children and put half of it in the refrigerator (see Pinch, Poke, Pull and Press, page 63).

2. Rub a small amount of oil in each toddler's hand.

3. Give each child a small amount of warm, freshly-made playdough. Talk to the children about the temperature and how it feels warm like food fresh from the oven or stove. Emphasize how people eat hot foods in winter to help them keep warm.

4. Next, give each child a handful of the playdough that has been stored in the refrigerator for about an hour. Compare the warm and cold temperatures. Emphasize that the coolness feels like the temperature outside in winter or foods in the refrigerator.

5. Let the toddlers play with the warm and cool playdough on their own as both change to room temperature.

Skills encouraged

fine motor
sensory exploration

Language to use with toddlers

ingredients
mix
cook
temperature
warm
cool
knead
hands
oil
feel

Materials

playdough ingredients
oil

Bundle Up!

While understanding the concept of seasonal changes is too abstract for toddlers, they do relate to the daily experience of dressing in warm clothing in the winter months. Use hats, mittens and heavy clothing to explore keeping warm in cold weather with toddlers.

Skills emphasized

sensory exploration
imaginative play

Language to use with toddlers

hat
scarf
mitten
gloves
boots
ear muffs
knitted
wool
warm
outside
cold

Materials

a variety of winter outer-
  wear
mirror
old camera

To do

1. Put out a variety of winter hats, scarves, mittens and gloves for the toddlers to try on. Ear muffs and winter boots are also fun for older toddlers.

2. Encourage the toddlers to look at themselves in the mirror. Pretend to take their picture with an old camera.

3. Talk with the children about the different articles of winter clothing, noting their colors and textures.

4. Look at pictures of people dressed up in winter clothing.

To do again

Have a "Warm Hat Day" and have each child wear a winter hat from home. Read *Old Hat, New Hat* by Stan and Jan Berenstain.

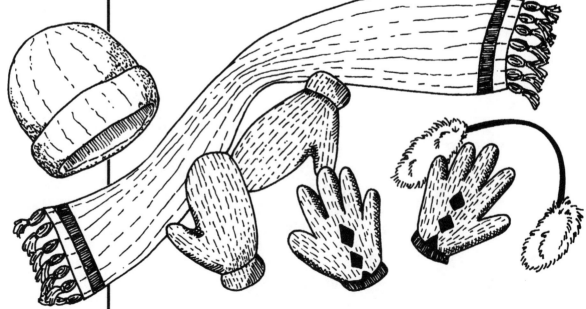

Sensations With Scarves

A wide variety of scarves can be explored in a number of playful ways.

To do

1. Collect a variety of old scarves, shawls and bandannas. Try to include some thinner, see-through ones as well as thick knitted scarves. Place in a basket.

2. Let the toddlers explore the scarves. Observe what they do on their own with the scarves.

3. Talk with the children about how scarves are used to keep peoples' heads warm like hats, to keep hair from getting blown in the wind, or for decoration and warmth around someone's neck.

4. Encourage the toddlers to explore the scarves in some of the following ways:

   Feel the scarf. Rub it against your cheek.

   What colors and designs are on the scarf? Which one matches your shirt?

   Look through the scarves. Which ones can you see through?

   What happens when you look through the scarf?

5. Dance or move around using the scarves. Wave the scarves in the air. Twirl the scarves in a circle. Wave the scarves up and down. Throw the scarf up and let it float down to the ground.

6. Play peek-a-boo with the scarf. With very young children, hide a favorite toy under the scarf.

7. Add the basket of scarves to the home living area for the children to use for dress-up or as blankets.

To do again

The older toddler may enjoy sorting the scarves by color into different piles or containers.

Skills emphasized

sensory exploration
gross motor

Language to use with toddlers

scarves
bandanna
shawls
knitted
thick
thin
yarn
wool
colors
head
warm
wind
feel
dance

Materials

scarves
bandannas
shawls
basket

They Found Their Mittens

Spend time in winter talking about keeping hands warm by exploring the textures and colors of mittens and gloves along with a familiar nursery rhyme.

Skills encouraged

language
creative movement

Language to use with toddlers

mittens
gloves
hand
thumb
fingers
warm
fuzzy
thick
kittens
three
rhyme

Materials

pairs of mittens and gloves

To do

1. Have a variety of adult-size mittens and gloves for the toddlers to feel and try on. Children's mittens and gloves can be used but they tend to be harder for the children to put on by themselves. Offer the smaller mittens and gloves as a challenge for older toddlers.

2. Talk to the older toddlers about the difference between the mittens (with a thumb place) and gloves ("places for all the fingers"). Emphasize the colors and textures of the gloves and mittens, as well as the warmth they provide.

3. As the children try on the mittens and gloves, chant the nursery rhyme "The Three Little Kittens." Encourage the children to clap the rhythm of the rhyme with the mittens on their hands.

4. With older toddlers, say the rhyme with three "mittened" children at a time. Count the three children before saying the rhyme and emphasize the word "three" each time it comes up in the verses.

5. Act out some of the verses in the following ways:

> *The three little kittens they lost their mittens,*
> *   (hide hands with mittens on behind back)*
> *And they began to cry, (sad look on face)*
> *"Oh Mother dear, we sadly fear our mittens we have lost."*
> *The three little kittens they found their mittens,*
> *   (hold up hands with mittens on and clap)*
> *And they began to sigh,*
> *"Oh mother dear, look here look here our mittens we have found."*

Act out other verses:

> *The three little kittens they soiled their mittens...*
> *   (look at mittens on hands in surprise)*
> *The three little kittens they washed their mittens...*
> *   (rub hands together to "wash" mittens)*

Teaching hints

This can be a long nursery rhyme for some toddlers, so say only as many verses as hold the children's attention.

To do again

Read a book version of this popular rhyme, such as the one by Paul Galdone

What a Pair!

Sorting mittens and socks into pairs makes for a simple matching activity for older toddlers.

To do

1. Have the child match two to four pairs of mittens by color or pattern.

2. Or let the child match pairs of mittens by size, such as adult, child and infant.

3. For a different activity, provide mittens and gloves for her to sort. Emphasize the difference between mittens ("whole hand with only a thumb place) and gloves ("places for each of the fingers").

4. Make a mitten matching game for older toddlers. Cut out a left and a right mitten shape from two to four different patterns of gift wrap, wallpaper or colored construction paper. Laminate the paper mittens or cover with clear contact paper. Store the mittens in a small shoe box. Add clothespins with which the toddler can clip the pairs together, if desired.

To do again

Do the same matching activities with pairs of socks.

Teaching hints

The toddlers may prefer to try on the mittens and gloves, so allow them to sort by putting the pairs on their hands and then finding a pair for you to wear. Vary the number of pairs according to the ability of the individual child. Most older toddlers will be able to easily match three different pairs.

Skills encouraged

visual discrimination

Language to use with toddlers

mitten
glove
same
different
pattern
color
match

Materials

pairs of mittens and gloves
pairs of socks
gift wrap, wallpaper or
  construction paper
scissors
clear contact paper
small shoe box
clothespins

Diddle Dumpling

The "Diddle, Diddle, Dumpling, My Son John" rhyme can be used when putting on toddlers' shoes to emphasize the concept of on and off.

Skills encouraged

language

Language to use with toddlers

son
daughter
bed
trousers
on
off
shoe
rhyme

To do

1. Say the following nursery rhyme with the toddlers during play or while putting on their shoes.

> *Diddle, diddle, dumpling,*
> *My son John,*
> *Went to bed with his trousers on!*
> *One shoe off and one shoe on,*
> *Diddle, diddle, dumpling,*
> *My son John.*

2. Substitute the children's names and what they are wearing.

> *Diddle, diddle, dumpling,*
> *My daughter Jane,/Big girl Jane*
> *Went to bed with her overalls on!*
> *One sneaker off and one sneaker on,*
> *Diddle, diddle, dumpling,*
> *My daughter Jane/ Big girl Jane.*

Teaching hints

With the advent of velcro, even toddlers have become proficient at taking off their shoes. Use the rhyme in a playful way to remind the toddlers to keep their shoes on when they are not in bed! Emphasize the importance of wearing shoes to keep their feet safe and warm.

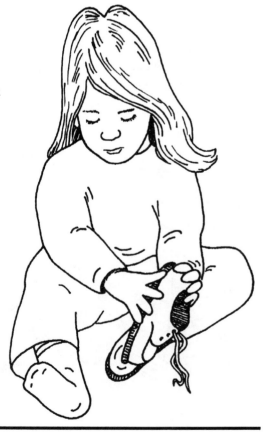

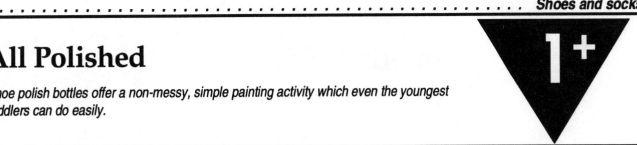

All Polished

Shoe polish bottles offer a non-messy, simple painting activity which even the youngest toddlers can do easily.

To do

1. Obtain empty shoe polish bottles with square sponge applicators.

2. Mix paint to the thickness of yogurt. (Thin paint will spill everywhere.) Pour into the empty shoe polish bottles.

3. Let the toddler choose what color of paper she wants to use.

4. Encourage the toddler to print on the paper with the shoe polish bottles.

5. Talk about the colors of the paint and the shapes made with the applicator tip.

To do again

With older toddlers, fill the shoe polish bottles with water. Let them pretend to polish an old pair of shoes with the water and a rag.

Teaching hints

Painting with the shoe polish bottles is an activity that can be done at a moment's notice with very little preparation or cleanup, so always have some bottles on hand. The bottles also work well for gluing activities with toddlers; simply add a little water to the glue to make it thinner. Bingo blotters can also be used.

Skills encouraged

fine motor
creative expression

Language to use with toddlers

shoe polish
bottle
paint
paper
print
squares
design
colors
shoes

Materials

empty shoe polish bottles with sponge applicator (bingo blotters will also work)
paint
paper
shoes

Smelly Socks

Toddler-style sachets can be made from infant socks.

Skills encouraged

sensory exploration

Language to use with toddlers

socks
smell
scent
nose

Materials

infant socks
pillow stuffing or cotton
 balls
potpourri
spices
ribbon

To do

1. Gather an assortment of infant socks (mismatched ones are fine).

2. Sprinkle spice on a ball of pillow stuffing or about five cotton balls. Suggested spices include: cinnamon, ground cloves, allspice, cardamon, star anise. Potpourri can also be used.

3. Place the scented stuffing inside the sock.

4. Double knot the ribbon or yarn around the sock opening to close the "toddler sachet."

5. Encourage the toddlers to smell the scent. These make wonderful gifts to take home for special occasions.

Teaching hints

Keep a few sachets near the diaper changing area for wiggly toddlers to smell during diaper changes.

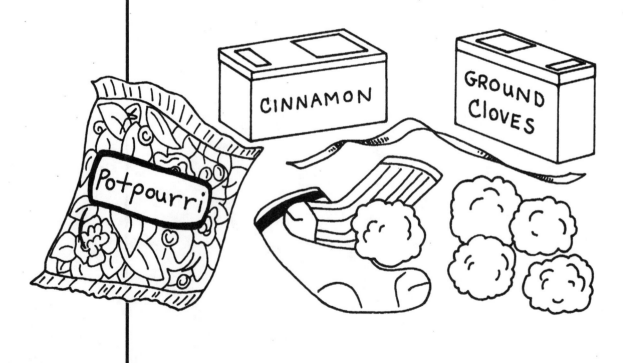

Sock It to Me!

Toddlers love playing with balls. Socks can be used to make soft balls for the toddlers to use indoors.

To do

1. Roll a pair of adult tube socks into a ball shape and turn it inside itself to hold the shape.

2. Toss the "sock ball" to a toddler. Encourage him to toss it back to you.

3. Make a ball out of a child's pair of tube socks. Compare the balls made from the adult and the child's size socks. Talk to the child about big and little, large and small.

4. Put out a bucket or basket for the toddlers to toss the sock balls into. Encourage the toddlers to stand back at a distance relative to their skill level.

To do again

Show the older toddlers how to roll up socks into a ball on their own. Provide three or so pairs of socks for the children to match into pairs and roll into balls or fold together.

Skills encouraged

gross motor

Language to use with toddlers

sock
ball
toss
catch
roll
up
down
big/large
little/small

Materials

adults' and children's tube
  socks
bucket or basket

Sizing Up!

While most classifying activities are too difficult for younger toddlers, they can practice their early sorting skills by matching shoes into pairs.

Skills encouraged

classification

Language to use with toddlers

shoes
pairs
small
large
feet
sizes
woman
man
baby
child
sandal
tennis shoes/sneakers
work boots
slippers

Materials

pairs of different kinds
  and sizes of shoes
shoe boxes

To do

1. Provide two to three different pairs of shoes of distinct sizes, such as baby, child and adult shoes for the toddlers to match into pairs.

2. Have the children put the pairs into shoe boxes.

3. Talk to the toddlers about the types of shoes, their sizes and who they would fit. Emphasize the importance of wearing shoes to protect their feet and keep them warm.

4. Let the toddlers match shoes into pairs according to type such as sandals, tennis shoes, boots, etc. Talk to the children about the purpose and special features of the shoes, such as comfort, running, work, dressing up, etc.

To do again

For older toddlers who are stable on their feet, add a few shoes and slippers to the dress up area. Flat-heeled shoes are the safest for toddlers. Keep the shoes in shoe boxes and encourage the toddlers to put the pairs together.

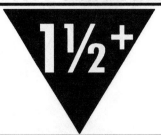

From the Bottom of My Sole!

Soles of shoes can be used for a fun and different painting activity.

To do

1. Gather two to three small shoes with designs on the soles. Beach sandals work well since they are easily washed.

2. Mix the paint to match the color of the shoe or soles, if desired.

3. Pour the paint into a flat container. Place one shoe in each dish of paint.

4. Let the toddler choose what color of paper she wants to use. Large sheets of paper work best.

5. Encourage the child to print with the shoes by "walking the shoes across the paper."

6. Talk to her about the colors, designs, etc. made by printing with the soles.

To do again

As a special activity, make feet prints with the children. Place a thin amount of paint in a flat container. Have the children walk in bare feet across a long sheet of butcher paper. Make an extra set of single footprints to send home to parents as keepsakes.

Skills encouraged

fine motor
creative expression

Language to use with toddlers

shoe
bottom
sole
pattern
design
print
paint
paper

Materials

old children's shoes
paint
paper
flat container

1½⁺

Sock Wash

Playing with water is a toddler favorite anytime during the year. Wash socks and mittens in winter to bring water play into the focus on warm clothing.

Skills encouraged

sensory exploration
fine motor

Language to use with toddlers

socks
dirty
clean
wash
water
bubbles
dry
scrub
squeeze

Materials

old socks
mittens or gloves
dish tub
dish soap
old bath towel or bath mat
scrub board, optional

To do

1. Add a small amount of mild dish soap to water in a dish tub or sensory table. Put an old bath towel or bath mat underneath to absorb any water that spills.

2. Give the toddlers socks to wash.

3. Encourage the children to squeeze, scrub and rub the socks together to get them clean. A small, old-fashioned scrub board is also fun to use.

4. Wash mittens on another day.

To do again

Let older toddlers wash socks and baby clothes outside in warmer weather.

Fabric Feel

The thicker fabrics of warm winter clothing offer an ideal time to explore the textures of different types of fabrics with toddlers.

To do

1. Collect a variety of swatches or scraps of thick fabrics like those used for winter clothing. Send a note home to parents to help obtain a wider variety.

2. Cut the fabric into squares the size of a scarf, if possible.

3. Place the fabrics into a basket for the children to explore on their own. Let the children use the fabrics for scarves or blankets to "keep the dolls warm."

4. Talk with the children about the colors, textures and types of fabric. Emphasize how the fabric is used to make clothing to keep us warm in the winter.

5. With older toddlers, include a sampling of thinner fabrics such as cottons, silks, etc. Show the children the difference between the thin and thicker fabrics.

To do again

Cut fabric samples into small strips and squares. Let the toddlers glue the fabric samples onto a piece of paper for a collage.

Skills encouraged

sensory exploration

Language to use with toddlers

feel
fabric
textures
color
thick
thin
wool
corduroy
flannel
warm
clothes

Materials

variety of fabrics
scissors
basket
paper
glue

Touch Boxes

Use old tissue boxes and fabric to make touch boxes for toddlers to explore textures.

Skills encouraged

sensory exploration

Language to use with toddlers

touch
feel
inside
fabric
smooth
furry
rough
bumpy

Materials

empty tissue boxes
glue
pieces of fabric
sandpaper
craft fur
shoe box
tape

To do

1. Collect empty tissue boxes. Rectangular ones with wide oval openings work best.

2. Cover the inside bottom with a fabric, such as corduroy, satin, velveteen, etc. Felt and craft fur also work well. Make one box for each different textured fabric.

3. Encourage the toddler to put his hand inside to feel the texture. Make comparisons for the toddler by saying such things as "smooth like satin on a night gown," "bumpy corduroy like pants," "furry like a teddy bear," etc.

4. Leave the boxes out for the children to feel on their own.

To do again

Place other textures inside the tissue boxes or on the outside of a box, such as sandpaper, bubble packing sheets, etc.

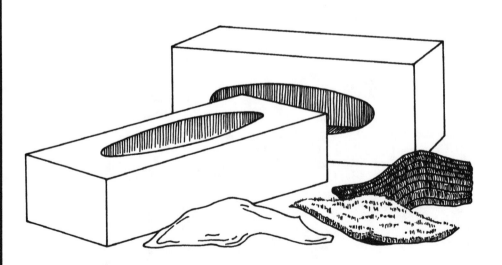

And Sew On

Recycle leftover rickrack and other sewing supplies to make "feely" boards so the toddlers can explore colors, patterns and textures.

To do

1. Make a variety of texture boards with leftover rickrack by:

   Gluing different colors of the same width of rickrack in rows across thick cardboard or posterboard to focus on colors.

   Gluing different widths and/or lengths of the same color of rickrack across the cardboard or posterboard to examine sizes.

   Gluing different pieces of rickrack into shapes, such as squares, stripes, crosses, etc. on a piece of cardboard to emphasize patterns.

2. Encourage the toddlers to feel the colors, textures, widths and shapes. Help the children identify the colors by relating them to an object, such as "red like an apple" or "blue like your shirt." Talk with the children about the thin/wide rickrack and the different shapes/patterns.

To do again

Attach a variety of craft and sewing items to a piece of cardboard, such as lace, fringe, hem tape. (Parents are often an excellent resource for leftover sewing items.) Talk with the toddlers about the different colors and textures.

Teaching hints

Encourage the children to just "rub the designs." If a child continually tries to pull up the rickrack or texture, place masking tape on the table for him to pull up as an alternative (see Pull It Up!, page 288).

Skills encouraged

sensory exploration

Language to use with toddlers

rickrack
design
zigzag
feel
colors
line
lace
fringe
ribbon
smooth
bumpy

Materials

rickrack
thick cardboard
posterboard
glue
various craft and sewing
  items

Strips and Stripes

While talking about the importance of wearing warm clothing in winter, spend time looking at the pattern of stripes in fabric.

Skills encouraged

sensory exploration
fine motor

Language to use with toddlers

strips
tape
paper
stripes
glue
design
pattern

Materials

colored tape
strips of paper, gift wrap
  and/or newspaper
edges of computer paper
wide ribbons
dish tub
small boxes and containers
tongs and tweezers
blunt scissors
paper
glue

To do

1. Show the toddlers warm clothing with stripes. See if anyone is wearing stripes. Look for other stripes around the room in pictures and on toys.

2. Cut scrap pieces of paper, gift wrap and/or newspaper into strips. A paper cutter works easily for this! The edges of computer paper are an excellent source of strips, too.

3. Place a variety of strips in a dish tub for the toddlers to explore. Add small boxes and containers for the children to put the strips into. Allow the toddlers to tear the strips into smaller pieces.

4. Providing tongs and tweezers to pick up the strips adds a challenge for the oldest toddlers. Provide blunt scissors, too, if desired.

5. Make collages with strips of paper of different widths. Talk to the children about the different colors and widths.

To do again

Let the children use masking and scotch tape to experiment with strips of tape. Put strips of colored tape on the table in plaid and striped patterns for the toddlers to explore. Let the children pull up the tape and then make their own patterns with the tape (see Pull It Up!, page 288). Designs with tape can also be made on long strips of construction paper.

Strips of M.I.M.s

Drawing on smaller pieces of paper encourages toddlers to use smaller hand movements to make their Most Important Marks (M.I.M.s).

To do

1. Cut long sheets of construction or manila paper into thirds to make strips of paper. Offer long and short strips of the paper for the toddlers to choose from.

2. Provide crayons and markers or pens and pencils for the toddlers to use to "draw" or "write."

3. Talk to the children about the colors being used. Point out any lines or zigzag patterns they may draw.

4. Display the strips of lines around the room.

To do again

Cut a long sheet of butcher paper into a strip for the entire class to make a picture together. Let each toddler color on the paper. Hang the class picture up in the room for all to enjoy.

Skills encouraged

fine motor
creative expression
pre-writing/emergen
  literacy

Language to use with toddlers

strip
lines
draw
write
color
marker
pencil
crayon
zigzag

Materials

manila or construction
  paper
scissors
markers
crayons
pencil

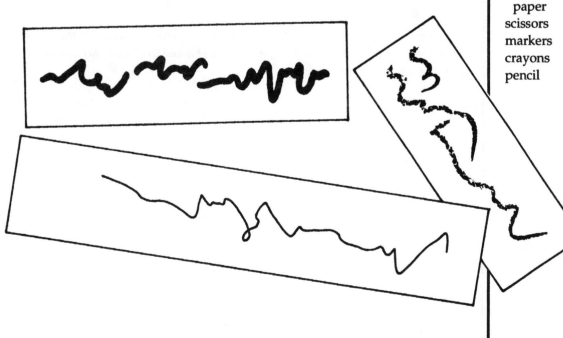

Block Patterns

Blocks can be used for printing different patterns and designs like those seen on clothing.

Skills encouraged

fine motor
eye-hand coordination
creative expression

Language to use with toddlers

blocks
print
paper
paint
design
rickrack
pattern
circles

Materials

wooden blocks
rickrack
glue
string
interlocking blocks
paint
flat containers
paper

To do

1. Obtain two or three wooden blocks in different colors.

2. Glue rickrack on the end of the block. Try to match the color of the rickrack to the color of the block.

3. Mix different colors of paint to match the colors of the blocks.

4. Pour the paints into flat containers. Stand one block with rickrack on the end in each corresponding color of paint.

5. Allow the toddler to choose the color of paper she wants to use for the activity.

6. Encourage the toddler to print with the blocks on the paper. Chant "paint-paper, paint-paper, look at that zigzag design," as she prints.

7. Talk with the toddler about the colors and designs she is making with the blocks.

To do again

Let the toddlers print patterns of circles with the tops of interlocking or bristle blocks. Match the paint to the color of the blocks.

Teaching hints

Expect that the toddlers will experiment with the blocks and paint rather than just printing with them. Have some blocks available that they can use for building when they are finished.

Pattern Day

Complete the unit on warm clothing and patterns with a day to celebrate stripes and plaids.

To do

1. Send home a note asking that the children wear striped or plaid clothing to school as the culmination of your clothing study. The teachers should wear stripes and plaids too!

2. During the children's play, say the following chant about the patterns on their clothing:

   > *Jeffrey is wearing stripes today,*
   > *Look at him and you will say,*
   > *Lots of, lots of, lots of stripes.*
   > *Jeffrey is wearing stripes today. (substitute other children's names)*

3. Put a collection of fabric pieces with striped and plaid patterns in a basket. Include pieces of corduroy, which have the stripes right in the fabric.

4. Let the toddlers explore the fabrics. Talk to them about the colors and patterns.

5. For a motor skills activity, put a "stripe" of tape on the floor that the toddler may walk along.

6. Have spaghetti or egg noodles that look like stripes for snack. Add butter and Parmesan cheese if desired.

Teaching hint

If there are children who do not wear plaids or stripes, let them wear one of the pieces of fabric as a scarf or ribbon.

Skills encouraged

sensory exploration
gross motor

Language to use with toddlers

stripes
lines
plaid
pattern
colors
fabric
clothing
wear

Materials

fabric pieces
basket
masking tape
spaghetti or egg noodles
bowls and spoons

1+

Hey Diddle Diddle

Nights are longer in winter, so focus a bit on nighttime fun with this familiar rhyme.

Skills encouraged

language

Language to use with toddlers

nursery rhyme
say
cat
fiddle
cow
moon
dog
laughed
dish
spoon

Materials

felt or construction paper
scissors
flannel board, optional

To do

1. Chant the following nursery rhyme with the toddlers:

   Hey diddle, diddle,
   The cat and the fiddle,
   The cow jumped over the moon.
   The little dog laughed to see such sport,
   And the dish ran away with the spoon.

2. Cut pictures of a cat, cow, moon, dog, dish and spoon out of felt or construction paper and hold them up or use them at the flannel board while saying the rhyme.

To do again

When the older toddlers are familiar with the rhyme, change the words to include the animal's sounds.

   Hey diddle, diddle,
   The "meow" and the fiddle. (pretend to fiddle)
   The "mooooo" jumped over the moon. (make arc motion with hand)
   The little "woof" laughed to see such sport, (pretend to laugh)
   And the dish ran away with the spoon. (make "running" sound by stamping feet)

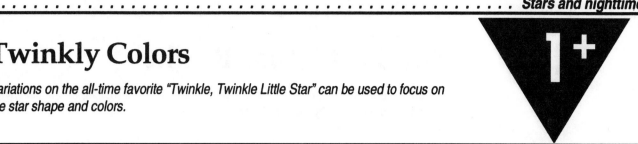

Twinkly Colors

Variations on the all-time favorite "Twinkle, Twinkle Little Star" can be used to focus on the star shape and colors.

To do

1. Sing the toddler favorite "Twinkle, Twinkle Little Star" with the children.

2. Encourage the children to hold their hands above their heads like "stars" in the sky while opening and closing their hands to the rhythm of the song.

3. Cut large star shapes out of construction paper. Laminate or cover with clear contact paper for durability if desired.

4. Give each child a star shape cut out of construction paper. Have them hold their stars up high while singing the song.

5. Use stars of all one color, e.g. blue, and change the words of the song to:

   > *Twinkle, twinkle blue stars,*
   > *How I wonder what you are?*
   > *Up above the world so high,*
   > *Lots of blue stars in the sky, etc.*

6. With older toddlers, give each child or small groups of children different color stars. Have each child or group stand up with their stars overhead as you sing the verse about their color star.

Skills encouraged

language
creative movement

Language to use with toddlers

song
star
sky
twinkle
colors
up high
sway
dark
night

Materials

construction paper
scissors
clear contact paper

Star Light, Star Bright

Introduce toddlers to colors and older toddlers to the notion of wishing for special things with a familiar nursery rhyme about stars.

Skills encouraged

language
color recognition

Language to use with toddlers

star
color
light
bright
wish
tonight
sky
rhyme

Materials

construction paper
scissors

To do

1. Pretend to look up at the stars in the sky and say the following nursery rhyme with the toddlers:

   > *Star light, star bright,*
   > *First star I see tonight.*
   > *I wish I may, I wish I might,*
   > *Have this wish I wish tonight.*

2. Cut stars out of different colors of construction paper.

3. Use two different colors of stars with the rhyme:

   > *Blue star, red star (hold up one star of each color)*
   > *First stars we see tonight.*
   > *We wish we may, we wish we might*
   > *Have this wish we wish tonight.*

4. Model making wishes for something special with older toddlers after saying the rhyme. For example, "I wish that it would stop raining so we can go outside to play," or, "I wish our friend Fay would get well so she can come back to play."

5. Substitute the children's names and encourage the older toddlers to make wishes after their names have been mentioned:

   > *Star light, star bright*
   > *First star I see tonight.*
   > *Fay wishes she may, Fay wishes she might*
   > *Have this wish she wishes tonight.*

Teaching hints

Use wishes to redirect toddlers' continual demands for something they cannot have. Acknowledge their desires by saying, "I know you want Mama. I wish she could be here, too!" or "I wish we could have more juice, but it is all gone."

Reaching for the Stars!

Toddlers use their large muscles as they stretch and jump to reach for the stars!

To do

1. Cut stars out of construction paper.

2. Using yarn, hang the stars from the ceiling at different lengths, all out of reach.

3. Encourage the toddlers to reach for the stars by stretching high on their tiptoes with hands up high. Participate with the toddlers. Using a dramatic voice, chant "Stretch, stretch, stretch up so high."

4. Have the toddlers jump to try to get one of the stars. Chant "Jump, jump, jump up to the sky."

5. Continue different stretching, reaching, jumping activities as the toddlers show interest.

6. To end the stretching and jumping, have the children lay down to look up at the stars. Sing the following to the tune of "Are You Sleeping?"

   > *See the stars, see the stars,*
   > *In the sky, so very high.*
   > *We tried hard to reach them,*
   > *But they're far away,*
   > *In the nighttime sky, in the nighttime sky.*

To do again

Sing other songs about nighttime, stars and/or the moon while lying under your indoor stars. Turn off the lights to pretend it is nighttime.

Skills encouraged

gross motor
creative movement

Language to use with toddlers

stars
sky
reach
stretch
tiptoe
almost
jump
arm
fingers

Materials

construction paper
scissors
yarn
tape

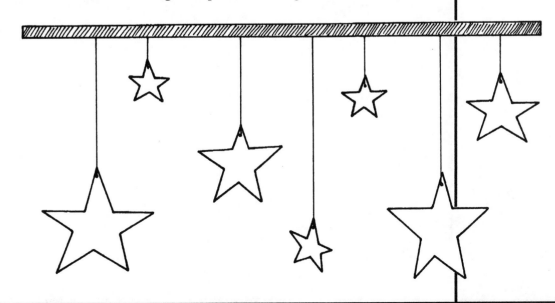

Star Search

Emphasize the star shape and colors with toddlers by playing a game with stars that have been hidden around the room.

Skills encouraged

language
color recognition

Language to use with toddlers

star
hidden
find
look
colors
Where is it?

Materials

construction paper
scissors
contact paper

To do

1. Cut large stars out of construction paper. If desired, cover with contact paper or laminate for durability.

2. Place stars of one color in conspicuous spots around the room before the children arrive.

3. During their play, encourage some of the toddlers to find the stars while singing the following to the tune of "Are You Sleeping?"

   Where are the blue stars, where are the blue stars?
   Can you find them, can you find them?
   They are hiding somewhere, in this room.
   When you see one, go and touch it.

4. Show excitement when the toddlers find the stars.

5. Look for stars of a different color on another day.

To do again

With older toddlers familiar with colors, place different colored stars around the room. Encourage the children to find stars of a specific color.

Teaching hints

Have enough stars hidden in order to have more than one star for each child who joins in the searching activity.

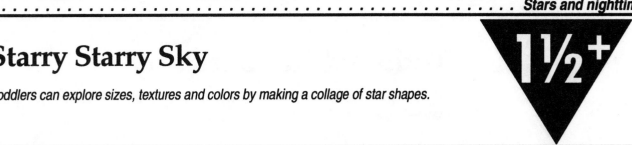

Starry Starry Sky

Toddlers can explore sizes, textures and colors by making a collage of star shapes.

To do

1. Cut out stars three to five inches in diameter from different colors of construction paper, gift wrap, wallpaper samples and/or foil. Provide big and little stars if desired.

2. Place the stars in an open container.

3. Let the child choose a dark color of paper for the background, such as blue or black. Also allow him to choose the number and types of stars he wants to glue on the paper.

4. Encourage the toddler to glue the stars on the paper.

5. Talk with him about the colors and the sizes of the star shapes. Sing "Twinkle, Twinkle Little Star" and say "Star Light, Star Bright."

6. Provide star stickers (available from office supply stores) for the child to add to the star collage on another day. Or, let him put only the star stickers on a piece of paper cut into a large star shape.

To do again

For another art activity related to stars, have the toddlers print with star-shaped cookie cutters and/or craft sponges cut into star shapes and dipped in yellow, blue or white paint.

Skills emphasized

fine motor
creative expression

Language to use with toddlers

stars
big
little
sky
night
colors
paper
glue
foil
stickers

Materials

construction paper
foil
gift wrap
wallpaper samples
star stickers
box or basket
glue
sponge
contact paper

2⁺

Toddler Slumber Party!

Simple props related to keeping warm at night added to the home living area promote toddlers' early social interactions.

Skills emphasized

social skills
imaginative play

Language to use with toddlers

nighttime
dark
sleep
comfortable
warm
blankets
slippers
pajamas
bed

Materials

old slippers
T-shirts
small blankets
books
old clock
quiet music
star and moon shapes

To do

1. Add some of the following to the home living area: slippers (adult size work best as they can easily be slipped over the children's shoes), large children's or small adults' T-shirts for pajamas, small blankets, books about bedtime, an old clock. Nap or exercise mats can be added for a pretend bed if desired.

2. Play quiet music in the background. Hang star and moon shapes from the ceiling or put them on the window.

3. Encourage the children to dress for bed and pretend to sleep. They can also cover each other, the teacher or dolls with the blankets. Emphasize how people keep warm at night with thick pajamas and blankets.

4. Read bedtime stories to the children or sing lullabies to them while they pretend to go to sleep. Be sure to include the all-time favorite, *Goodnight Moon*, by Margaret Wise Brown.

5. Emphasize the importance of rest and a good night's sleep for healthy bodies and growth.

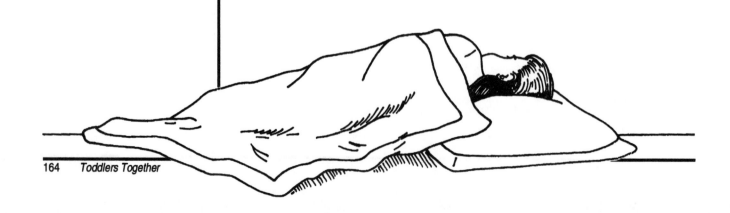

Pet Care

1½+

Pets require extra attention on cold winter nights so the winter months offer an ideal time to talk about pets and pet care with the toddlers.

To do

1. Set up a pet area in the room with various stuffed animals, such as dogs, cats, turtles, birds, etc. Be sure to have the toddlers help you name the pets.

2. Add some of the following for the children to use while they care for the animals: small animal carriers or small boxes for cages, small blankets, plastic bowls, empty pet food boxes, dog brush, collar/leash, small balls, plastic pet toys, "dog bones" cut from thick cardboard.

3. Encourage the toddlers to take care of the pets. Emphasize how to keep the animals warm on cold winter nights.

4. Look at pictures and read stories about pets with the children.

5. Have the children bring in pictures of their own pets to display in the pet area. Talk with the children about their animals and how they help care for them at home.

6. Play marching music and have a pet parade of stuffed animals.

To do again

Let the toddlers make a collage of magazine pictures of pets. Also use magazine pictures to also make a "Pet Book" (see Toddler Books, page 48).

Skills encouraged

imaginative play
social interaction

Language to use with toddlers

pets
care
feed
groom
dog
cat
bowl
bird
fish

Materials

stuffed animals
plastic bowls
pillows
small blankets
small boxes
dog brush
pet toys
empty animal food boxes
leash
animal carrier

Pet Supply Match

A simple color and size matching game for toddlers can be made with pet shapes and their related supplies.

Skills encouraged

language
matching skills

Language to use with toddlers

colors
sizes
big
medium
little
dog
dog bone
cat
ball
fish
food
bird
cage
same
match

Materials

felt
scissors
construction paper
clear contact paper
small box or large enve-
  lope

To do

1. Make any or all of the following matching games for the toddlers. If construction paper is used, laminate or cover with clear contact paper for durability.

   Cut out three to five different colored dogs from felt or construction paper. Cut out matching bones. Encourage the toddlers to feed each dog the same color of bone.

   Cut a big and little dog out of one color of construction paper or felt. Cut a big and little bone out of the same color. Have the toddlers feed the dogs the matching size of bone.

   Some toddlers may be ready to match dogs and bones of three different sizes.

2. Store the pieces in a small box or large envelope.

3. Make similar matching games of colors and sizes with any or all of the following: cats and balls of yarn, fish and box of food, bird and cage.

4. Talk with the children about the specific types of pets and their care, as well as the colors and sizes.

Teaching hints

Make the games according to the skill level of individual children. Some toddlers may need just two sizes or colors to match, while others may be able to match five colors with little difficulty.

Who Is in the Dog House?

1½⁺

Toddlers love boxes. Provide large boxes for the toddlers to crawl in and out of as they pretend to be dogs.

To do

1. Show the toddlers different pictures of dogs. Emphasize the different colors and sizes.

2. Encourage the toddlers to pretend to be dogs. Ask them to crawl around the room, wag their tail, bark, stand on their hind legs to beg, chase their tail (crawl in a circle) or curl up to go to sleep.

3. Provide a large box for the toddlers to use as a "dog house."

4. Place stuffed dogs in the block area. Encourage the toddlers to build dog houses and fenced yards for the pets.

To do again

Although they can be difficult to obtain, large appliance boxes can be used as trains, buses, houses or just about anything.

Teaching hints

Using boxes requires closer supervision when more than one toddler is in the box. Cut out large squares on three sides to help with supervision. It is best to have at least two boxes, preferably three, as the boxes are popular with toddlers. Use the boxes outside for more space.

Skills encouraged

imaginative play
gross motor

Language to use with toddlers

dog house
box
inside
outside
sleep
colors
big
little
bark
tail

Materials

large boxes
pictures of dogs

White-On

White is the color of winter in many regions of the country. Let toddlers explore white items to introduce them to the wonderful world of snow and winter.

Skills encouraged

sensory exploration
fine motor

Language to use with toddlers

squeeze
white
bag
guess
cold
warm
inside
toothpaste
shaving cream
hand lotion
thick
creamy
squishy

Materials

thick resealable freezer
  bags
toothpaste
shaving cream
hand lotion
duct tape or masking tape
tempera paint

To do

1. Add to separate resealable freezer bags one of the following: white toothpaste, shaving cream, white hand lotion, etc.

2. Seal bag and tape closed with duct or masking tape.

3. Encourage the toddlers to feel the bags. Talk about the different sensations of the items, such as the "thick and gooey toothpaste," "the creamy shaving cream," etc. As you speak, emphasize the color white which reminds us of the snow.

4. Chill the bags in the freezer or refrigerator before you use them.

5. Talk about and compare them to the temperature outside. As they become warmer, they are more like the temperature in the room.

6. Tape the bags to a wall or window for the children to continue to feel on their own.

7. Replace or refill the bags as needed.

Teaching hints

Avoid emphasizing snow in regions of the country where it rarely, if ever, snows. This concept is not "real" for those children. Use this "White-On" activity just to explore textures and the color of white for toddlers living in warmer areas.

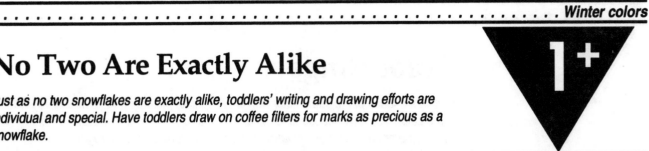

No Two Are Exactly Alike

Just as no two snowflakes are exactly alike, toddlers' writing and drawing efforts are individual and special. Have toddlers draw on coffee filters for marks as precious as a snowflake.

To do

1. Provide washable markers for the toddlers to draw on coffee filters.

2. Talk with each toddler about the round shape of the coffee filter, the types of lines, colors, etc. Emphasize how the coffee filter looks like a snowflake.

3. Hang the "snowflake drawings" on the window or use a yarn to hang them from the ceiling. Have the toddler show you where she wants her snowflake to hang.

To do again

Let older toddlers paint with watercolors on the coffee filters.

Skills encouraged

fine motor
creative expression
pre-writing/emergent
  literacy

Language to use with toddlers

coffee filter
white
round
draw
write
circles
lines
precious

Materials

coffee filters
washable markers
yarn

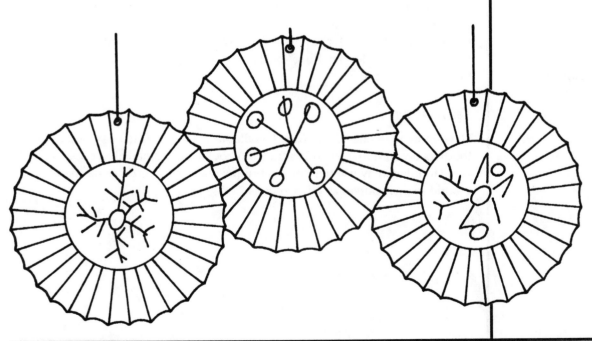

Color Rings

Highlight shades of the same color with collections of pictures and textures all in the same color. You may choose to focus on the colors of the winter season, for example, white, blue or purple. Or use whatever seems appropriate for your region.

Skills encouraged

language
sensory exploration

Language to use with toddlers

color
shape
food
fabric
felt
feel
smooth

Materials

magazines
stickers
felt
fabric scraps
ribbon scraps
posterboard
glue
scissors
hole punch
book rings
clear contact paper or
  laminating film

To do

1. Using magazines and catalogs, collect small pictures of foods and miscellaneous items in one of the winter colors. Stickers can also be used.

2. Find scraps of fabric and ribbon in the specific color.

3. Cut basic shapes such as circle, square, triangle and heart out of felt in the same color. Make the shapes approximately two inches tall. Cut out the shape of a small hand and/or foot for variety.

4. Cut posterboard into circles approximately five inches in diameter.

5. Glue the pictures, felt shapes, fabric and ribbon scraps onto the circles.

6. Write the name and color of the object underneath the item, such as purple grape or purple circle.

7. Laminate the circles or cover with clear contact paper for durability.

8. Punch a hole in the top of each circle. Use book rings to put the circles together into a "Color Ring" of pictures and textures.

9. Place the "Color Rings" out for the toddlers to look through and feel. Talk with the toddlers about the colors, shapes and textures.

To do again

Make "Rainbow Rings" to explore different colors. Cut the circles out of different colors of construction paper or posterboard. Put one picture or sticker on the same color of paper. Add colored felt shapes and fabric scraps too. Or, make a "Holiday Ring" of stickers, small pictures and shapes related to an annual event.

Teaching hints

Have more than one "Color Ring" available as they tend to be popular with toddlers because they are different from books and a small object. Expect that some toddlers may use the rings in unique ways, such as carrying them around in their purses as "checkbooks."

Shades of Most Important Marks

Toddlers can explore the shades of a winter color as they draw with various writing and drawing media all in the same color.

To do

1. Collect different media of one color, such as blue markers, blue chalk, blue coloring pencils, blue pens and blue crayons. Place the items in a basket for the toddlers to use.

2. Give the toddler a piece of drawing paper and encourage the toddler to draw with the different items.

3. Talk with him about the different drawing implements, the lines, colors and shades on the paper.

To do again

Place a large sheet of butcher paper on the wall, floor or on the concrete outside for the toddlers to make a group mural using the different drawing utensils in the same color.

Skills encouraged

fine motor
sensory exploration
pre-writing/emergent
  literacy

Language to use with toddlers

marker
crayon
chalk
pencil
same colors
different shades
lighter
darker
draw
lines
circles
paper

Materials

various drawing media,
  all in the same color
basket
paper

Color Changes

Enjoy mixing colors without any mess by filling resealable freezer bags with contrasting colors of fingerpaint or shaving cream mixed with food colors. Squeeze the bag and a new color is created.

Skills encouraged

sensory exploration
fine motor

Language to use with toddlers

color
mix
new
see
lighter
bag
rub
changes
creamy
squish

Materials

resealable freezer bags
fingerpaint
masking tape or duct tape

To do

1. Fill large, heavy-duty resealable freezer bags with fingerpaint in a winter color. Add white fingerpaint. Freezer bags are better than resealable sandwich bags as they are much thicker.

2. Seal the end with masking or duct tape. Place inside a larger bag if desired for extra durability.

3. Let the toddler mix the paint by squishing the bag and rubbing her hand over the top.

4. Talk to the toddler about the changes in color and the lighter shade being formed.

5. Fill another bag with the same color and a different primary color.

6. Talk with the child about the changes in color.

7. Recycle the paint mixture for fingerpainting the next day. Or, tape the bags to the wall or window for the toddlers to continue to mix and observe the changes in colors.

To do again

Place a small amount of shaving cream into the freezer bag and add a few drops of a food coloring. Seal the bag. Encourage the toddlers to mix the color.

Teaching hints

This is a terrific and easy activity for younger toddlers to do while sitting at a table or in a high chair before or after their meal.

Great Balls of Snow

1½+

Pretend "snow" cotton balls provide lots of sensory fun for toddlers.

To do

1. Fill a dish tub or sensory table with cotton balls. Add plastic containers and cups for the toddler to fill with cotton.

2. Encourage the toddlers to play with the cotton balls and containers.

3. Talk with them about the soft textures and white color of the cotton balls. With toddlers who are familiar with snow, pretend that the cotton balls are like snow.

4. Let older toddlers practice their fine motor skills by providing tongs and tweezers for picking up the cotton balls.

To do again

Make a collage of cotton balls by gluing them on a white circle like a "snowball." Offer the toddlers choices of large and small circles.

Skills encouraged

sensory explorations
fine motor

Language to use with toddlers

snowballs
cotton balls
soft
feel
white
pick up
put inside
small
large

Materials

cotton balls
dish tub
plastic cups and containers
tongs
tweezers

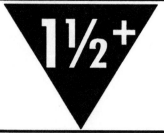

Cotton Ball Painting

Cotton balls can be used for painting and making a collage all in one step when glue is added to the paint.

Skills encouraged

fine motor
creative expression

Language to use with toddlers

cotton balls
paint
glue
paper
leave
stick
cotton swabs

Materials

cotton balls
paint
glue
paper
aluminum pie tin
clothespin
cotton swabs

To do

1. Add a small amount of glue to two or three different colors of paint. Be sure to include white as one of the options. Colored cotton balls can be found in some drug and variety stores. If colored cotton balls are used, choose paint that matches the color of the balls.

2. Pour a thin layer of paint into the pie tin. Add a small amount of glue to the paint. Place five or so cotton balls to the paint.

3. Let the toddler choose the color of paper he would like to use and the color of paint he would like to start with.

4. Show the toddler how to print up and down or paint side to side with the cotton balls. Use a clothespin to hold the cotton ball if desired.

5. Since glue has been added to the paint, encourage the toddler to leave the cotton balls on the paper to make a collage.

6. Let the toddler paint with more cotton balls and colors of paint if he desires.

To do again

Do the same activity with cotton swabs instead. With older toddlers, offer swabs and balls at the same time.

Teaching hints

Some toddlers may be confused about leaving the cotton balls on the paper since they are more familiar with having to put paintbrushes back into the paint container. Once they catch on, toddlers enjoy using lots of cotton balls for the painting collage.

For Toddlers in Spring: March, April and May

Springtime heralds an emerging freshness in the environment, providing the natural opportunity to explore new life and growth through the following themes:

- ◆ *Rain*
- ◆ *Birds*
- ◆ *Bees, Butterflies and Bugs*
- ◆ *Ducks and Other Pond Animals*
- ◆ *Green Creatures like Frogs and Turtles*
- ◆ *Picnics*
- ◆ *Spring Cleaning and Fixing Up*
- ◆ *The Spring Colors of Green and Pastel Shades*

Rain, Rain Go Away

Explore the common weather phenomenon of spring rain with a traditional nursery rhyme.

Skills encouraged

language
creative movement

Language to use with toddlers

rain
umbrella
open
dry
head
hold
up and down
play

Materials

umbrella
assorted colors of posterboard

To do

1. Show the toddlers an umbrella. Talk with them about the colors or design on the umbrella. Open the umbrella and talk about how it keeps people dry from the rain.

2. Chant "Rain, rain go away." Hold the umbrella up and move it up and down to the rhythm of the rhyme.

   Rain, rain go away,
   Come again another day.
   All the children want to play,
   Rain, rain go away.

3. Hold the umbrella over one or two children's heads and chant the rhyme with their names.

   Rain, rain go away,
   Come again another day.
   Tara and Sunny want to play,
   Rain, rain go away.

4. Repeat as many times as the toddlers seem to show interest. For variety, say the rhyme fast and then slowly.

To do again

Encourage older toddlers to pretend to hold up an umbrella. Talk to them about the colors of their pretend umbrellas. Have them move their "umbrellas" up and down to the beat of the rhyme. Or cut umbrella shapes out of different colors of posterboard for the children to move up and down to the rhythm of the rhyme. Encourage the children to follow you around the room to take a "walk in the rain."

Rainy Day Songs

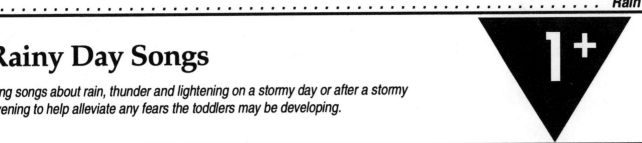

Sing songs about rain, thunder and lightening on a stormy day or after a stormy evening to help alleviate any fears the toddlers may be developing.

To do

1. Sing the following to the tune of "London Bridge," emphasizing the raining words:

   It is raining, raining, raining,
   Really raining, really raining.
   It is raining, raining, raining,
   All day long!

2. Sing the following to the tune of "Are You Sleeping?"

   See the rain fall, see the rain fall,
   From the clouds, in the sky.
   Lots of, lots of raindrops, lots of, lots of raindrops,
   Everything is wet, except (or including) me!

   Hear the thunder, hear the thunder,
   Crash boom bang, crash boom bang,
   It is loud, it is loud,
   Oh so loud, and so exciting!

   See the lightening, see the lightening,
   Across the sky, across the sky,
   Zip zip zap, zip zap zap,
   Did you see it, just a flash!

3. Use your imagination to make up other songs about rain to familiar tunes.

Teaching hints

It is important to show a calm interest in the rain or storm so the children do not become too frightened. Adults must try not to show any uneasiness or fears they may have to the children, for toddlers pick up on them so easily. Stress to the children that the rain is needed to provide water to the grass, trees and plants.

To do again

Read *Rain* by Robert Kalan and illustrated by Donald Crews to the children, especially on a rainy day.

Skills encouraged

language

Language to use with toddlers

rain
thunder
lightening
loud
storm
water
grow

Materials

none needed

Rain Maker

Toddlers can pretend to be in control of making rain when they play with strainers in water.

Skills encouraged

sensory exploration

Language to use with toddlers

water
rain
stream
up
strainer
grass
grow

Materials

dish tub, baby bath tub or
  sensory table
newspapers or old towels
strainers
strainer-type toys
plastic food containers
smocks

To do

1. Fill a dish tub, baby bath tub or sensory table with water. Put newspaper or old towels underneath to absorb any water that may spill.

2. Place a wide variety of strainers and toys with strainers in the water.

3. Make strainers by poking holes in the bottom of empty plastic food containers, such as cottage cheese or yogurt cups.

4. Put on smocks.

5. Encourage the toddlers to fill the strainers with water and then hold them up high to make the "rain."

6. Chant the "Rain, rain go away" nursery rhyme as the toddlers play with the strainers.

7. Sing the following to the tune of "Are You Sleeping?"

    See the rain, see the rain,
    Drip drip drip. In a stream.
    I can make rain, with the strainer.
    Just like this, drip drip drip.

To do again

Take strainers and a tub of water outside on a warm day. Encourage the children to hold the strainer over grass to rain on the grass to help it grow.

Mud Splash

Toddlers and mud attract each other like magnets. Let toddlers have the time of their life in mud and puddles after a rain.

To do

1. After a rain on a warm spring day, let the children play in a safe area outside that has a few puddles, wet sand or even mud.

2. Take off the children's shoes and socks. Roll up their pants if needed.

3. Encourage the children to drop a rock or ball in the puddle to make a splash. Chant "Splash, splash, make a big splash."

4. Let the toddlers feel wet sand or mud with their feet. Talk to the children about the squishy feeling of the mud. Encourage the toddlers to make feet prints in the mud or sand.

5. Wash off their feet when finished.

6. With older toddlers, let them dig or make designs in the sand or mud with a shovel or a stick.

To do again

On a hot day in the late spring or summer, plan a "Messy Day" for the toddlers. Wet down the sand and/or make mud with garden hoses. Have shovels, scoops, plastic containers, etc. available. Leave the water from the hose on at a low pressure for the children to use. Let the parents know in advance so they can dress their children in old clothes and send an extra set of clothing.

Teaching hints

Some toddlers do not enjoy getting dirty and may prefer to watch. In time, they too may join in the messy fun with gentle encouragement.

Skills emphasized

sensory exploration

Language to use with toddlers

mud
wet
sand
dry
rain
splash
puddle
feel
squishy

Materials

sticks
rocks
balls
towels

Rainbow Salad

A rainbow of colors appears when each child brings a different fruit for a group salad.

Skills encouraged

sensory exploration
fine motor

Language to use with the children

fruit
colors
bananas
apples
strawberry
grapes
cut
stir
spoon
knife
bowl

Materials

large plastic bowl
plastic knives
large spoon
small paper cups
spoons
vanilla yogurt, optional

To do

1. Ask each child/parent to bring a specific fruit for a group salad. Try to make certain different colors and types of fruit will be represented.

2. Show all the different fruits to the children, emphasizing the various colors.

3. Wash hands.

4. Have each child find the fruit he brought from home. Talk to the child about the fruit he brought.

5. Encourage the child to help wash his fruit. Older toddlers may be able to help cut some soft fruits, such as bananas, peaches, melon, cored apple quarters, etc.

6. Once cut, have the child help add the fruit to the bowl. Let him stir the fruit salad.

7. When all pieces of fruit have been added, serve portions into paper cups for each child. Enjoy the salad as is or add vanilla yogurt.

8. Talk with the children about all the different colors, tastes and types of fruit in the "Rainbow Fruit Salad."

9. Show the children pictures or items with rainbows. Talk to the children about all the colors.

To do again

Have each child bring in a vegetable for a community soup or raw vegetable tasting party with older toddlers.

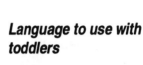

Rain Drops

Toddlers practice their fine motor skills as they pretend to make rain drops with eyedroppers.

To do

1. Collect plastic eye or medicine droppers. Turkey basters and/or nasal syringes work fine too.

2. Place the eyedroppers in a small amount of water in a dish tub or sensory tub.

3. Show the toddlers how to squeeze the bulb to fill and empty the eyedropper. Let them experiment with the different droppers.

4. Encourage the toddlers to make "rain drops" by gently squeezing the eyedroppers so that just a few drops come out at a time.

To do again

Use the eyedroppers with colored water in muffin tins. Fill three to four sections with a different primary color (red, yellow, blue). Add clear water to one of the cups. Leave the other sections empty. Let the toddlers experiment with mixing the colors with the eyedroppers. Change the water after each child.

Skills encouraged

fine motor

Language to use with toddlers

eyedropper
squeeze
water
drops
empty
fill
baster
syringe

Materials

eyedroppers
turkey baster
nasal syringe
dish tub or sensory tub

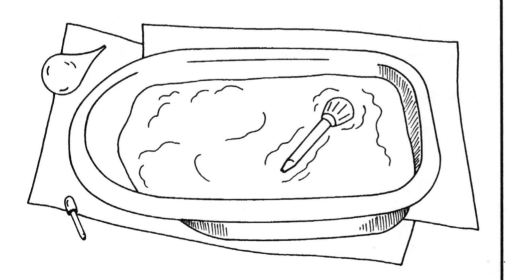

Two Little Blackbirds

A traditional nursery rhyme introduces toddlers to the freedom of flying birds.

Skills encouraged

language
fine motor

Language to use with toddlers

two
blackbirds
hill
fly away
come back
yellow ducks
grass
waddle

Materials

felt
scissors
black construction paper
stuffed animals
clear contact paper
craft sticks

To do

1. Chant the following nursery rhyme:

   Two little blackbirds sitting on a hill, (place fists on leg)
   One named Jack and one named Jill. (raise one fist at a time)
   Fly away Jack, fly way Jill. (one at a time, "fly" hands behind back)
   Come back Jack, come back Jill. (one at a time, "fly" hands back to hill)

2. While saying the rhyme, use two birds and a green hill cut out of felt or construction paper at the flannel board. Stuffed animals or plastic birds can also be used.

3. Cut two small birds for each child out of black construction paper. Laminate or cover the bird shapes with clear contact paper. Attach to craft sticks, if desired. Encourage each child to hold one bird puppet in each hand as you say the rhyme.

4. Change the rhyme to use with other colors of birds. Use different colored construction paper birds to emphasize the colors.

5. Focus on ducks in the following rhyme.

   Two yellow ducks sitting in the grass, (place hands on floor)
   One named Lucky and one named Cass. (raise one hand at a time)
   Waddle away Lucky, waddle away Cass. (one at a time, "waddle" hands behind back)
   Come back Lucky, come back Cass. (one at a time, "waddle" hands back)

6. Use two ducks and a blue pond cut out of felt or construction paper at the flannel board while saying the rhyme. Or, for variety, use bathtub ducks.

7. Cut out two ducks for each child to hold while saying the rhyme.

To do again

Use other springtime animals with the verse, such as frogs or butterflies.

The Birds and the Bees

The words to a traditional fingerplay about bees can be changed to a chant about birds.

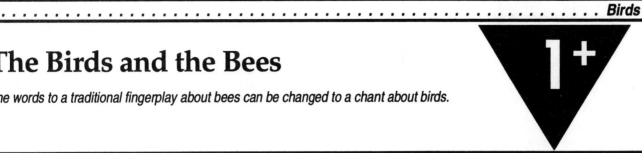

1+

To do

1. Chant the following traditional rhyme with the toddlers:

   Here is the beehive. (hold hands together)
   Where are the bees? (look puzzled)
   Hidden away where nobody sees. (shake head no)
   Soon they'll come buzzing out of their hive.
   1, 2, 3, 4, 5. (hold up one finger at a time)
   Buzzzz! (wiggle fingers like bees flying)

2. Cut five bees and a yellow hive shape out of felt or construction paper to use with the chant. at the flannel board.

3. Change the words of the rhyme to refer to birds:

   Here is the bird's nest. (cup two hands together)
   Where are the birds? (look puzzled)
   Sleeping there quietly for a good rest.
      (rest head on shoulder)
   Soon they'll come flying out of their nest.
   1, 2, 3, 4, 5. (raise fingers one by one)
   Now they can fly away, just like the best.
   ("fly fingers" away)

4. Cut a brown nest and five birds out of construction paper or felt to use with the verse.

Skills emphasized

language
fine motor

Language to use with the children

beehive
bees
honey
bird's nest
young birds
where
hidden
see

Materials

felt
construction paper
scissors

Light as a Feather

Toddlers can explore textures, colors, and sizes with all sorts of feathers.

Skills encouraged

sensory exploration
fine motor

Language to use with toddlers

soft
stiff
long
small
tickle
color
design
pillow
heavy
light
squish
firm
soft
thick

Materials

a variety of feathers
craft feathers
dish pan

To do

1. Show the toddlers the feathers. Try to have a variety such as small feathers from a down pillow and large peacock feathers. Talk about the colors, textures and sizes.

2. Tickle the toddlers on their cheeks or under their chins with the feathers.

3. Place feathers longer than four inches in a dish pan or basket for the toddlers to explore on their own.

4. Give two feathers to each child to hold, one in each hand. Have them pretend to fly around the room flapping their wings like a bird.

To do again

Show the older toddlers a feather pillow and a foam pillow. Let them feel how one is "soft," "light" and "squishy" and how the foam pillow is "thick," "heavy" and "firm." Leave out a few pillows for the children to lay on, sit on or use as beds for stuffed animals and dolls.

Teaching hints

Wash the bird feathers in soapy water with a small amount of bleach prior to allowing the children to handle them.

For the Birds

Bird seed offers a unique sensory substance for toddlers to explore outside.

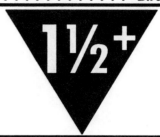

To do

1. Fill the baby bath tub, dish tub or sensory tub with bird seed.

2. Add in plastic cups, containers, scoops and sand sifters. Plastic and stuffed birds can be a fun addition.

3. Let the toddlers explore the texture of the bird seed as they fill, empty, stir and scoop the seed. Encourage them to "feed" the birds if some have been added.

4. With older toddlers, have them pick the sunflower seeds out of the feed and place them in a small container for an extra fine motor challenge.

To do again

Add plastic eggs and containers with covers. Show the children how to fill the containers to make shakers.

Teaching hints

Bird seed can be very messy and slippery so it is best to do this activity outside. The birds can then be responsible for cleaning up the seed that spills!

Skills encouraged

sensory explorations
fine motor

Language to use with toddlers

seeds
tiny
bumpy
feed
full
empty
pour
stir
scoop
shake
sunflower seeds

Materials

bird seed
baby bath tub, dish tub or
  sensory table
scoops
spoons
small cups and plastic containers
sand sifters
plastic or stuffed birds

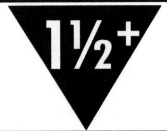

Feather Painting

For a different type of art activity, let toddlers paint with feathers.

Skills encouraged

fine motor
creativity

Language to use with the children

feather
color
paint
side to side
up and down

Materials

craft feathers
plastic tray or plate
paint
glue
paper

To do

1. Obtain two to three different colors of craft feathers.

2. Mix paint the same color as the craft feathers. Add a small amount of glue to the paint.

3. Let the toddler choose the color of paper she wants to use.

4. Have the child pick out a feather and then dip it into the same color of paint. Encourage the child to paint with the feather. Describe her actions as she paints (up and down, side to side, etc.).

5. When finished with the feather, encourage the child to leave the feather on the paper for a collage. Tell her that the glue in the paint helps it stick to the paper.

6. Let the toddler choose another color of feather and paint. Allow the toddler to use as many feathers as she wants for her painting.

7. Comment on the colors and the strokes used.

To do again

Make a feather collage without painting.

Teaching hints

While it may seem tempting to cut out the shape of a bird for the children to glue or paint on, it is best to let the children use an open ended shape (rectangle, square, long strip of paper, etc.) as a background. Toddlers and young children are interested in the process of painting with the feathers rather the completed product of a "bird" or "turkey" that has been designed by the teacher. Emphasize creative exploration in all art experiences with young children.

Feathered Friends

Take toddlers out for a walk to look for birds in their natural environment.

1½⁺

To do

1. Take the toddlers on a walk to "look" for birds.

2. Find a tree to sit under and "listen" for the birds. Look up into to the tree to see if there are any nests.

3. With older toddlers, taste a few shelled, unsalted sunflower seeds. Talk with the children about how the birds eat sunflower and other seeds with their beaks.

4. Read a story, sing or chant songs about birds while sitting under the tree.

5. Leave some bird seed under the tree for the birds to enjoy later.

6. Pretend to fly back to the classroom when finished.

Teaching hints

While the group may not actually come upon a flock of birds. Use dramatic actions (for example, hands placed over the eyes to look, hands cupped on the ears to listen, tiptoeing and walking quietly) while looking and listening for the birds to maintain the children's interest. Visit the tree a few days later to see if the birds found the seeds.

Skills encouraged

gross motor
sensory exploration

Language to use with toddlers

look
listen
see
hear
walk
taste
sunflower seeds
beaks
tree
up
nest

Materials

shelled, unsalted sunflower seeds

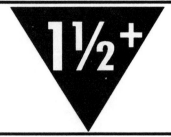

Bird's Nest

Toddlers are fascinated with natural materials like leaves and twigs. Bird nests provide an ideal opportunity to explore these items and how they can be used with scraps of paper and string to make something beneficial.

Skills emphasized

sensory exploration
fine motor

Language to use with toddlers

nest
home
twigs
leaves
trash
string
paper
tree
build
eggs
young

Materials

dish tub, baby bath tub or
  sensory tub
small plastic bowls or
  microwave dinner trays
an old bird's nest
nature items
pieces of string and yarn
scrap pieces of paper
plastic or stuffed birds

To do

1. Show the toddlers an old bird's nest if possible. Talk to the toddlers about the nature items and scrap materials in it and how the birds make their nests by collecting items outside. Emphasize how the nest is the home where birds raise their young.

2. While outside, have the toddlers pretend to be birds with you collecting nature items, such as small sticks, twigs, leaves, grass, etc. to make a nest.

3. Add the nature materials to a sensory or dish tub.

4. Let the toddlers explore the materials.

5. After the children have explored the "nesting" materials, add the small bowls and plastic or stuffed birds. Encourage the children to fill the bowls with the twigs, leaves, paper, etc. to make a nest for the birds.

To do again

Let the toddlers make a "nest" of their own. Have the children spread a thick layer of glue on the bottom of a paper or styrofoam bowl or plate. Or staple contact paper sticky side up on top of a disposable plate to act like glue (see Sticky Side Up, page 61). Provide nesting items such as twigs, leaves, scrap paper, string, etc. for the children to place on top of the glue or contact paper.

Teaching hints

Refer to the offspring as young birds rather than "babies" or "birdies" to provide accurate language for the toddlers.

My Nest or Yours!

Small wading pools filled with soft items and books offer a cozy area in which to relax in a busy classroom. Make a "bird's nest" with these items so that toddlers may pretend to be young birds sleeping or playing.

1½⁺

To do

1. Depending on the size of the classroom, put out one or two small wading pools. If you will be doing the activity outside, put out two or more wading pools.

2. Fill the pools with stuffed birds, bird puppets, books about birds and pillows.

3. Cut out pictures of birds and glue them onto cardboard or posterboard. Laminate or cover with clear contact paper. Add the bird pictures to the "nest" and hang some from the ceiling above the nest.

4. Encourage the toddlers to get into the "nest" and pretend to be birds sleeping in the nest. Or have the children pretend to be mother or father birds caring for their young. For older toddlers, provide pieces of yarn for "worms" if desired.

5. Play nature music in the background. Read books and sing songs about birds.

To do again

See if one of the families has a pet bird that they could bring to the classroom for the toddlers to see.

Teaching hints

Older toddlers will vary greatly in their level of imaginative play. Participate with the toddlers to help them initiate their play if needed, but also take time to observe the children and follow their lead in the activities they come up with on their own.

Skills encouraged

social interaction
imaginative play

Language to use with toddlers

nest
home
rest
sleep
warm
tree
flock worms
young

Materials

small wading pools
stuffed birds
bird puppets
books about birds
nature magazines with
  pictures of birds
pillows
scissors
glue
clear contact paper
yarn

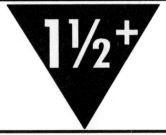

Empty Nest

Toddlers can practice their visual discrimination skills when they help birds return home to an empty nest.

Skills emphasized

visual discrimination
eye-hand coordination
matching

Language to use with toddlers

color
same
different bird
nest
home
slide
inside

Materials

posterboard
scissors
construction paper
glue
laminating film or clear
  contact paper
utility knife
resealable bag
double faced tape

To do

1. Cut two to five birds out of different colors of construction paper, fewer for young toddlers and more for older toddlers.

2. Cut out a corresponding number of nests in the same colors as the birds.

3. Attach the nests to the posterboard by using glue. Leave the top edge of the nest open so that the birds can be slipped into the nest.

4. Laminate or cover both the birds and the nests on the posterboard with clear contact paper.

5. Store the birds in a resealable bag which you attach to the back of the posterboard with double faced tape.

6. Show the toddlers how to slide the bird into the nest. Encourage them to help the bird return home to the nest which is the same color as his feathers.

To do again

Cut out a large bird, small bird, large nest and small nest. Have the toddlers match the birds to the appropriate nest by size.

Teaching hints

Younger toddlers may prefer to experiment with sliding the birds in and out of the nest for some time before working on accurately matching the birds and nests. Allow for this exploration.

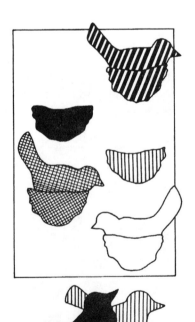

Fly Young Birds, Fly!

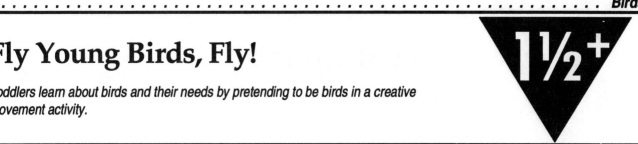

Toddlers learn about birds and their needs by pretending to be birds in a creative movement activity.

To do

1. Sit on a large blanket or sheet. Have the toddlers huddle around by sitting or squatting down and holding their legs. Tell them they are all young birds in the nest.

2. Encourage them to pretend they are hungry by looking up and making bird sounds. "Peep, peep." Pretend to "feed" each young bird with a "worm" (piece of yarn).

3. Tell the young birds that it is time for them to learn how to fly. Have the toddlers stand flap their arms for "wings." Chant "up and down, up and down....". Remind the birds to stay in the nest until their wings are strong.

4. When the young birds are ready, encourage them to continue to flap their wings and walk on their tiptoes as they move around the room practicing flying. Give the young birds lots of encouragement about how strong they are growing.

5. Chant and move arms up and down to the rhythm of the following verse:

    Fly young birds, fly.
    Fly like this, up in the sky.
    Fly young birds, fly.
    Fly, fly oh so high.

6. Have the young birds fly back to the nest to rest to bring an end to the activity.

To do again

Use scarves or craft feathers while flying. Play environmental music in the background.

Teaching hints

Flying like birds is a wonderful activity to use as a transition when going outdoors to keep toddlers from running.

Skills encouraged

gross motor
creative movement
language

Language to use with toddlers

wing
fly
soar
up
sky
flap
feathers
land
down
ground

Materials

scarves or feathers
blanket or sheet
yarn

Feed the Birds

Challenge older toddlers' fine motor skills with a stringing activity to make a bird feeder.

Skills encouraged

fine motor
eye-hand coordination

Language to use with toddlers

feed
hungry
eat
beak
string
thread
through
hole
pull
hang

Materials

yarn or string
scissors
round oat cereal
circular pretzels
tape

To do

1. Cut the string or yarn into approximately six inch lengths. If desired, make a "point" by wrapping tape around one end. Tie a knot at the other end.

2. Show each child how to string the oat cereal. Give him some oat cereal to try to string on his own. Continually give encouragement.

3. If the oat cereal is too difficult for the child, give him circular pretzels to string. He may want to string both the oat cereal and pretzels.

4. When finished, tie the ends to make a loop.

5. Hang the bird feeder on tree branches outside for the birds to enjoy. Watch the birds eating from the classroom window if possible.

6. Eat the leftover pretzels and oat cereal for snack, just like the birds.

Teaching hints

Toddlers vary widely in their fine motor skills. Some will be able to string the oat cereal pieces with little or no difficulty and may spend a great deal of time making bird feeders. Other toddlers may enjoy stringing the larger holed pretzels while others may not yet be at the appropriate level of fine motor development to find any part this activity rewarding. Respect these differences.

Shoo Fly

Warmer weather brings all kinds of winged insects so sing a traditional song about the pesky nature of these creatures.

To do

1. Look at pictures of different insects, such as flies, mosquitos, bees and butterflies.

2. Sing the traditional "Shoo Fly" verse with the children.

   > *Shoo fly don't bother me!*
   >   *(make shooing action with hand then point to self)*
   > *Shoo fly don't bother me!*
   > *Shoo fly don't bother me!*
   > *For I belong to somebody! (hug self)*

3. Repeat the verse, each time singing it differently, such as slowly, quickly, loudly, softly, etc. Toddlers enjoy emphasizing the "shoo fly" words in the song.

To do again

Change the "fly" in the song to refer to other insects, such as mosquitos, bees, ants, etc.

Skills encouraged

language

Language to use with toddlers

shoo
away
fly
bother
me
I
feel
hug

Materials

pictures of insects

Fly Like a Butterfly

Saying the same chant with different actions allows toddlers to explore the many ways they can move their bodies like a butterfly.

Skills encouraged

language
gross motor
creative movement

Language to use with toddlers

butterfly
fly
wings
up
down
graceful
quiet
hand
arm

Materials

pictures of butterflies
scarves
ribbons
felt

To do

1. Look at pictures of butterflies. Talk about the different colors in the wings and that butterflies are fragile and quiet. Read *The Very Hungry Caterpillar* by Eric Carle

2. Chant the following in sing song fashion:

    > *Butterflies, butterflies fly all around. (put hands together at the thumb, move fingers up and down gently like wings fluttering)*
    > *Their wings move up and their wings move down. (hold hands high, then down to the ground)*

3. Repeat the chant as the toddlers show interest.

4. Cut small butterfly shapes out of felt. Give each child a felt butterfly to fly up and down to the rhythm of the verse.

5. With the toddlers sitting, have them extend their arms like butterfly wings. Move up and down to the rhythm of the chant. Leave hands down for the ending.

6. Encourage the toddlers to pretend to be butterflies flying around the room with you. On the down ending to the verse, have the children "land" by squatting to the floor. Remind the toddlers that butterflies are graceful and move quietly.

7. Use scarves or ribbons for butterfly wings with the chant if desired.

To do again

Use butterflies cut out of different colors of felt at the flannel board. Change the chant to include the addition of color:

> *Yellow butterfly, yellow butterfly all around, (take the yellow felt butterfly off the flannel board and move it around)*
> *Your wings move up (hold felt butterfly high)*
> *Then they go down. ("land" the felt butterfly back on the flannel board)*

Bumblebee Tickle

A simple chant about a bee landing on the children can be used to help toddlers learn the names of parts of their bodies.

To do

1. Chant:

   Bumble, bumble, bumblebee buzz
   Flew out of his hive
   And landed right under Laura's chin
   Buzzzzzzz, buzzzzzzz, buzzzzzzz! (softly tickle child under her chin)

2. Repeat chant for different children.

3. Substitute different areas of the body as the place for the bumblebee to land, such as on the arm, behind the ear, under the knee, etc. Change the wording of the chant accordingly.

4. Use a bumblebee puppet or make a bee out of felt to use with the chant.

5. Change the words to another similar verse, "Squirrels Visit," page 116 in the Fall chapter to refer to bees.

To do again

Say both of the chants with other flying creatures, such as butterflies, hummingbirds, mosquitos, etc.

Teaching hints

Keep the tickles soft and stop the activity if the child does not want to be tickled.

Skills encouraged

language

Language to use with toddlers

bumblebee
buzz
flew
barn
tickle
names of parts of the body
on
under
behind

Materials

bee puppet or felt and
  scissors

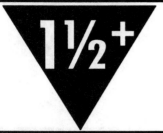

Bee My Honey

Toddlers can explore the relationship between bees and honey through simple chants and matching activities.

Skills encouraged

visual discrimination
language
eye-hand coordination

Language to use with toddlers

bee
color
same
different
small
large
honey
beehive

Materials

honey
spoons
posterboard
construction paper
scissors
laminating film or clear
  contact paper
utility knife
resealable bags
double face tape

To do

1. Let each child taste a small amount of honey on the tip of individual spoons. Talk about the sweet taste and that bees make honey in their hives.

2. Chant about bees in the hive with "Where is the Beehive?" (see The Birds and the Bees, page 183).

3. Cut two to five bees out of different colors of construction paper. Cut hives out of the same colors. Adjust the number of bees/hives to be matched to the abilities of the toddlers.

4. Attach the hives to the posterboard by gluing only the top and sides. Leave the bottom edge open so the bees may enter the hive.

5. Laminate or cover the bees and posterboard with clear contact paper. Slit the bottom of the hives open with a utility knife.

6. Attach a resealable freezer bag to the back side of the posterboard with double face tape for storing the bees.

7. Encourage the toddlers to have each bee fly inside the hive of the same color. Talk to the children about the colors.

To do again

Cut out a small bee, small hive, large bee, large hive for the children to match according to size.

Buzz! Buzz!

Toddlers have fun buzzing around and walking on their tiptoes as they pretend to be bees looking for flowers.

1½⁺

To do

1. Encourage the toddlers to squat down near you. Tell them you are the queen bee and they are your helpers in the hive. Make buzzing sounds.

2. Have the bees fly in little circles walking on their tiptoes around the room looking for beautiful flowers. Continue to make buzzing sounds.

3. Squat down to land on a flower. Pretend to taste the nectar.

4. Tell the toddlers that it is time to fly back to the hive. Fly around the room in circles on tiptoes making buzzing sounds again.

5. "Land" back in the hive for the night to end the activity.

To do again

Place large flower or circle shapes cut out of felt or construction paper on the floor for the children to land on.

Teaching hints

Pretend to be bees when leaving the classroom as a group to reduce random pushing and running behaviors.

Skills encouraged

gross motor
creative movement

Language to use with toddlers

hive
queen
fly
buzz
flower
nectar
honey

Materials

none needed

Animal, Animal

A repetitive chant used with puppets introduces toddlers to the names and colors of any number of animals.

Skills encouraged

language

Language to use with toddlers

duck
yellow
puppet
chant
animals
nose
knee
shoulder
body

Materials

duck and frog puppets or
   stuffed animals

To do

1. Move a puppet up and down to the rhythm of the following chant

   Yellow duck, yellow duck,
   Yellow duck, yellow duck,
   Yellow duck, yellow duck,
   Yellow duck, DUCK! (emphasize the duck)
   Quack!

2. Repeat as the toddlers show interest, but end with a child's name and a kiss to that child.

   Green turtle, green turtle,
   Green turtle, green turtle,
   Green turtle, green turtle,
   Green turtle, Richard Thomas! (have the turtle kiss the child's nose)

3. Pretend to "feed" the puppet. Talk to the toddlers about the animal, where it can be found, what it eats, etc.

4. Say the chant and mention a part of the body as the ending. Have the puppet touch that part of the body.

   Green frog, green frog,
   Green frog, green frog,
   Green frog, green frog,
   Green frog, on your knee (touch child's knee)
   Ribbet!

To do again:

Any stuffed animal or puppet can be used with the chant. Just change the words accordingly.

Life at the Pond

Toddlers love making animal sounds, especially with variations on a very familiar tune.

To do

1. Change the words of the all time favorite, "Old MacDonald," to a song about pond animals. The name of Old MacDonald can be changed also to the teacher's name or the class' name if desired. For example:

   The terrific toddlers went to the pond, E—I—E—I—O
   And at this pond they saw some ducks, E—I—E—I—O
   With a "quack, quack" here and a "quack, quack" there.
   Here a "quack," there a "quack,"
   Everywhere a "quack, quack."
   The terrific toddlers went to the pond, E—I—E—I—O.

2. Substitute in other pond animals, such as:

   fish—fff, fff (pucker lips to make a fish sound)
   turtles—snap, snap (clap hands)
   frogs—ribbet, ribbet
   birds—-tweet, tweet
   mosquitoes—buzz, buzz

   Use your imagination for other animals or let the toddlers suggest them.

3. At the flannel board sing the song with pictures of the animals or animal shapes cut from felt or construction paper. Stuffed animals, puppets, and/or plastic animals can be used as well.

To do again

Use the song with other groupings of animals and their sounds. For a pet store use puppies—woof, woof; kittens—meow, meow; parrots—squawk, squawk; fish—fff, fff; snakes—sss, sss; etc. For a zoo, lions—roar, roar; monkeys—chatter, chatter; bears—growl, growl; seals—arf, arf; alligators—snap, snap; etc. Your imagination is the only limit!

Skills encouraged

language

Language to use with toddlers

pond
duck
quack
turtles
snap
fish
frogs
mosquitoes
buzz
butterflies
pet store
animals
zoo

Materials

animal pictures
plastic animals
stuffed animals
felt or construction paper
scissors

Little Turtle

A simple fingerplay about turtles and their shells emphasizes their hiding nature which fascinates children.

Skills encouraged

language
fine motor

Language to use with toddlers

turtle
shell
house
inside
hand
finger
fist
thumb
circle
hide
feed
kiss

Materials

none needed

To do

1. Show the toddlers a picture of a turtle. Talk about the shell being the animal's house that it hides in and carries around on his back.

2. Hold one hand in a fist, with the thumb tucked in. Tell the toddlers that it is a pretend turtle. Encourage them to make a "turtle" too.

3. Chant the following verse in a sing song fashion. Rub the top of your fist with the other hand in a circular motion to get the "turtle" to come out to play. At the end of the verse, pop the thumb out like the head of a turtle.

    Little turtle come out to play.
    Don't stay in your house all day.

4. Pretend to feed the turtle or give her a kiss. Let the turtle kiss each child's cheek or knee.

5. Have the turtle go back "home" with the following verse:

    Little turtle go back inside,
    That's where you like to hide. (Tuck thumb back inside fist).

6. Repeat as the toddlers show interest. Encourage the toddlers to do the actions with the verse.

7. Substitute snail, tree crab or hermit crab to use with the verse.

To do again

Bring a real turtle, snail or tree crab into the class for the children to observe. Perhaps someone in the class has a pet turtle or tree crab which could visit. A rectangular glass fish tank with a cover would allow the children to observe the creature's safely. After the children have seen a real turtle or tree crab, pretend to be one with older toddlers. Sit on the floor with your head tucked down on your knees. Say the first verse, then hold your head up. Crawl around very, very slowly looking for a plant to eat. Say the second verse and tuck your head back inside your shell.

Gagunck, Quack and All That

A catchy verse explores rhyming words, animal sounds and actions with toddlers in a playful way.

To do

1. Sing or chant the following traditional verse:

    Gagunck went the little green frog.
    Gagunck went the little green frog.
    Gagunck went the little green frog.
    As he sat upon his little wooden log!
    Gagunck! (hop or sit and "look" like a frog)

2. Substitute other animals, sounds and actions. Try to rhyme the ending if possible.

    Quack, quack went the little yellow duck.
    Quack, quack went the little yellow duck.
    Quack, quack went the little yellow duck.
    As she waddled to the bread truck!
    Quack, quack! (waddle like a duck)

    Peep, peep went the young chick....
    As he climbed over the stick (tiptoe like a chick)

3. Have the toddlers suggest other animals.

4. Cut out shapes of the animals from felt or construction paper to use at the felt board for a visual stimulus. Pictures, stuffed animals and puppets can also be used.

Skills encouraged

language

Language to use with toddlers

frog
green
log
gagunck
duck
yellow
truck
quack
cat
meow
hat

Materials

pictures of animals
felt
construction paper
scissors

Freckled Frogs

A traditional counting verse about frogs can be shortened to make it a more appropriate length for the shorter attention spans of toddlers.

Skills encouraged

language
fine motor

Language to use with toddlers

frogs
green
one
two
three
log
bug
pool
water
cool

Materials

none needed

To do

1. Sing the traditional song, "Three Little Speckled Frogs" with the toddlers, except change the number of frogs from five to three (or even two for the youngest of toddlers if needed). Chant or say the words in a sing-song fashion if you are not familiar with the tune.

   > *Three (or two or one) green speckled frogs,*
   > *Sat on a speckled log.*
   > > *(sit three fingers of one hand on one horizontally held finger of other hand)*
   > *Eating a most delicious bug. (pretend to eat by smacking lips)*
   > *Yum, yum! (rub tummy)*
   > *One jumped into the pool, (jump one finger down into "pool")*
   > *Where it was nice and cool, (hug body)*
   > *Then there were only two (one, no) green speckled frogs.*
   > > *(hold up appropriate number of fingers)*

2. Repeat the verse for two frogs, then for one frog.

To do again

Use the song as a flannel board activity with three frogs and a log shape cut out of felt or construction paper.

Teaching hints

With any counting song that repeats the verse with one less item each time, reduce the number to around three rather than five or ten. This is more appropriate for the attention span of most toddlers.

Sir Crocodile

Toddlers love to say "No!" A chant about a snapping crocodile gives them the opportunity to say "No" in a playful way.

To do

1. Show the toddlers a picture of a crocodile. Talk about the many teeth, long tail, bumpy hide, etc.

2. Chant the following verse.

   > *Sir-rr Crocodile, crocodile, crocodile, (Cup hands together like the mouth of an crocodile, open and close the mouth to the rhythm)*
   > *NO! Don't you snap at me! (Clap hands loudly to make a big snap)*
   > *Sir-rr Crocodile, crocodile, crocodile, (repeat above directions)*
   > *NO! I am not for thee! (shake head no and point to self)*

3. Sing about a little crocodile and do the chant in a quiet voice to a quick tempo.

4. Next, do the chant about a large crocodile. Say the chant loudly and slowly.

5. Substitute in the children's names. If possible, have the ending rhyme with the child's name.

   > *Sir-rr crocodile, crocodile, crocodile,*
   > *No! Don't you snap at Amanda.*
   > *Sir-rr crocodile, crocodile, crocodile,*
   > *She is not a panda.*

To do again

Say the chant about a "Lady Alligator."

Skills encouraged

language
fine motor

Language to use with toddlers

crocodile
big teeth
snap
long tail
no
don't
me
alligator
turtle

Materials

none needed

Duck Pond

Toddlers are drawn to water just like ducks. Rubber ducks placed in the water of your sensory table will be a guaranteed success with toddlers.

Skills encouraged

sensory exploration

Language to use with toddlers

ducks
yellow
white
webbed feet
wings
beak
tail
quack
swim
float
frog
fish
turtle

Materials

dish pan
old towels or shower
  curtain
plastic or rubber ducks

To do

1. Fill a dish pan, baby bath tub or sensory table with a small amount of water. Place on the floor with old towels or an old shower curtain underneath to catch any water that may spill.

2. Place plastic and/or rubber ducks in the water.

3. Let the toddlers play with the ducks.

4. Talk with the children about the ducks floating, their wings, their beaks, etc

5. Take the "pond"outside on a warm day..

To do again

Add plastic frogs, turtles or fish if desired. Talk to the children about the animals that live at the pond.

On Toddlers' Pond

Create a toddler-style pond for the children to visit with blue fabric and stuffed animals.

To do

1. Place a large piece of blue fabric or a blue sheet on the floor to be a pond.

2. Put stuffed animals, such as ducks, frogs, turtles, birds, fish and others related to pond life on or around the sheet.

3. Put pictures of pond animals on the wall nearby and display related books as well.

4. Let the children visit the "pond."

5. Encourage the toddlers to pretend to be some of the animals in the water. Have them move like and make the sounds of the ducks, turtles, frogs, etc. while they "sit" in the pretend water.

6. Talk with the children about life on the pond and sing songs about frogs, turtles, ducks, etc. Read *Have You Seen My Duckling?* by Nancy Tafuri.

Skills encouraged

imaginative play
language

Language to use with toddlers

pond
water
fish
ducks
turtles
frogs
birds
butterflies
feed
walk
boat

Materials

blue fabric or sheet
stuffed animals

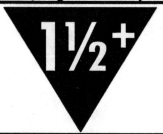

Duck Prints

Toddlers can paint with spatulas to make webbed feet type prints.

Skills encouraged

fine motor
creative expression

Language to use with toddlers

duck
wide
webbed feet
walk
waddle
swim
spatula
print
paint
paper

Materials

spatulas
forks
paper
paint
flat container

To do

1. Mix orange and/or yellow paint. Pour the paint into a flat container.

2. Place one or two spatulas on top of each color of paint.

3. Offer large, different colored sheets of paper for the toddler to choose from for painting.

4. Encourage the toddler to print with the spatula to make "duck feet." With older toddlers, encourage them to "walk" two spatulas across the paper.

5. Talk about the patterns made by the different spatulas. Emphasize how they make a shape like a duck's webbed feet.

To do again

Print with forks to make chick's feet.

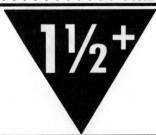

Animal Cracker Picnic

Spring is a time of newborn animals. Plan a day with a special snack and activities to celebrate animals and their young.

To do

1. Send a note home to the parents asking them to dress their child in something that has some type of animal on it. Have animal stickers on hand for any children who forget.

2. Talk with each child individually about the animal(s) on her shirt, pants, sock, etc. Discuss the sounds the animal makes, where it lives, the name of its young, special features of the animal, etc.

3. Pretend to move like the various animals on the children's clothing.

4. Sing a version of "Old MacDonald" substituting the children's names and the animals on their clothing. For example:

    > *Shawn wore green frogs*
    > *Oh yes, oh yes, oh yes,*
    > *With a ribbet, ribbet here and a ribbet ribbet there*
    > *Here a ribbet, there a ribbet, everywhere a ribbet ribbet*
    > *Shawn wore green frogs*
    > *Oh yes, oh yes, oh yes*

5. Have a picnic snack outside. Eat animal crackers with all the "animals!"

To do again

Have the toddlers bring a favorite stuffed animal for an "Animal Cracker Parade."

Skills encouraged

language
creative movement

Language to use with toddlers

animal
different
same
tail
head
ears
feet
eyes
wear

Materials

animal crackers
stickers

Picnic Picnic

With the arrival of more pleasant weather in springtime, picnic snacks offer an easy way to bring new life into the classroom routine. Older toddlers also enjoy having pretend picnics in class with a few simple props.

Skills encouraged

language
imaginative play

Language to use with toddlers

picnic
eat outside
nice weather
finger foods
blanket
basket
paper plates
park

Materials

blanket or sheet
finger foods
baskets
picnic plates and cups
old thermoses
lunch boxes
plastic fruits

To do

1. On a nice day, have a picnic of finger foods for snack. Take along a blanket to sit on and eat outdoors on the playground or around the school.

2. Talk with the toddlers about what they see and hear going on around them outside.

3. Set up a pretend picnic area in the classroom for older toddlers. Include some of the following: blanket or sheet on the floor, picnic plates and cups, old thermoses and lunch boxes, plastic foods, vegetables and/or fruits, baskets, etc.

4. Encourage the toddlers to sit on the blanket for a pretend picnic lunch with their friends.

5. Let the toddlers bring dolls and/or stuffed animals with them to the picnic area.

Paper Plate Expressions

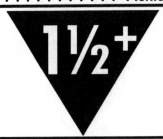

Paper plates can be used instead of construction paper for toddlers' Most Important Marks (M.I.M.s) and painting activities.

To do

1. Provide inexpensive white paper plates with markers or crayons. Have the toddlers make their **Most Important Marks** on the plates. The ridges on the edge provide an interesting texture effect. Talk to the children about the lines they are making.

2. Mix two to three different colors of paint.

3. Let the toddlers paint on top of a paper plate with a paintbrush or print with craft sponges shaped like fruits. Cookie cutters can also be used.

4. Talk with the toddlers about the colors of the paint, the fruit shapes, etc.

5. Let the toddlers glue pictures of fruits and foods from magazines on top of a paper plate. Give them a variety from which to choose and talk about the different foods.

To do again

Use paper sacks instead of paper plates in the above activities.

Skills encouraged

fine motor
creative expression
pre-writing/emergent
 literacy

Language to use with toddlers

paper plate
draw
crayon
lines
paint
smell
scent
print
pictures

Materials

paper plates
crayons
markers
paint
paintbrushes
fruit-shaped craft sponges
magazines
scissors
glue

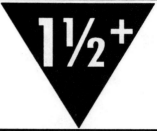

Paper Plate Boogie

Paper plates introduce fun into dancing activities.

Skills encouraged

gross motor
creative expression

Language to use with toddlers

dance
music
beat
paper plate
circle
wave
up high
down low
clap
noise

Materials

paper plates
recorded music

To do

1. Play music with a definite dancing rhythm.

2. Give each toddler interested in dancing two paper plates. The thin inexpensive ones work better than thicker plates.

3. Encourage them to use the paper plates while they dance. Model how to wave the plates, move them up and down, around in circles, from side to side, etc.

4. Have the children clap the plates to the rhythm of the music.

5. Use your imagination in other ways to dance with the plates.

Let's Hammer

Springtime is a perfect time for cleaning and repair activities. Introduce toddlers to fixing things with a song about hammering.

To do

1. Chant the traditional verse of "Johnny Hammers" while pounding the rhythm on the floor. Use "Let's," "we," "I" or the children's names in the verse.

> *Let's hammer with one hammer, one hammer, one hammer,*
> *Let's hammer with one hammer, all day long.*
> *(pound one fist on the floor)*

2. Add the following additional verses as desired, depending on the interest and ability of the children:

> *We hammer with two hammers, two hammers, two hammers,*
> *We hammer with two hammers, all day long.*
> *(pound two fists on the floor)*
> *We hammer with three hammers, three hammers, three hammers,*
> *We hammer with three hammers all day long.*
> *(pound floor with two hands and one foot)*
> *We hammer with four hammers....*
> *(pound floor with two hands and both feet)*
> *We hammer with five hammers....*
> *(use two hands, both feet and move head up and down to beat)*

To do again

As a toddler plays with a pounding bench or with playdough, sing the first verse using the child's name and color of the hammer or playdough.

> *Daniel uses the blue hammer, blue hammer, blue hammer,*
> *Daniel uses the blue hammer, on the pounding bench.*
> *Amelia pounds the purple playdough, purple playdough, purple playdough,*
> *Amelia pounds the purple playdough with her fist.*

Teaching hints

Use the chant when toddlers are playing with the pounding bench to encourage them to use the hammer on the pegs rather than on the wall or table. Don't expect toddlers to be able to do all the motions associated with the more difficult verses. They take a lot of coordination!

Skills encouraged

language
gross motor

Language to use with toddlers

hammer
one
two
three
four
five
build
pound
color

Materials

none needed

Pokey Fun

Toddlers enjoy peg boards but often the pegs are too numerous or too small for younger toddlers to use. Use egg cartons and clothespins to make a peg board just for toddlers.

Skills encouraged

fine motor
eye-hand coordination

Language to use with toddlers

clothespin
inside
hole
poke

Materials

egg cartons
wooden craft clothespins

To do

1. For younger toddlers, use egg cartons from a half-dozen eggs and six craft clothespins. For older toddlers, use a regular dozen carton and twelve non-clipping clothespins.

2. Turn the egg carton upside down and cut or punch small holes in the bottom of each cup-section. The clothespins should just fit into the holes.

3. Place the clothespins in the holes and let the toddler experiment with taking the clothespins out and putting them back in.

To do again

Use the egg cartons to hold markers or large crayons to help keep them from rolling off the table while toddlers are coloring. The cartons can also be used to hold individual toddlers' sets of markers or crayons thus eliminating sharing conflicts.

Clothespin Challenge

Clothespins placed around the edge of a can provide a wide variety of activities from "dump and fill" for the youngest toddlers to a fine motor challenge for the oldest toddlers.

To do

1. Smooth down the rim of the can with a spoon and cover the inside edge with duct or electrical tape to eliminate any rough edges. Cover the can with contact paper. Plastic food storage containers at least three inches tall can be used instead of cans.

2. Place three to six craft clothespins (non-clipping) around the edge.

3. Younger toddlers will use the clothespins and cans as a "dump and fill" activity.

4. Encourage the toddlers to take the clothespins off and then put them back on the side of the can.

5. For older toddlers, provide both craft and clipping clothespins for variety and challenge. Show the older toddlers how to pinch open the clothespins.

To do again

Turn the clothespin challenge into a game of matching for older toddlers. Prepare three cans. Cover each one with a different primary color of contact or construction paper. Use plastic clothespins of different colors. If wooden clothespins are used, color them with a permanent marker or crayons or attach ribbons to make them the same colors as the cans. Encourage older toddlers to match the color of the clothespins to the can as they put them around the edge.

Teaching hints

Some older toddlers may not yet have the fine motor skills to use the clipping clothespins so watch that they do not become too frustrated. Use the craft clothespins with these children.

Skills encouraged

fine motor
visual discrimination

Language to use with toddlers

clothespin
inside
edge
clip
pinch
slip on
match
color

Materials

large juice can, tin can or
  plastic container
spoon
construction or contact
  paper
electrical or duct tape
craft clothespins
clipping clothespins
ribbon

Squish Squish Squish

Squeezing objects helps toddlers develop their hand grasp and is also relaxing.

Skills encouraged

fine motor
sensory exploration

Language to use with toddlers

sponge
squeeze
water
bubbles
hand
strong
muscles
feel

Materials

sponges
mild dish soap
dish tub
old towels or plastic
  covering
smocks

To do

1. Add a very small amount of mild dish soap to a small amount of water in a dish tub. Place the tub on a low table or on the floor on top of old towels or a plastic covering to catch any spills.

2. Put on smocks.

3. Place an assortment of sponges in the water.

4. Encourage the children to squeeze the sponges to make bubbles. Provide thick and thin sponges to require different amounts of pressure.

5. Chant "squish, squish, squishy squeeze" while showing the toddlers how to squeeze the sponges.

To do again

Use craft or bath sponges cut into specific shapes. Talk to the toddlers about the colors and shapes of the sponges.

Teaching hints

Once older toddlers are familiar with wringing out water, they can help wipe off tables or clean up with just a reminder to squeeze out the water. Toddlers enjoy participating in adult chores and most can be encouraged to do so during transition times to help with classroom management.

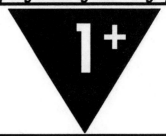

Spic and Span

Toddlers enjoy working hard as they help adults with simple chores. Cleaning props allow toddlers to help "spring clean" in the room.

To do

1. Collect a variety of cleaning supplies to use for "Spring Cleaning" in the classroom, such as old buckets, cloths, different sizes and types of scrub brushes, sponges, feather duster, empty squirt bottles, child-size broom, mop, or vacuum, other types of safe cleaning supplies.

2. Have parents donate some of the items if needed. Make sure all of the items are safe for toddlers to use.

3. Encourage the toddlers to help you clean the shelves, walls, floors, windows, etc. Model the appropriate use of the materials.

4. Leave some of the cleaning supplies in the home living area so that they can be incorporated into the children's play.

To do again

Clean toys, structures and even windows on the playground on a warm day. Fill the squirt bottles, buckets, etc. with water for outside cleaning.

Teaching hints

It is best to keep the amount of water available for indoor cleaning to a minimum. Dusting, sweeping and damp cloths should be sufficient. You can be more generous with the water when cleaning outdoors.

Skills encouraged

gross motor
imaginative play

Language to use with toddlers

scrub
dirty
sweep
sponge
wall
clean
mop
dust
rag
floor

Materials

toddler-safe cleaning
  supplies

Scrubba Dub Dub

A wide variety of scrub brushes allows toddlers to explore colors, sizes and textures.

Skills encouraged

fine motor
sensory exploration

Language to use with toddlers

scrub brushes
toothbrushes
clean
bristles
handle
shiny
dirty
back and forth

Materials

scrub brushes
toothbrushes
items to scrub
squirt bottles
buckets

To do

1. Collect a variety of scrub brushes and toothbrushes.

2. Let the toddlers explore the brushes. Talk about the sizes, bristles, colors, use of the items, etc. Have the toddlers gently rub the brushes over their hand or legs to feel the bristles.

3. Encourage the toddlers to scrub the wall, sink or table with the brushes by chanting "back and forth, back and forth, that is the way we scrub." Give them an empty squirt bottle to use with their scrubbing.

4. Sing the following to the tune of "Here We Go 'Round the Mulberry Bush."

   This is the way to scrub the sink, scrub the sink, scrub the sink,
   This is the way to scrub the sink, to get it nice and clean.

5. Add some of the brushes to the water play table or dish tub with a small amount of water. Provide plastic toys, pieces of wood, or plastic containers that could use some cleaning.

To do again

Take the scrub brushes outside on a warm day to use with squirt bottles and buckets filled with a small amount of water to clean the playground equipment, wheel toys or sand toys.

Teaching hints

Tell the toddlers that the toothbrushes are old and are used for cleaning small things and in corners but not for their mouths.

Washing Up!

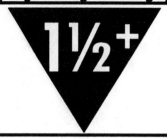

Toddlers take pride in helping with adult chores. Cleaning the classroom toys builds their self-esteem while helping the teacher!

To do

1. Place a small amount of water in a dish tub on the table or floor on top of an old towel or shower curtain. Add only as much as you are willing to clean up.

2. Add a small amount of mild dish detergent to the water with sponges, cloths and/or scrub brushes.

3. Put on smocks.

4. Put dishes or toys in the water for the toddlers to wash. Talk to the toddlers about the process of cleaning the dirty things. Emphasize how much they are helping you.

5. When finished, place the items out on a towel to dry. Older toddlers may also enjoy drying the toys.

To do again

Over a period of days, let the toddlers wash the other toys in the room by adding different objects each day.

Teaching hints

This is a perfect activity to do periodically throughout the year to keep your toys clean!

Skills encouraged

fine motor
sensory exploration

Language to use with toddlers

help
wash
clean
dirty
bubbles
dishes
toys
cloth
sponge

Materials

dish tub
mild dish soap
old towels or shower
  curtains
sponges
cloths
smocks
towel

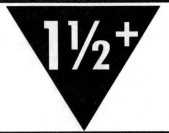

Sponge Prints

Sponges provide a simple printing activity for toddlers.

Skills encouraged

fine motor
creative expression

Language to use with toddlers

sponge
shape
colors
paint
paper
print
bubbles

Materials

thick sponges
scissors
craft sponges
clothespins
paint
mild dish soap
flat container or pie tin
paper

To do

1. Cut a thick sponge into fourths.

2. Attach a clothespin to each section for a handle.

3. Mix two to three different colors of paint. Add dish soap to the paint so it will make bubbles as the children print.

4. Pour the paint into a flat plastic container or pie tin. Place the sponges in the paint.

5. Let the toddler pick what color of paper he wants to use for the painting activity.

6. Encourage the toddler to print with the sponges by chanting "paint paper, paint paper, see the sponge prints." Show excitement if bubbles start to appear.

7. Allow the toddler to use a different color of paint if desired.

8. Talk with him about the prints he is making on the paper, the colors, etc.

9. Sponges cut into a variety of shapes can be purchased at craft stores. Shaped sponges may be used to relate to a certain topic.

To do again

Paint with other cleaning supplies, such as dish washing sponge wands or feather dusters (see Bushy Tails, page 118).

Teaching hints

Some toddlers may use more of a painting action with the sponges instead of printing with them. Allow for the children to experiment with sponges rather than insisting on printing.

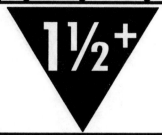

Scrub Painting

Toddlers strengthen their fine motor skills as they scrub back and forth while painting with scrub brushes and old toothbrushes.

To do

1. Collect two to four toothbrushes, preferably of different colors, for the children to use for painting.

2. Mix paint to match the color of the brushes. Add a small amount of dish detergent to the paint for easy cleanup.

3. Pour the paint into a flat container. Place each brush in the corresponding color of paint.

4. Let the toddler pick what color of paper she wants to use.

5. Show the toddler how to paint with the brush by moving it "back and forth" or "side to side" on the paper. Chant while the child paints to encourage the scrubbing action. For example, "back and forth, back and forth, look at you, scrubbing with the brush."

6. The dish detergent may make bubbles in the paint as the child scrubs. Talk with her about the bubbles as they appear.

7. Let the child switch to another color of paint if she desires.

To do again

Use different types of scrub brushes or vegetable brushes. With larger brushes, use big sheets of paper to encourage large hand arm movements.

Teaching hints

This is an excellent alternative to splatter painting with brushes and screens, which very few toddlers have the patience or skill to do.

Skills encouraged

fine motor
creative expression

Language to use with toddlers

scrub
back and forth
side to side
bristles
paint
lines
design
bubbles
paper

Materials

toothbrushes
paint
dish detergent
flat container
paper

Toddler Painting Crew

Build motor skills and self esteem by letting the toddlers help "paint" the walls as part of the spring cleaning.

Skills encouraged

imaginative play
gross motor

Language to use with toddlers

paint
paintbrush
bucket
roller
cap
drop cloth
drip
stroke
up and down
wall
shelf
work

Materials

old sheet
paintbrushes
small paint rollers
paint trays
buckets
sheet
cap

To do

1. Place an old sheet (folded up if necessary) on the floor near a wall that the toddlers can "paint."

2. Put empty buckets, paint trays, short-handled paintbrushes and small rollers on the sheet.

3. Show the toddlers how to "paint" the wall by taking "long strokes up and down."

4. Tell the toddlers the sheet is on the floor so the "paint" does not get on the floor or carpet. Encourage them to put on a cap so they don't get "paint" in their hair.

5. Let the toddlers "paint" other walls or toy shelves around the room.

To do again

On a warm day outside, fill the buckets with water and let the children paint the fence, playground structures or wall with the wet paintbrushes. Refill the buckets as the water spills or runs out. Very young toddlers enjoy this activity.

Rollers

Toddlers can paint with rollers just like a real house painter.

To do

1. Place a large sheet of butcher paper on the floor or outside on the sidewalk. A very long sheet of paper can be used for a group mural if desired. Place newspapers or an old sheet on the floor next to wall as a "drop cloth."

2. Pour a small amount of paint in a flat dish or tray.

3. Have the toddler dip his paint roller in the paint.

4. Encourage the toddler to roll the paint roller around on the paper by chanting "back and forth" or "up and down" according to his actions.

5. Talk with the toddler about the lines he makes on the paper and how he is painting just like a house painter.

To do again

Glue rickrack, ribbon or string to the roller. It will make interesting designs on the paper as the children paint.

Teaching hints

The smaller paint rollers work best with toddlers.

Skills encouraged

fine motor
creative expression

Language to use with toddlers

paint roller
paint
roll
paper
back and forth
up and down
lines
design

Materials

small paint rollers
newspapers or old sheet
flat tray
butcher paper
paint

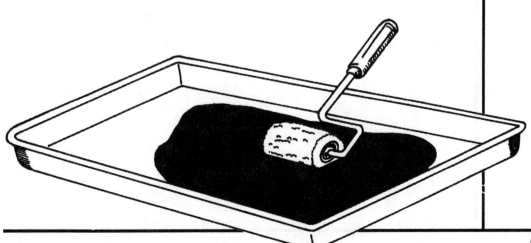

Painting Match

Matching paintbrushes to the same color of paint is a simple matching activity for toddlers.

Skills encouraged

visual discrimination
fine motor

Language to use with toddlers

paint can
paintbrush
colors
match
put inside
same
different

Materials

plastic cups
small plastic paintbrushes
juice cans
contact paper
construction paper
scissors
posterboard
glue
clear contact paper
utility knife
resealable plastic bag
double face tape

To do

1. Find two or three plastic cups or tumblers in different colors and two or three plastic paintbrushes which are the same colors. Or cover empty juice cans with two to three different colors of contact paper. Cover the handles of the paintbrushes in the same colors of contact paper.

2. Encourage the toddlers to put the paintbrush in the cup of the same color for a matching activity.

3. Make a size matching activity. Cut a large and small paintbrush out of one color of construction paper. Do the same with a paint can pattern.

4. Attach the paint cans to the posterboard by using glue only on the bottom and sides so that the top remains open.

5. Laminate or cover both the paintbrushes and cans on the posterboard with clear contact paper for durability. Cut open the top of the paint can with a utility knife.

6. Attach a resealable freezer bag on the back with double face tape for storing the paintbrushes.

7. Show the toddlers how to slide the paintbrush into the can of the same size.

To do again

Make a game of matching three or more sizes or colors for toddlers needing a more challenging activity.

Teaching hints

Try to have the brush or object used for painting match the color of the paint for a matching activity within art activities.

Toddler Carpentry

$1\frac{1}{2}^+$

Tools fascinate toddlers. Toddler-style carpentry can be introduced safely with pounding benches, sand paper and styrofoam blocks.

To do

1. Provide a pounding bench for younger and older toddlers to use. Chant "pound pound pound" or sing "Johnny Hammers" as they use the bench (see Let's Hammer on page 211).

2. Put out golf tees with a large styrofoam block. Encourage the toddler to push or hammer the tees into the styrofoam.

3. A large mound of playdough can be used in the same way with the golf tees.

4. Show the toddlers tools which they may safely explore *with supervision*, such as a hammer, clamp, wrench, pliers, etc. Tell the toddlers the names of the tools and their use.

5. Let the toddlers pretend to use the tools with blocks of wood.

6. Invite a parent with carpentry skills to show hand electric tools to the children. They are fascinated with the sounds. Perhaps the carpenter could make something simple while the children watch, such as a small shelf or bookcase for the classroom, or repair something that is broken.

To do again

Let the toddlers feel different grades of sandpaper. Encourage them to rub the sandpaper over wood to make it smooth. Have them experience coloring on old pieces of sandpaper with crayons.

Teaching hints

Pounding benches are an item that should be provided at all times for toddlers. Hammering fulfills their interest in noise and develops their eye-hand coordination. As with woodworking with all ages, these simple activities for toddlers require close supervision.

Skills encouraged

fine motor
eye-hand coordination

Language to use with toddlers

hammer
pounding bench
peg
push
styrofoam
tee
tools
wrench
pliers
sand
sandpaper
wood
smooth
rough

Materials

pounding bench
large styrofoam packing
  block
golf tees
playdough
toy hammer
real hammer
clamps
pliers
wrench

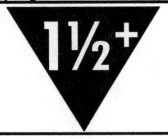

Color Creations

Toddlers experiment with creating new shades and colors as they fingerpaint with various colors of paint. Spring, with its abundance of pastel shades in nature, is the perfect time to focus on shades of color.

Skills encouraged

fine motor
sensory exploration

Language to use with toddlers

fingerpaint
hand
color
white
mix
lighter
see

Materials

smocks
fingerpaint
fingerpaint paper or tray
construction paper

To do

1. Put on smocks.

2. Place a spoonful of fingerpaint on fingerpaint paper or a flat tray.

3. Encourage the toddler to use her hands and fingers to spread the paint. Talk about the feel and color of the paint.

4. Add in a spoonful of white fingerpaint.

5. Show surprise as the original color begins to lighten. Talk with the child about the changes in colors.

6. For the older toddler, add in a spoonful of a primary color to further change the original color. Talk about the new color created.

7. If the toddler fingerpainted on a tray, make a magic print with a piece of construction paper (see Magic Print, page 66).

To do again

When focusing on secondary colors such as green, purple or orange, let older toddlers fingerpaint with the primary colors needed to create that color. For example, to make:

green—use blue and yellow

orange—use red and yellow

purple—use red and blue

Show excitement as the new color emerges in the paint.

Color Collage

A unique collage can be created from a wide variety of scrap items of the same color.

To do

1. Collect a variety of collage items all in the same color, such as ribbons, bows, tissue paper, fabric pieces, construction paper scraps, yarn, plastic milk jug tops, etc.

   Use your imagination.

2. Let the toddler choose the color background paper he wants to use.

3. Mix glue with a small amount of water. Have the toddler dip a sponge in the glue, then spread the glue all over his paper. Or use the sticky side up technique with contact paper (see Sticky Side Up, page 61).

4. Let the toddler choose various collage items to place on his paper.

5. Talk with the toddler about the collage items, the color and the different shades of the same color.

To do again

Older toddlers can do a multi-media activity that builds over a few days. Have them paint or draw with the specific color one day then add collage items of the same color on another day.

Teaching hints

Glue sticks will also work very well with some items and keep glue mess to a minimum.

Skills encouraged

fine motor
creative expression

Language to use with toddlers

color
same
different
lighter
darker
glue
paper
stick
collage

Materials

collage materials in one
  color
construction paper or
  contact paper
glue
sponge

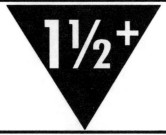

Keeping in Shape

It is best not to focus on different colors and different shapes at the same time as this can be too many variables for most toddlers. Rather, emphasize different shapes in all one color or the same shape in different colors.

Skills encouraged

language
fine motor

Language to use with toddlers

shape
color
circle
square
triangle
heart
star
big
little
paper
glue
collage

Materials

construction paper
gift wrap
wallpaper samples
glue
contact paper
bowl or basket

To do

1. Cut out different basic shapes (square, circle, triangle, heart, star) out of construction paper in just one color. Wallpaper samples and gift wrap scraps with the focus color as the predominate color can also be used.

2. Place the shapes together in a bowl or basket.

3. Talk with the toddler about the different shapes. Let her pick out which shapes and how many she wants to glue to make a shape collage.

4. Have her pick out a background paper and encourage her to glue the shapes on the paper. Identify the shapes with the toddler while she makes her shape collage.

To do again

Once the toddlers are familiar with the different shapes, introduce the element of size by providing large and small shapes.

Teaching hints

Compare the two-dimensional shape to a three dimensional object. For example, tell the toddlers "circle like a wheel," "square like a piece of bread," "triangle like a piece of pizza."

For Toddlers in Summer:
June, July and August

The free-spirited, slower paced days of summer provide the ideal time to explore all the objects of outdoor fun and travelling with the following themes:

◆ *Summer Fruits and Ice*

◆ *Water, Shells and Sand*

◆ *Going Places*

◆ *Balls*

◆ *Circles*

◆ *Summer Colors—Bright Shades of Red, Yellow and Blue*

Tooty Fruity

Introduce toddlers to the fruits of summer with melon and berry tasting parties.

Skills encouraged

sensory exploration

Language to use with toddlers

melon balls
round
juicy
taste
red watermelon
green honeydew melon
orange cantaloupe
white crenshaw melon
rind
bumpy
smooth
seeds
red strawberry
red raspberry
blueberry
blackberry
fruit

Materials

assorted melons
melon ball utensil
berries

To do

1. Show the children two to three different types of melon. Let them feel the rinds. Talk about the bumpy or smooth textures and colors of the rinds.

2. With a small group of toddlers, cut open the melons. Talk about the colors of the fruit inside.

3. Cut the melons into bite size pieces or make melon balls.

4. Let the toddlers enjoy a melon tasting party for snack. Emphasize how the melons are filled with good things to help them grow strong.

To do again

Have a berry tasting party with different kinds of berries. Read *Jamberry* by Bruce Degen and *The Big Hungry Bear* by Don and Audrey Wood.

BRRR!

Ice makes a cool addition to outside play on hot summer days. The ice will melt quickly and the toddlers will have a chance to get cool.

To do

1. Add ice cubes to a small amount of water in a water table or dish tub.

2. Let the toddlers first feel the ice cubes and the cold water. Talk to the children about the cold temperatures and the ice slowly melting.

3. Provide spoons, plastic scoops and containers for the children to use with the melting ice. Older toddlers can also use tongs to practice picking up the ice cubes.

4. For variety, big blocks and different shapes of ice can be made by freezing water in various plastic containers.

To do again

Add one or two drops of food coloring to the water in the ice cube tray before putting it in the freezer. Place cubes of all one color or different colors in the water and observe what happens when the cubes melt.

Skills encouraged

sensory exploration
fine motor

Language to use with toddlers

ice
water
frozen
cube
big
little
melt
cold
brr!
hand

Materials

dish tub
spoons
tongs
plastic containers
ice cubes

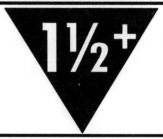

Berry Baskets

Berry baskets can be recycled with paint to print unique patterns.

Skills encouraged

fine motor
creative expression

Language to use with toddlers

berry basket
green
plastic
container
paint
print
design
lines
square

Materials

plastic pint-sized berry
  baskets
paint
paper
pie tins or flat containers

To do

1. Mix two to three different colors of paint.

2. Pour a small amount of paint into pie tins or similar flat containers.

3. Place one berry basket, bottom down, in each different color of paint.

4. Let the toddler choose the color of paper and paint she wants to use.

5. Encourage her to print with the baskets. Chant: "Paint-paper, paint-paper, look at the patterns I am making."

6. Talk to the child about the colors and design as she prints with the basket.

To do again

Cut the baskets into flat pieces for gluing on a collage.

Basket Weaving

Challenge the toddlers' fine motor skills with a lacing activity using berry baskets.

To do

1. Tie the end of an approximately twelve inch piece of thick yarn or ribbon to the side of a berry basket.

2. Show the toddlers how to string the yarn or ribbon in and out of the sides of the basket. If needed, wrap tape around the end of the yarn to make a needle-point.

3. Allow the toddlers to thread the yarn or ribbon around the berry basket in any pattern.

Teaching hints

A few toddlers enjoy stringing activities at eighteen months while many may not show interest or ability until closer to the second birthday or later. Offer stringing activities for those who are interested.

Skills encouraged

fine motor

Language to use with toddlers

berry basket
yarn
string
thread
in
pull
out
pattern
weave

Materials

strawberry baskets
thick yarn or ribbon
scissors
tape

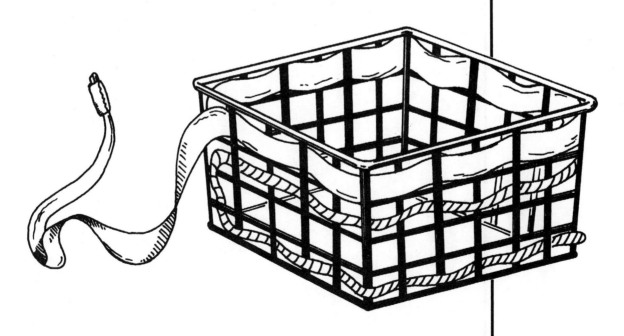

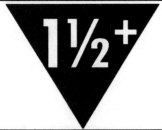

Sweet and Sour

Explore citrus fruits with tasting and painting activities.

Skills encouraged

sensory exploration
fine motor

Language to use with toddlers

orange
yellow lemon
green lime
smaller
larger
cut in half
sour
sweet
juice
paint
print

Materials

citrus fruits
paint
paper
flat container
paintbrushes

To do

1. Show the toddlers the lemons, limes and oranges. Talk about the differences in sizes and colors.

2. Cut up the fruits and taste a small section of each. Talk about the sweet and sour tastes.

3. Mix orange, green and yellow paint. Pour the paint into separate flat containers.

4. Let the toddler choose what color of paint and paper he wants to use.

5. Encourage the toddlers to paint pictures with these citrus-colored paints.

To do again

Make fresh squeezed lemonade or orange juice with a juicer.

Ice Cream Social

Ice cream is the traditional treat of summer for many families. Let toddlers serve their friends at a pretend ice cream social.

2⁺

To do

1. Loosely crumple white, brown and pink tissue paper into individual balls to resemble scoops of ice cream. Place the balls of "ice cream" into empty containers.

2. Provide scoops and plastic bowls so that the toddlers may pretend to serve "ice cream" to each other.

3. Make a pretend freezer out of a box.

4. Encourage the toddlers to put the ice cream away in the freezer before it melts.

5. Enjoy ice cream or fruit pops outside one day for snack.

Skills encouraged

social skills
imaginative play

Language to use with toddlers

ice cream
vanilla
chocolate
strawberry
scoop
ice cream scoop
dish
cold
freezer
melt
container
top

Materials

empty ice cream containers
ice cream scoops
tissue paper
plastic bowls
box

In the Good Ole' Summertime

Water fascinates toddlers. Lots of water play outside is ideal in the summer to help everyone keep their cool.

Skills encouraged

sensory exploration

Language to use with toddlers

wet
water
hot
cool
splash
sand
mud
sprinkler

Materials

soaker hose
sprinkler
dish tubs
water toys
shovels

To do

1. As often as possible, provide dish tubs, baby bath tubs or sensory tubs filled with water outside for the children to explore and to help them stay cooler in the heat. Provide plastic cups, strainers, sponges, water toys, etc. to use with the water.

2. Set aside a special day for the parents to send their toddlers in old clothes or a swimsuit, with a diaper if needed. Ask that they send a towel too.

3. Put out a sprinkler on low, sprinkler toy, and/or a soaker hose for the toddlers to play with outside on the playground or in a safe area on the school grounds.

4. Wet down the sand area and provide buckets of water for the children to play in with the sand.

5. Let the toddlers get wet and messy. Have a snack of watermelon or fruit juice popsicles outside. What a cool treat!

6. Before going inside, rinse the toddlers off with water from the hose or buckets.

Teaching hints

Enjoy the messy, wet day with your toddlers. While it does require more work and possibly extra help, it is a terrific summertime treat for the teachers and children.

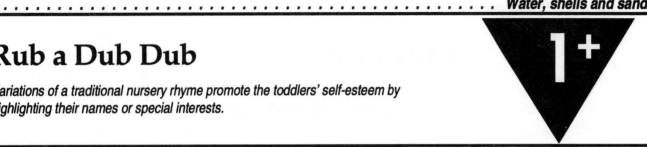

. . . . **Water, shells and sand**

1+

Rub a Dub Dub

Variations of a traditional nursery rhyme promote the toddlers' self-esteem by highlighting their names or special interests.

To do

1. Say the following traditional nursery rhyme with the toddlers.

    > *Rub a dub dub,*
    > *Three friends in a tub.*
    > *And who do you think they be?*
    > *The butcher, the baker, the candlestick maker,*
    > *Send them out to sea,*
    > *All three. (rock back and forth to the rhythm as though in a boat)*

2. With older toddlers, have three children sit by each other to say the rhyme. Use the children's special interests in place of the butcher, baker, and candlestick maker in the verse.

    > *Rub a dub dub,*
    > *Three friends in a tub.*
    > *And who do you think they be?*
    > *The tractor driver, the duck feeder and the outdoor player,*
    > *Send them out to sea,*
    > *All three! (encourage the group to hold hands and rock back and forth like on a boat)*

3. Say other variations using the children's full names or naming an article of their clothing in the fourth line.

Skills encouraged

self-esteem
language

Language to use with toddlers

rub a dub dub
tub
who
sea
three
friends
special
chant

Materials

none needed

Row Row

Use a traditional song about boats for a movement activity, to explore fast/slow and to promote the toddlers' interaction with their peers.

Skills encouraged

language
gross motor
social interaction

Language to use with toddlers

boat
row
stream
dream
back and forth
hands
legs
slowly
quickly

Materials

none needed

To do

1. Sing the traditional song, "Row, Row, Row Your Boat," with the toddlers.

   Row, row, row your boat,
   Gently down the stream.
   Merrily, merrily, merrily,
   Life is but a dream. (encourage the children to rock back and forth to the rhythm of the song or pretend to row with their arms)

2. Pretend to be on a large boat and sing the song very slowly in a deep voice. Row slowly.

3. Pretend to be on a small boat and sing the song quickly and in a high voice. Row quickly.

4. Have a toddler sit facing you with both legs outstretched. Hold the toddlers' hands and rock back and forth while singing the song.

5. Have older toddlers make "rowing pairs" with each other. Sing "Row, Row, Row Your Boat" as the pairs row back and forth together to the rhythm.

Teaching hints

When doing activities in which you vary the speed from slow to fast, it is helpful to end with the slower variation as this helps calm and focus the children for what will come next.

Never, Never Sinking

Toy boats and variations on a familiar song allow toddlers to examine colors, sizes and types of boats.

To do

1. Cut a large oval shape out of blue fabric or felt for water. Place the "water" on the floor.

2. Place a variety of boats in the "water" for the toddlers to play with. Fish shapes cut out of felt can also be added if desired.

3. Talk to the toddlers about the types of boats, the colors and the different parts of a boat.

4. As they play with the boats in the "water," sing the following to the tune of "Are You Sleeping?"

   Big ships, little boats,
   Big ships, little boats,
   Watch them float, watch them float,
   All around the water,
   Never, never sinking,
   Get on board, let's get on board.

5. Change the words of the song to relate to the colors or types of ships and boats (sail, speed, fishing, cargo, etc.) with older toddlers. Show pictures of the different types while singing the verse.

Skills encouraged

language
fine motor

Language to use with toddlers

ships
boats
colors
sizes
floating
sinking
sail
motor
fishing
water

Materials

blue fabric or felt
other colors of felt
scissors
toy boats
pictures of boats

Catch of the Day

Introduce toddlers to colors, sizes and types of fish and sea life with a simple fingerplay about fishing.

Skills encouraged

language

Language to use with toddlers

fish
fins
eyes
colors
swim
water
trout
catfish
sea horse
shark
crab

Materials

pictures of fish and sea life
felt or construction paper
scissors

To do

1. Show the toddlers pictures of different colors of fish. Talk about the names of the fish, colors, fins, etc.

2. Chant or say in a singsong fashion:

    > *Ruthie rides in a boat, (cup hands together)*
    > *Ruthie goes out to sea. (make wave motions with hands)*
    > *Ruthie caught a big fish, (show size with hands)*
    > *But she didn't catch me! (point to self)*

3. Substitute a child's name and the color, size, or kind of fish they want to catch. With younger toddlers, choose the color of the fish to match the clothing they are wearing.

4. Cut fish shapes out of different colors of felt or construction paper to use as a visual stimulus with the rhyme.

5. To emphasize sizes, sing the verse slowly for a "huge" fish, in a regular voice for a "medium size" fish, and quickly for a "teeny tiny" fish.

6. With older toddlers, show pictures of other kinds of sea life, such as sharks, sea horses, crabs and turtles they can catch. Use the pictures as a visual stimulus with the rhyme.

7. Read *The Owl and the PussyCat* by Edward Lear and illustrated by Jan Brett for wonderful pictures of fish and ocean animals.

Shell Collections

In summer, toddlers explore the colors and textures of nature with shells, as they did with rocks in the fall.

1½⁺

To do

1. Let the toddlers explore a variety of shells in a bucket. Talk about the rough/smooth texture, the colors, the size, etc. with the children.

2. Leave the shells out in a basket or bucket for the toddlers to explore on their own. Make sure the shells are large enough to pass the choke test.

3. Put out small empty buckets or containers for a "dump and fill" activity with the shells. Or encourage the toddlers to make shakers with the shells and containers with lids.

4. Place sand with a small amount of water in a dish tub or sensory table. Place shells in the wet sand like at the beach.

5. Encourage the toddlers to feel the wet sand, to hide the shells in the sand, to scoop the sand with the shells, etc.

6. Take the wet sand and shells outside.

To do again

Sort two or three different types or sizes of shells.

Teaching hints

The activities done with rocks earlier in the year can easily be adapted into activities with shells. See the following fall activities for additional ways to explore shells with toddlers:

Rock Polishing, page 107
Hard as a Rock, page 110
Splash, page 111
Natural Sorting, page 113
NaturalSculptures, page 115

Skills encouraged

fine motor
sensory exploration

Language to use with toddlers

shells
rough
smooth
beach
collect
sand
dry
wet
water
scoop

Materials

shells
basket or bucket
small containers with lids
sand
dish tub or sensory table
shovels

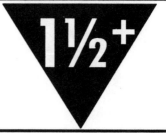

Little Squirt

Toddlers practice their fine motor skills by figuring out how to use squirt bottles filled with water.

Skills encouraged

fine motor

Language to use with toddlers

squirt
squeeze
water
spray bottle
wash
empty
full

Materials

spray bottles
water
cloths and sponges

To do

1. Provide empty squirt bottles for the toddlers to explore the squeezing action of the handle. Provide cloths and dry sponges for them to use with the bottles for pretend cleaning in the classroom.

2. Add water to the squirt bottles for the toddlers to use outside on a hot day.

3. Encourage the toddlers to mist the trees and plants outside. Provide cloths for the toddlers to use with the water for cleaning the windows, doors, playground structures, etc.

Teaching hints

Younger toddlers will enjoy just carrying the bottles around and may not quite have the skills to squeeze the handle. Older toddlers will develop this skill over time.

Bubble Mania

Blowing bubbles can be difficult for many young children, but shaking fly swatters dipped in a bubble mixture allows toddlers to be successful at making bubbles.

To do

1. Blow bubbles for the toddlers to chase out on the play yard. Let the toddlers try to blow some with your help if they desire.

2. Mix the following bubble mixture:

    1 cup water
    1 tablespoon glycerine
    2 tablespoons of dish detergent

3. Pour the bubble mixture into a flat tray. Lay fly swatters in the bubble mixture.

4. Encourage the toddlers to make bubbles by waving the fly swatter side to side or shaking it up and down. Small bubbles appear easily, especially if there is a breeze.

Teaching hints

Not all dish soaps work for making the bubble mixture. Experiment with the proportions as more water or more dish detergent may be needed.

Skills encouraged

sensory exploration

Language to use with toddlers

bubbles
wand
lay flat
wave
shake
up and down
back and forth
tiny
blow away

Materials

bubbles
fly swatters with small
  holes
flat trays
glycerine
dish detergent

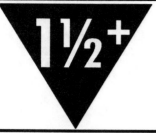

Fun in the Sun

Many children spend time at the beach and/or pool in the summer with their families. Provide simple props for the toddlers to play "at the beach" with their fellow toddlers.

Skills encouraged

imaginative play
social skills

Language to use with toddlers

beach
sand
sun
water
towels
sunglasses
hats
sunscreen
burn
sandals
bags
beach ball
bucket
shovel
T-shirt

Materials

large towels
yellow construction paper
scissors
tape
sand and water toys
beach clothing
tote bags
empty bottles of sunscreen
optional, recording of
  ocean waves

To do

1. Set up a "beach area" in the classroom with large towels on the floor. Hang a large sun cut from yellow construction paper on the wall or from the ceiling.

2. Add some of the following for the toddlers to use at the beach: sunglasses, hats, sandals, large T-shirts and swimsuits that the toddlers can fit over their clothing, tote bags, beach, balls, buckets, shovels, shells, etc.

3. Play a recording of ocean waves if possible.

4. Encourage the toddlers to play that they are at the beach. Provide empty bottles of sunscreen and remind them to rub the cream on so they don't get burned from too much sun!

Fishing Harbor

Boats and fish make natural additions to summer water play activities for toddlers.

To do

1. Fill a large dish tub, baby bath tub or sensory table with water. This will be the "harbor."

2. Add plastic boats and fish to the harbor.

3. Show the toddlers how to catch some fish with a small strainer or goldfish net.

4. Talk to the toddlers about the boats, fish, colors.

5. Sing a version of "Michael, Row Your Boat Ashore" substituting the names of the children who are playing with the boats.

   Ronnie steer the yellow boat ashore, Alleluia.
   Ronnie steer the yellow boat ashore, Alleluia.

6. Take the water with the boats and fish outside on a hot summer day.

To do again

With close supervision, add some plastic fishing worms for the toddlers to explore.

Skills encouraged

fine motor
sensory exploration

Language to use with toddlers

harbor
boats
fish
catch
people
water
float
sink
under
row
steer
ashore

Materials

dish tub, baby bath tub or
  sensory table
plastic boats
plastic fish
small strainers and/or
  goldfish nets

All Around the Town

Summer is a time of going places. Sing about travelling all around the town with a song that is an all-time favorite with toddlers because of its repetitive quality and hand actions.

Skills encouraged

language
fine motor

Language to use with toddlers

bus
big
wheels
around and around
town
people
up and down
wipers
swish
horn
beep
baby
mommies
daddies
rock
children
wiggle

To do

1. Sing "The Wheels on the Bus."

   The wheels on the bus go 'round and 'round, (roll hands)
   'Round and 'round, 'round and 'round.
   The wheels on the bus go 'round and 'round,
   All through the town.

2. Sing some or all of the following verses with the children.

   The horn on the bus goes beep, beep, beep...
   (pretend to honk horn)
   The wipers on the bus go swish, swish, swish... (move hands and arms back and forth
   like windshield wipers)
   The people on the bus go up and down... (raise hands up and down or stand up and
   down)
   The babies on the bus go waa, waa, waa... (pretend to cry)
   The mommies and daddies rock the babies, rock the babies, rock the babies...
   (pretend to rock a baby)
   The children on the bus go wiggle, wiggle, wiggle... (wiggle fingers or entire body)

3. Use your imagination for other verses!

To do again

Read a book version of the song such as the one illustrated by Sylvie Kantorovitz Wickstrom.

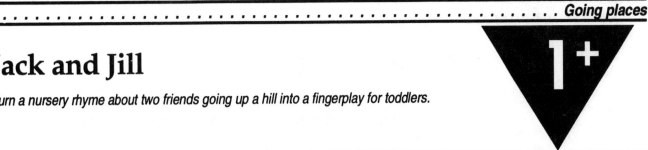

Jack and Jill

Turn a nursery rhyme about two friends going up a hill into a fingerplay for toddlers.

1+

To do

1. Chant this traditional nursery rhyme with the toddlers.

    Jack and Jill went up the hill, ("walk" two fingers up a hill)
    To fetch a pail of water.
    Jack fell down, (hit the ground with one hand)
    And broke his crown, (touch head)
    And Jill came tumbling after. (roll hands to ground)

2. Substitute the names of the toddlers.

Teaching hints

This rhyme can also be used when comforting a child who has fallen by using the child's name, body part bumped, etc.

Skills encouraged

language
fine motor

Language to use with toddlers

friends
Jack
Jill
hill
water
pail
down
broke
crown
tumbling

Materials

none needed

Pack Your Bags

Toddlers love to dump and fill. Provide backpacks and other soft suitcases for the toddlers to empty and fill as they pretend to pack for a summer vacation.

Skills encouraged

language
fine motor

Language to use with toddlers

backpack
suitcase
tote bag
pack
full
empty
take out
vacation
car
plane
train

Materials

tote bags
backpacks
soft suitcases
large, empty detergent
  boxes
contact paper

To do

1. Gather old tote bags, backpacks, and small soft suitcases for the toddlers to use.

2. Make "suitcases" from large, empty laundry detergent boxes with a handles. Cover the boxes with contact paper.

3. Encourage the children to pack their bags with toys, dress up clothes, etc. from around the room.

4. Talk to them about what they are putting in their bags. With older toddlers, discuss where they are pretending to go and how they will get there.

To do again

Add the bags and suitcases to a pretend bus, train, plane, boat, or car made out of a large box (see Down by the Station, page 249).

Teaching hints

To avoid pinched finger use suitcases with zippers. If the suitcases have locks, make sure you know the combination or have the key just in case a toddler locks his favorite bear inside. It can happen!

Toddler Freeway

Toy cars can be an important teaching tool. Use the cars to promote social interaction, sequencing, eye-hand coordination, and gross motor skills.

To do

1. Provide toy cars and trucks for the toddlers to explore on their own. Talk to the toddlers about the colors, types and parts of the cars.

2. Put wide tape on the floor or draw a wide line on a long sheet of butcher paper for the toddlers to "drive" their cars on the "road."

3. Encourage them to put the cars in a line or in a row. Talk about which one is in front, which one is in the back and which cars are next to each other.

4. Encourage the toddlers to follow you as you crawl around the room pushing a car. Older toddlers may initiate this on their own so follow them. Make car "noises."

5. Sit facing a young toddlers. Roll a car to him and have him roll it back to you. Encourage older toddlers to roll cars back and forth to each other. This can help children learn to share. Sing "Roll the Car" (see Roll the Ball, page 257).

To do again

Change the words to "Wheels on the Bus" to apply to cars and trucks (see All Around the Town, page 244).

Skills encouraged

fine/gross motor
language
social interaction
eye-hand coordination

Language to use with toddlers

cars
colors
wheels
track
follow
crawl
road
drive
line up
in front
behind
in back
next to
paint
back and forth
together

Materials

toy cars and trucks
wide tape or butcher
  paper
marker

1+

The Whistle on the Train

Create a new song for toddlers by changing the words to the toddlers' favorite "The Wheels on the Bus" to a song about trains. The verses of the song introduce toddlers to the special features of trains.

Skills encouraged

language
fine motor

Language to use with toddlers

train
cars
engine
front
caboose
back
wheels
clickety clack
engineer
all aboard
whistle
cows
cattle car
people
dining car
children
sleeping car

Materials

pictures and books about
  trains

To do

1. Show the toddlers pictures and books about trains. Talk about the different cars, engine, caboose etc. with the children.

2. Change the words of "The Wheels on the Bus" to apply to the parts of a train with the following song.

   The whistle on the train goes whoo, whoo, whoo, (pretend to pull whistle)
   Whoo, whoo, whoo, whoo, whoo, whoo.
   The whistle on the train goes whoo, whoo, whoo,
   All around the country.

3. Sing other verses about the train as the toddlers show interest.

   The engineer on the train says, "All aboard"... (motion hand to come)
   The wheels on the track go clickety clack... (bend arms at elbow, fists forward and
       move in a circle like train wheels)
   The engine on the train is in the front... (point ahead)
   The caboose on the train is always in the back... (point behind back)
   The people in the dining car say yum, yum, yum... (rub stomach)
   The children in the sleeping car go to bed... (rest head on hands and close eyes)
   The cows in the cattle car say moo, moo, moo... (moo)

4. Use your imagination to make up additional verses.

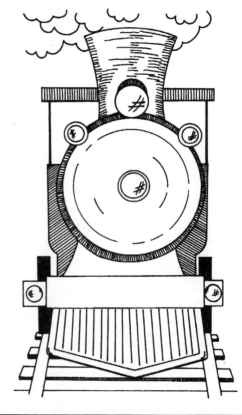

Down by the Station

Toddlers enjoy playing inside big boxes. Turn a large box into a "train" for the children to get in and out of and pretend to take a trip.

To do

1. Let the toddlers explore toy trains appropriate for their age. Read books and look at pictures of trains.

2. Find three or four boxes that toddlers can fit into. Cover with foil or contact paper if desired. Line the boxes up like a train.

3. Three to four chairs can also be lined up like train cars.

4. Encourage the toddlers to get in the train for a ride.

5. While the children take a ride, sing the following song to the tune of "Are You Sleeping?"

    Let's go on a train, let's go on a train.
    All aboard, all aboard.
    Choo, choo, whoo, whoo, choo choo, whoo, whoo.
    You can ride too, you can ride too.

6. Sing other songs about trains.

7. Provide some of the following props for older toddlers to pretend to take trips on the train: small suitcase, purses, vests, hats, etc.

8. Encourage the toddlers to "pack" their bags for the train trip (see Pack Your Bags, page 246).

To do again

Use large boxes as a bus, boat or car.

Skills encouraged

gross motor
imaginative play
social skills

Language to use with toddlers

train
engine
caboose
track
box
inside
All aboard!
suitcase
cap
ride

Materials

toy train
backpacks
small suitcases
purses
hats
vests
large boxes or chairs
optional, foil or contact
  paper

Making Tracks

Use cars for making tracks in a fun and easy painting activity.

Skills encouraged

fine motor
creative expression

Language to use with toddlers

car
wheels
tracks
paint
paper
roll
back and forth

Materials

cars and trucks
paint
paper
pie tins or flat containers

To do

1. Collect two to four different colors of cars and trucks, especially any with interesting tire patterns.

2. Mix paint to match the colors of the vehicles. Pour the paint into flat containers.

3. Place each vehicle in the paint of the same color.

4. Let the toddler pick out the color of paper she wants to use for making car tracks. Black is a good option as it looks like a "road," but also offer lighter colored paint.

5. Encourage the toddler to roll the car or truck back and forth on the paper.

6. Talk about the color and kind of tracks made by the wheels, the child's actions, etc.

7. Let the toddler paint with another vehicle if she desires.

To do again

Provide a large sheet of butcher paper on the floor or table for the toddlers to make tracks for a group picture.

We're Going

Toddlers use a wide variety of motor skills as they pretend to move like different forms of transportation.

To do

1. Show the toddlers pictures of different forms of transportation. Talk with the toddlers about the special features of each.

2. Pretend to move like various forms of transportation with some or all of the following verses sung to the tune of "Farmer in the Dell"

   > *We're going in the car.*
   > *We're going in the car.*
   > *Get in and buckle up.*
   > *We're going in the car. (sit down and pretend to drive)*

   > *We're going in the boat.*
   > *We're going in the boat.*
   > *Put on your life vest.*
   > *We're going in the boat. (pretend to row)*

   > *We're going on the train.*
   > *We're going on the train.*
   > *Find your car and climb aboard.*
   > *We're going on the train. (walk around room on knees with*
   >   *arms moving back and forth)*

   > *We're going in the big truck... (sit down and bounce upper body)*
   > *We're going on the plane... (walk around the room with arms outstretched)*
   > *We're going on the helicopter... (spin around with arms on hips)*

3. Be sure to include the most basic form of transportation—walking!

   > *We're going on a walk.*
   > *We're going on a walk.*
   > *Come on and join us.*
   > *We're going on a walk.*

4. Sing the following to end the movement activity and to refocus the toddlers' energy.

   > *We're back at home/school.*
   > *We're back at home/school.*
   > *Lay down and take a rest.*
   > *We're back at home/school. (lay down)*

To do again

Extend any of the verses into more of a "trip" with a pretend story about brakes, hills, landing, moving fast, coming to a stop, etc. according to the form of transportation.

Skills encouraged

gross motor
language

Language to use with toddlers

move
car
truck
train
boat
plane
helicopter
walk
spin
steer
bounce

Materials

pictures of different forms of transportation

Wheel Toy Wash

Stay cool outside with a car wash for wheel toys!

Skills encouraged

fine motor
sensory exploration

Language to use with toddlers

wheels
tires
steering wheel
dirty
muddy
clean
wash
water
soap
scrub
sponge
cloths
bucket
squirt bottle
wipe
shiny

Materials

wheel toys
squirt bottles
sponges
buckets
dish soap
cloths
small cloths
toothbrushes
dish pan or sensory table

To do

1. Gather squirt bottles filled with water, buckets with soapy water, rags, sponges, etc. and take outside.

2. Bring wheel toys over to the "wheel toy wash station."

3. Encourage the toddlers to wash the wheel toys. Talk to them about the supplies and their actions. Emphasize how helpful they are being.

4. For an indoor "car wash," let the toddlers use the sponges, small cloths and toothbrushes to wash and dry toy cars and trucks. Place the items in a small amount of water at the sensory table or in a dish pan on the floor.

To do again

Wash and groom animal riding toys, such as rocking horses. Remember to "feed" the animals too!

Park It Please!

Make a matching game for toddlers with cars and boxes, two of their favorite toys!

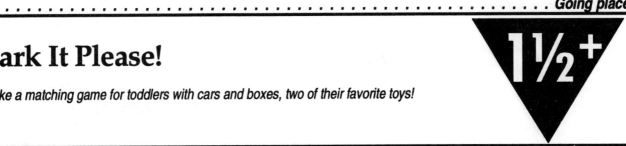

To do

1. Collect three to four cars of different colors.

2. Find boxes that the cars will easily fit into. Shoe boxes work fine for smaller cars.

3. Take the tops off the boxes. Cut a "garage door" that the car to fit through in one side of each of the boxes.

4. Cover the sides and bottom of the boxes with construction or contact paper in the same colors as the cars.

5. Turn each box upside down so it resembles a garage with a roof.

6. Place the cars near the boxes. Encourage the toddlers to "park" the cars in the garage of the same color.

To do again

Make a big garage for big cars and a small garage for smaller cars for a sorting by size activity.

Skills encouraged

language
visual discrimination

Language to use with toddlers

car
garage
park
match
same color
different color
inside

Materials

boxes
cars
scissors
construction or contact
  paper

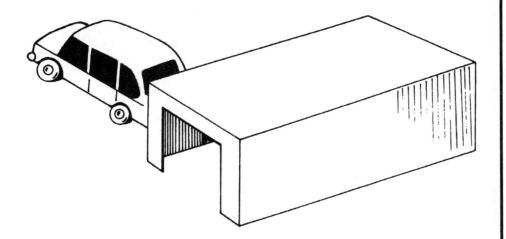

All Aboard!

Toddlers are fascinated by the sounds, parts and movements of trains. Pretending to be trains provides an opportunity for creative movement and promotes social interaction among pairs of toddlers.

Skills encouraged

gross motor
social skills
creative movement

Language to use with toddlers

train
caboose
engine
friend
waist
choo choo
whistle
whoo whoo
depot
stop
all aboard

Materials

recorded music

To do

1. Have older toddlers be "train friends" with you or another child. One person will be the engine while the other is the caboose. Have the caboose hold on to the waist of the engine. Teachers will need a train friend to provide a model of the actions.

2. Play music with a definite rhythm or a recording of a song about trains.

3. Shout "All aboard" before starting!

4. Have the "train friends" move around the room to the music. Make "choo, choo" sounds and blow the whistle "whoo, whoo" now and then.

5. At the end of the recording or when ready to end the activity, have the trains come to a stop at the "depot."

6. Have the engine and caboose switch places and repeat the activity.

To do again

Sing the following song to the tune of "Are You Sleeping?"

> *We are trains, we are trains.*
> *One is the engine, the other is the caboose.*
> *Chugga, chugga, choo, choo, chugga, chugga, choo, choo.*
> *Watch us go, watch us go.*

Teaching hints

Rather than forming the group into one large train, smaller units of two, maybe three, "cars" work best with children under three. When pairing children for the activity, encourage more active toddlers to pair off with more tentative children to provide a balance.

Ball Pool

Placing balls in the sensory table offers an extremely easy and fun way for toddlers to explore a traditional toy of the summer season.

To do

1. Collect a variety of balls. Place the balls in a small, dry wading pool on the playground.

2. Let the toddlers explore the balls.

3. Describe the properties of the balls as the children play with them. For example, "Emily has the red, white and blue ball."

4. Sing a verse of "Mary Wore Her Red Dress" in relation to who is playing with what ball:

   Who has the big furry ball, big furry ball, big furry ball?
   Who has the big furry ball in their hands?
   Chris has the big furry, big furry, big furry ball.
   Chris has the big furry ball in the pool.

5. Provide smaller, softer balls for the toddlers to explore inside in a sensory table or dish tub. The "ball pool" can also be used inside if there is enough space in the room.

6. Add containers with lids that the balls fit inside. Encourage the children to put the balls inside the containers and shake.

Teaching hints

The toddlers will most likely take the balls away from the tub or table. Allow them to do this with a reminder to "put the ball away" in the tub when they are finished.

Skills encouraged

sensory exploration

Language to use with toddlers

balls
round
size
light
heavy
names of colors and/or
  patterns

Materials

dish tub or sensory table
balls
small wading pool
containers with lids

See Them Roll

Examine sizes and colors with toddlers in a song about all the different kinds of balls.

Skills encouraged

language

Language to use with toddlers

balls
big
small
roll
round
circle
names of colors and types
  of balls

Materials

a variety of balls

To do

1. Sing the following to the tune of "Are You Sleeping?"

    Big balls, small balls, big balls, small balls, (show size difference with hands)
    See them roll, see them roll. (roll hands)
    Round and round in circles, round and round in circles.
    Just like this, just like this.

2. Substitute other characteristics of balls. Sing about colors, sizes or types of balls. Use real balls as a visual stimulus.

3. Have a variety of balls available around the room or on the playground. Sing the verse as the children play with the balls.

To do again

With older toddlers, sort balls by color or other characteristics using the song to emphasize the differences.

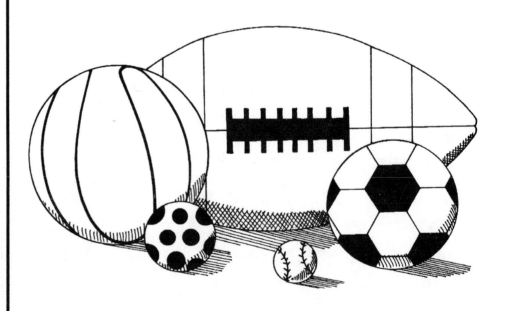

Roll the Ball

Rolling a ball back and forth with peers and teachers helps toddlers develop a sense of turn-taking and promotes early social interactions.

To do

1. Have a toddler sit facing you with legs open to help "catch" the ball. Older toddlers can sit facing each other in pairs or in small groups while the teacher says the chant to help guide the activity.

2. While rolling the ball back and forth, chant the following in a singsong fashion.

   > *Roll the ball to Jenny, like I do!*
   > *Roll it back to me, thank you!*

3. Continue to say the chant, substituting the name of each child involved in the activity.

To do again

With older toddlers, provide a basket of balls of different colors, patterns and sizes. Have the child find a specific ball and roll it to you by chanting the following in a singsong fashion.

> *Find the big orange ball (substitute different colors, patterns and sizes)*
> *And roll it over to me, thank you!*

Skills encouraged

social interaction
gross motor

Language to use with toddlers

roll
to
back and forth
ball
names of colors of balls

Materials

balls

Ball Wash

Toddlers can explore sinking and floating properties and other characteristics of balls with a washing activity.

Skills encouraged

fine motor
sensory exploration

Language to use with toddlers

ball
dirty
clean
wash
cloth
water
soap
color

Materials

balls
dish tub or sensory table
dish soap
cloths
sponges
squirt bottles

To do

1. Add a small amount of gentle dish soap to water in a dish tub or sensory table.

2. Place balls in the water. Smaller balls work fine indoors while larger balls are best washed outside in a baby bath tub or sensory table.

3. For variety, include balls that float, golf balls that sink and sponge balls the absorb water.

4. Provide sponges or cloths so that the children may wash the balls. Squirt bottles can be fun for older toddlers to use outside. They also provide a fine motor challenge.

5. Encourage the older toddlers to dry the balls when they are finished.

6. This is a perfect outside activity on a hot summer day.

Throw, Catch and Roll

Use a simple action song to introduce toddlers to the various ways that balls can move.

To do

1. Sing the following verses to the tune of "Here We Go 'Round the Mulberry Bush."

   This is the way we throw the ball, (pretend to throw the ball)
   Throw the ball, throw the ball.
   This is the way we throw the ball
   When we play with our friends.

   This is the way we catch the ball... (pretend to catch ball with two hands)
   This is the way we roll the ball... (pretend to roll the ball)
   This is the way we bounce the ball.. (pretend to bounce ball)

   This is the way we hold the ball (pretend to hold ball close to the chest)
   Hold the ball, hold the ball.
   This is the way we hold the ball,
   When we are finished playing with our friends.

2. For older toddlers, substitute other actions, such as:

   kicking the ball
   tossing the ball (with two hands overhead)
   bouncing like a ball
   spinning like a ball

To do again

Use the song with real balls outside.

Teaching hints

Exaggerate your actions as though you were using a very large ball to help illustrate the movements. Adjust the number of verses sung according to the age level and interest of the children.

Skills encouraged

language
gross motor
creative movement

Language to use with toddlers

throw
catch
roll
bounce
hold
kick
toss
ball
play
friends

Materials

none needed

Ball Game

Challenge the motor abilities and coordination of toddlers as they swat at a ball that is hanging from the ceiling or a tree.

Skills encouraged

gross motor
eye-hand coordination

Language to use with toddlers

ball
swat
hit
reach
finger
head
kick
foot
watch
swings
stretch
reach

Materials

beach ball
yarn or thick rope
pillowcase
newspaper
paper sack
tape

To do

1. Inflate at least two beach balls. Attach yarn or thick rope to the balls.

2. Hang the balls from the ceiling at two different lengths, one at eye level and the other just within the reach of most of the toddlers so they would have to stand on their tiptoes to reach it.

3. Encourage the toddlers to swat at the balls. Show excitement as they hit the balls. Remind the children to swat at the balls rather than pulling on them.

4. Encourage older toddlers to hit the balls back and forth to each other or with you.

5. Hang another ball down low for the toddlers to kick at if desired.

6. Outdoors, hang some balls from a porch or tree for the toddlers to swat.

To do again

Pillowcases and paper sacks filled with torn newspaper can be used in place of balls.

Teaching hints

Avoid using balloons as they present a serious choking hazard for toddlers. Use the ball game with hanging balls to redirect toddlers who are hitting to an appropriate activity that will also challenge their eye-hand coordination.

Magic Balls

Here's a magical painting activity for toddlers using two basics: balls and boxes.

To do

1. Gather boxes that have a lid, such as those for school supplies. Empty diaper wipe containers also work well.

2. Cut construction paper to fit either in the bottom of the box or around the edges of the container.

3. Mix two to three different colors of paint. White is a good color to use as it mixes well with any other color.

4. Pour the paints into separate pie tins or flat containers. Place one ball in each color of paint.

5. Let the toddler choose the color of paper he wants and the color of paint he wants to use first.

6. Carefully take the ball out of the paint and drop it into the box. Close the lid and shake. Tell the toddler that he is making "magic."

7. While shaking the ball in the container, chant or sing the following to the tune of "The Farmer in the Dell."

   Shake, shake, shake,
   Magic we will make.
   Heigh ho, the derry-o,
   Shaking magic make.

8. Let the toddler use a ball from another color of paint if he wants.

9. Remove the paper when the toddler is finished. Show excitement and surprise over the "magic" of the painting.

Teaching hints

Avoid using marbles as is traditionally done with this type of activity since they are extremely difficult for toddlers to pick up when covered with paint and could pose a choking hazard.

Skills encouraged

fine motor

Language to use with toddlers

box
lid
close
size
balls
inside
paint
colors
shake
magic
design
surprise

Materials

small boxes with lids
paint
construction paper
scissors
ping pong, golf or similar
  type of ball
pie tins or flat containers

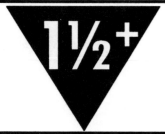

Toddler Slam Dunk!

Challenge toddlers' eye-hand coordination with toddler-style basketball fun.

Skills encouraged

gross motor
eye-hand coordination

Language to use with toddlers

basket
ball
drop
inside
reach
throw

Materials

ball
laundry or other type of
  large basket

To do

1. Place two to three balls near a laundry basket.

2. Encourage the toddlers to drop the balls into the basket.

3. Show excitement and clap when the children make a "basket."

To do again

Cut the bottom out of an old, round laundry basket. Attach the basket to the wall or tree outside so the brim is within the toddlers reach, even if they have to stand on their tiptoes. Encourage the children to make baskets by dropping the balls over the edge.

Teaching hints

Young toddlers will need to stand close to the basket while older toddlers can be encouraged to stand back from the basket to provide more of a challenge. Be very flexible about the distance they are required to stand so that all toddlers can be successful.

Spotty Marks

Balls can be used for printing activities and allow the toddlers to mark their "spot."

To do

1. Mix paint to match the colors of the sponge balls.

2. Pour the paint into separate pie tins.

3. Place the sponge balls in the same color of paint.

4. Cut large circles out of construction paper.

5. Let the toddler choose the colored paper circle she wants to use and the colored ball she wants to paint with first.

6. Encourage the child to print with the ball by chanting: "Paint paper, paint paper, we're making spots with the ball."

7. Let the child print with another color if she desires.

8. Talk to the toddler about the colors used and the "spots" made by printing with the ball.

9. Print with other types of balls, such as ping-pong, tennis or rubber balls.

To do again

Add the sponge balls to water with dish soap so the toddlers may practice squeezing to make bubbles (see Squish Squish Squish, page 214).

Skills encouraged

fine motor
creative expression

Language to use with toddlers

paint
paper
print
color
dots
spots
balls

Materials

inexpensive sponge balls
construction paper
paint
foil pie tins

Toddler Ping-Pong

The unpredictable movements of ping-pong balls on a hard surface keep toddlers intensely involved as they explore the balls in a number of ways.

Skills encouraged

fine motor

Language to use with toddlers

ping-pong ball
small
bounce
light
white
colors
hold
drop
throw
inside

Materials

ping-pong balls
plastic containers or cups
egg containers

To do

1. Give the toddlers ping-pong balls to explore on their own. Watch what the children do with the balls, especially on a hard surface outside.

2. Provide plastic containers for the children to use with the balls. Put one ball in each container. Encourage the child to drop the ball inside.

3. Cut an egg carton in half. Place six ping-pong balls near the carton. Encourage the toddlers to place the balls in each cup of the carton for a simple one-to-one correspondence activity.

To do again

Place white ping-pong balls in a dish tub with white cotton balls so the toddlers may compare hard and soft. Or, place white ping-pong balls and white golf balls in a water play table for float/sink and heavy/light comparisons.

Teaching hints

While the ping-pong balls do pass the choke test, they work best with toddlers over fifteen months of age and/or out of the highly oral stage of early toddlerhood.

Balls and Tubes

Dropping balls through tubes is a trial and error activity of experimenting with sizes and making objects disappear and reappear.

1½⁺

To do

1. Gather ping-pong balls, golf balls and other small balls that pass the choke test.

2. Collect the tubes from paper towels, gift wrap and toilet paper. Be sure to include large tubes such as those from big rolls of gift wrap and packing tubes for posters.

3. Cut some of the tubes into different lengths.

4. Place the tubes and balls together in a box, basket or dish tub on the floor for the children to explore on their own.

5. Show the toddlers how to drop a ball through the tube. Some balls will not fit through some tubes. This will promote more experimentation. Talk to the toddlers about the "too big" and "just right" sizes.

6. Observe what the toddlers do. They will come up with new ideas for the tubes and balls on their own!

To do again

Let the toddlers use the tubes with "match box" or other small cars. Provide proper supervision if the cars are very small. Encourage them to roll the cars through the tubes.

Teaching hints

Most older toddlers will grasp the idea of using one "tool" such as the tube with another "tool" like a ball to make something new. Younger toddlers may have difficulty using the two separate objects together at first and may prefer to explore the balls and tubes independently. Keep this in mind. Always follow the lead of the toddlers in their explorations.

Skills encouraged

fine motor
object permanence

Language to use with toddlers

ball
tube
inside
outside
roll
disappear
wide
long
short
too big
too small
just right

Materials

small balls
paper tubes
small cars
box or dish tub

Marking Around the Circle!

Activities with circles follow naturally from the focus on balls and the wheels of vehicles. Introduce the round shape simply with paper cut into circles for painting and the toddlers' most important marks.

Skills encouraged

fine motor
creative expression
pre-writing/emergent
  literacy

Language to use with toddlers

circles
round
color
draw
marker
crayon
pencil
write
lines
around
paint

Materials

construction paper
crayons
markers
paint
paintbrush

To do

1. Cut different colors of paper into circles. Have the toddler choose the color of paper he wants to use.

2. Provide markers and/or crayons for the toddlers to color on the circle.

3. Talk to the child about the straight/round/wavy lines that he is making and the circular shape on his paper.

4. If desired, chant: "Round and round, round and round, marking around the circle" as the child colors.

5. Provide large circles cut out of butcher paper for the toddlers to use with the paints or markers at the table or easel another time.

To do again

Provide other basic shapes (square, triangle, heart) for the children to draw on.

Teaching hints

Smaller circles encourage smaller, wrist movements while larger circles tend to produce larger, whole arm movements. Over time provide both small and large sizes of paper for the children.

OOO Circles

Toddlers can explore colors and sizes by making a collage of circles.

1½⁺

To do

1. Let the toddler choose the color of circle that she wants to use.

2. Give the toddler a page of dot stickers. If needed, show the child how to peel off the sticker and place it on the paper. Let the toddler put on as many dots as she desires.

3. For another type of collage, cut small, medium and large circles out of construction paper, gift wrap or wallpaper samples.

4. Let the toddler choose the color of an extra-large circle she wants for a backing for her circle collage.

5. Place the different sizes of circles in front of the child. Let her choose how many (even one is fine!) and which ones she wants to place on the extra large circle.

6. Encourage her to glue the circles on the biggest circle.

7. Dot stickers can also be used with the gluing activity.

8. Talk to the child about the size and colors of the circles she is gluing on the paper.

To do again

Make collages of different sizes and colors of one specific basic shape, such as squares, triangle, hearts or stars.

Teaching hints

This activity can focus just on sizes by using only one color of paper. Or colors can be emphasized by having circles of the same size in a variety of colors. With the younger toddlers, focus on either a few sizes or a few colors. Older toddlers can benefit from more choice in both.

Skills encouraged

fine motor
creative expression

Language to use with toddlers

circles
small
medium
large
color
pattern
glue
stick
pull up

Materials

dot stickers (available at office supply stores)
construction paper cut into circles
scissors
gift wrap
wallpaper samples
glue

Lots of Spots

Recycle odds and ends for toddlers to use for printing all kinds of circles.

Skills encouraged

fine motor
creative expression

Language to use with toddlers

circular
circles
shape
round
top
print
paint
paper
big
little
names of colors

Materials

circular objects
dish tub
paint
pie tins
paper
scissors

To do

1. Collect a variety of circular objects, such as plastic tops to spray cans, toilet paper tubes, yogurt containers, margarine tubs, etc.

2. Place the items in a dish tub or sensory table for the toddlers to explore on their own.

3. Mix two to three colors of paint.

4. Pour the paint into separate pie tins or flat containers.

5. Add two to three circular objects to each color of paint, trying to match the colors of the items to the color of the paint.

6. Cut paper into a large circle. Let the child pick the color of paper he wants to print on.

7. Encourage the child to print with the circular objects provided. Chant: "Paint paper, paint paper, look at all the circles" as he prints.

8. Talk to the child about the objects, colors and process of printing during the activity.

9. For another printing activity, print with the tops of interlocking blocks or bristle blocks. They make a neat design of lots of little circles (see Block Patterns, page 156). Match the color of the paint to the colors of the blocks.

To do again

Use bingo blotters for an easy printing activity for young toddlers (see All Polished, page 145).

Teaching hints

For younger toddlers, limit the number of objects for printing to two to three items. Older toddlers can handle more.

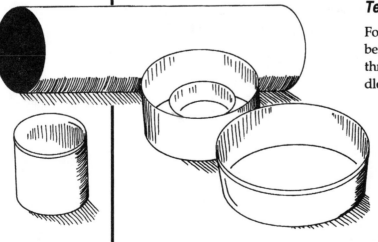

Polka Dots!

Celebrate balls and circles with a special day when everyone wears polka dots!

To do

1. Set a day for "Polka Dot Day". Send a note home to the parents asking them to dress their child in something with polka dots. Remember to wear polka dots yourself.

2. Have sticker dots on hand to put on clothing in case a child forgets to wear polka dots.

3. Talk to the children individually about their polka dots in terms of sizes, colors and numbers. Count some of the polka dots on the child's clothing.

4. Chant the following during the day.

   > *We are wearing polka dots.*
   > *Look at us and you will see,*
   > *Lots of polka dots.*
   > *We are wearing polka dots! (substitute the names of individual children and the colors or sizes of their polka dots)*

5. Have a circle snack, such as melon balls and/or round crackers or cereal.

6. Have fabric, ribbons, and/or scarves with polka dots available for the toddlers to explore and to use with dancing.

7. Do lots of activities with circles and other round objects like balls and wheels. Use your imagination!

Skills encouraged

sensory exploration
language

Language to use with toddlers

polka dots
circles
balls
shirt
pants
small
large
tiny
names of colors

Materials

sticker dots
fabric, ribbon or scarves with polka dots
melon balls, round crackers or cereal

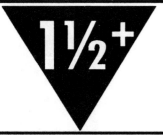

Tube Tops

Toddlers can use three-dimensional objects to make an interesting collage.

Skills encouraged

fine motor
creative expression

Language to use with the children

circles
names of colors
plastic
paper tubes
cut
short
long
glue
circle
round
stand up

Materials

shoe box tops or cardboard
glue
pie tin
round tops to cans, con-
    tainers and milk jugs
paper tubes
construction paper circles

To do

1. Collect three-dimensional circular objects such as the tops of spray cans, milk jugs and jars. Make sure tops pass the choke test.

2. Cut the paper tubes from toilet paper, paper towels, gift wrap, etc. into different lengths.

3. Pour glue into a pie tin or flat container.

4. Place the tubes and tops in separate bowls near the glue.

5. Have the children dip the tubes and tops into the glue then place them on the cardboard or inside the box top.

6. Talk to the toddlers about the colors of the tops, the lengths of the tubes and the circular shape of all the objects.

7. Provide circles cut out of construction paper for the children to glue on if they desire.

To do again

Combine this activity with printing circles with objects. First have the children print with paint. Then, on another day, have them glue on the circular objects and pieces of paper to make a collage.

Going in Circles!

Spinning helps young children develop a sense of balance. Explore circles with toddlers by finding ways to spin and go in circles!

1½⁺

To do

1. Show the children a toy top and how it spins around until it stops. Spin a ball for them also.

2. Encourage the children to spin like a ball or top with the following verse sung to the tune of "Are You Sleeping?"

   Spin with me, spin with me,
   'Round and 'round, 'round and 'round.
   Moving in a circle, moving in a circle,
   Touch the ground and sit down.

3. Repeat the spinning as long as the children show interest. For variety, change the last line to:

   Touch the ground and lay down.

4. Move in different circular and spinning ways with the children.

   make big and little circles with arms outstretched
   roll hands
   move feet in a circle at the ankle
   move hands in a circle at the wrist
   crawl in a circle
   spin in a circle while sitting down

5. Play "Ring Around the Rosie" or another circle game in pairs or small groups.

To do again

Show the toddlers a dreidel (or a top) used for a Hanukkah game. Encourage the toddlers to spin like a dreidel. Change the words to the verse to:

   Spin with me, spin with me,
   'Round and 'round, 'round and 'round.
   Just like a dreidel (or top), do the same,
   Now sit down, to end this Hanukkah (or spinning) game.

Teaching hints

Emphasize the "down" endings to refocus the toddlers so they do not continue to spin until they fall for they seem to have an innate desire to spin repeatedly, long after the adults have given up with dizziness.

Skills encouraged

gross motor

Language to use with toddlers

spin
circles
round and around
touch
ground
sit
dance
top
dreidel
Hanukkah

Materials

toy top or dreidel
ball

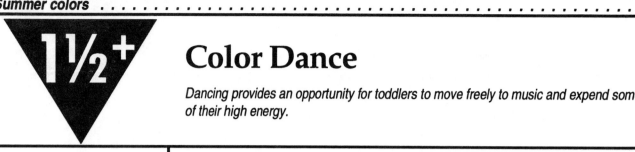

Color Dance

Dancing provides an opportunity for toddlers to move freely to music and expend some of their high energy.

Skills encouraged

gross motor
creative expression
social skills

Language to use with toddlers

dance
move together
side to side
up and down
in a circle
music
ribbons
scarves
blanket
sheet
towel
hoop
ball
center
grow
shake

Materials

blanket, sheet or large
  towel
hula hoop
scarves or ribbons
ball

To do

1. Play a variety of music without words that has a definite rhythm. Ethnic music, waltzes and polka music can be fun. Remember that the tempo of the music will control the tempo of the dance. High energy music will produce high energy dancers. More gentle, quiet music will have the opposite effect.

2. Dance with scarfs and/or ribbons in a summer color. Wave them side to side, up high and down low, around and around, etc. to the music.

3. Encourage two toddlers to hold opposite ends of the scarf or ribbon while they dance together.

4. Have two or three toddlers hold a hula hoop (preferably one that is a summer color). Encourage them to dance in a circle to the music.

5. Using a blanket or large towel, have a small group of at least four toddlers hold on to the corners. Encourage the group to move the blanket or towel up and down to the rhythm of the music. Or, have them move in to the center to make the blanket small and back out to make it grow.

To do again

Put a ball of the same color on top of the blanket or sheet. Encourage the toddlers to shake the cloth to make the ball move around.

Teaching hints

The teacher may have to join in with the group dances to helpguide the interaction process. Once the toddlers are familiar with the activity, they will often come up with new ways to use the props on their own.

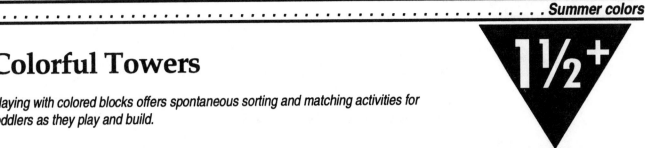

Colorful Towers

Playing with colored blocks offers spontaneous sorting and matching activities for toddlers as they play and build.

To do

1. Provide colored wooden or plastic blocks as a choice for the toddlers.

2. Encourage the toddler to find and separate out all the blocks of the focus color.

3. Talk with her about the colors, the process of sorting and building.

4. Encourage the toddler to build a tower or building with just the blocks of the focus color. Pretend with her and say this is a "red tower where spaghetti sauce is made", a "blue tower where blueberry jam is made," etc. with each color.

To do again

Build two or three different "garages" or fenced areas with blocks in all the same color. Have the toddler match cars of the same color to the garage as she parks the vehicles.

Teaching hints

When cleaning up blocks with the toddlers, turn it into a game of "I'll pick up all the red blocks and you do the green ones." Or count the blocks with the toddlers while putting them away. Clean up games like these centered on colors and counting work especially well with some toddlers who refuse to help put away blocks or other toys.

Skills encouraged

visual discrimination
fine motor

Language to use with toddlers

blocks
color
same
different
stack
tower
up high
garage

Materials

colorful wooden or plastic
  blocks

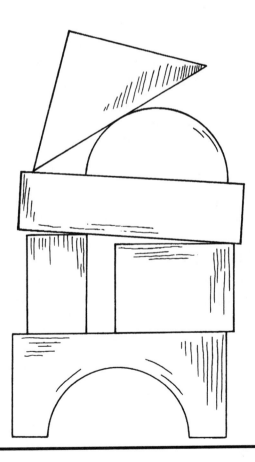

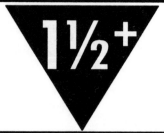

Color My World

Set aside a day at the end of the week to celebrate a specific color with clothing, food and a parade. Have a colorful, festive time!

Skills encouraged

sensory exploration

Language to use with toddlers

color
all
same
different
shades
shirt
pants
socks

Materials

construction paper
bulletin border paper
tissue paper
scarves
ribbons

To do

1. Have a "Color Day" and encourage each child to wear clothing in a particular color. Send a reminder home to the parents the day before. The teachers should wear the color as well!

2. Have on hand scraps of fabric, ribbons and/or scarves in the focus color in case a child forgets to wear the color of the day. Hats work too!

3. As the children arrive and throughout the day, chant:

   Mitchell is wearing yellow today.
   Look at his clothes and you will say,
   Yellow, yellow, yellow.

   Vary the chant for each child's name and article of clothing.

4. Talk with the older toddlers about the light, dark and different shades of the one color seen on all the clothing.

5. Have a colorful snack of juice, fruits, vegetables or other foods in the focus color.

6. Have a color parade with everyone wearing the same color. Wave ribbons and scarfs too! Or make crowns to wear in the parade from large sheets of paper or bulletin border in the focus color. Allow the children to take their color crowns home.

7. Fill the day with any of the color activities in this book (look at the end of each seasonal chapter) to help celebrate the color. Use your imagination to come up with more colorful ideas.

To do again

For a unique sensory effect, cover the ceiling lights with tissue paper in the focus color and/or hang streamers in that color around the room.

Teaching hints

Plan activities around a single color each month, related to the season or holiday. Focusing on colors in isolation helps toddlers learn about specific colors.

For Toddlers Celebrating: Holidays, Birthdays and Special Occasions

Simple, daily opportunities arise to celebrate toddlers' accomplishments and their joy in the newness of life. Tone down the hype of seasonal events, which can be overstimulating for toddlers, by relating the occasions to their daily lives with simple activities based on the following themes:
- ◆ *Signs of Celebrations*
- ◆ *Boxes and Gift Wrap*
- ◆ *Musical Instruments and Parades*
- ◆ *Teddy Bears*
- ◆ *Birthday Fun*

Occasional Greetings

Toddlers can be a part of the tradition of enjoying and sending greeting cards and notes for special occasions.

Skills encouraged

fine motor
pre-writing/emergent
  literacy

Language to use with toddlers

card
letter
note
pencil
pen
write
color
lines
name
envelope
picture
design

Materials

old, recycled cards and
  stationary
envelopes
small pads of paper
basket
pencils, pens or crayons

To do

1. Collect different types of cards (Christmas, Hanukkah, Welcome Baby, Birthday, etc.), old stationary, envelopes and small pads of paper. Parents are an excellent source of these items.

2. Place the greeting cards in a basket for the children to look through and enjoy on their own. Talk to the children about the designs or pictures on the cards. Provide envelopes for older toddlers to use with the cards.

3. Let the toddlers use pencils, pens or crayons to write notes on the old cards or stationary.

4. Talk with the children about their "writing" on the card. With older toddlers, discuss how people send cards to each other for special occasions.

5. Encourage older toddlers to give a "letter" to their teacher, friend or parent.

To do again

Let the children color and add stickers to construction paper folded in half to make a card to give to someone special. This could be done anytime during the year.

Useful Junk Mail

Let toddlers open their own mail by putting the often unwanted multitude of flyers, bulk letters and catalogues to a good use.

To do

1. Save unopened junk mail and catalogues from home and school. Send a note home to the parents to send in their junk mail and you will have more than an ample supply.

2. Place the mail in a basket or small box.

3. Encourage the toddlers to look through the catalogues for specific items. Talk with the children about the different pictures.

4. Show older toddlers how to open the letters. Younger toddlers will enjoy just sifting through the papers.

5. Encourage the children to put the mail back in the basket and/or throw away the unwanted pieces in the trash when they are finished. Or, better yet, place them in a box to be recycled.

To do again

Let the toddlers use the pictures from the catalogues for a picture collage (see Magazine Collages, page 49). The catalogues are also a good source of pictures for making books (see Toddler Books, page 48).

Skills encouraged

fine motor
eye-hand coordination
pre-cutting

Language to use with toddlers

mail
letter
envelope
open
tear
read
catalogue
pictures
look
trash

Materials

unopened junk mail
catalogues
basket or small box

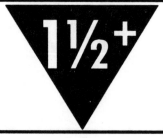

Cookie Cutter Symbols

Certain shapes are synonymous with specific holidays and celebrations. Toddlers can explore the symbols of the seasons and special events with the shapes from cookie cutters.

Skills encouraged

fine motor

Language to use with toddlers

cookie cutters
print
paint
design
symbol
special occasion
holiday
shape
spice
scents

Materials

cookie cutters
paint
paper
flat containers or pie tins

To do

1. Collect cookie cutters related to a holiday season or special occasion. The shapes can also be related to a theme.

2. Mix two to three colors of paint related to the holiday or event.

3. Pour the paint into separate flat containers or pie tins. Place two or more cookie cutters in each color of paint.

4. Let the toddler choose the color of paper he wants to use to print.

5. Encourage the toddler to print with the cookie cutters by chanting: "Paint paper, paint paper, look at the bell" (or other shape).

6. Talk to the toddlers about the shape/symbol and how it relates to the holiday or event. For example, "The heart says "I love you.""

To do again

Use cookie cutters to make prints in wet sand outside or in a sensory table in the room.

Cookies Anyone?

Toddlers enjoy making pretend cookies with seasonal-shaped cutters.

To do

1. Make playdough according to the following recipe. Add:

    1 cup flour
    1 tablespoon oil
    1 cup water
    1/2 cup salt
    2 teaspoons cream of tartar

    Combine all ingredients in a saucepan or electric frying pan. Cook over medium heat, stirring constantly, until the mixture forms a ball. Oil hands and knead until smooth. Store in a covered container.

2. Let the toddlers use cookie cutters related to a holiday, special event or theme with the playdough. Older toddlers can also use small rolling pins and plastic knives with the dough if desired.

3. Pretend to make cookies with the toddlers. Encourage them to make some for their friends. Talk to the children about the shapes, the process of cutting cookies and how families make cookies for special celebrations.

To do again

Have each toddler choose a favorite cookie to dry and take home. It can also be made into an ornament or special gift by making a hole for a ribbon or yarn.

Teaching hints

Remind the toddlers that these are pretend cookies and are not to eat. Expect that most toddlers will taste playdough at least once as part of their experimentation. Most stop after the first few bites of this salty substance.

Skills encouraged

fine motor
creative expression

Language to use with toddlers

dough
roll
cookie cutter
shape
cook
knife
cut
eat
pretend
seasonal symbol

Materials

flour
oil
water
salt
cream of tartar
saucepan or electric frying pan
cookie cutters
small rolling pins
plastic knives

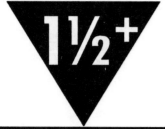

Toddlers Treats

Many toddlers experience lots of baking in their homes during holidays and special gatherings. Let them be gourmet bakers as they pretend to make treats for each other.

Skills encouraged

imaginative play
fine motor
social interaction

Language to use with toddlers

bakery
bake
oven
hot
cakes
cookies
muffins
batter
stir
ingredients
sugar
flour
treats
delicious
recipe

Materials

non-glass baking utensils
  and equipment
empty food containers
optional, large cardboard
  box

To do

1. Collect a variety of "toddler-safe" metal or plastic baking items, such as muffin and pie tins, wire whisks, bowls, spatula, cookie sheets, empty cake or muffin boxes, empty spice containers, measuring cups and spoons, hot pads, aprons, etc.

2. Make sure all the items pass the choke test and are non-breakable.

3. A few paper muffin cups with the muffin tins and plastic eggs with an egg carton can be fun too. Even consider an old cookbook and/or recipe box.

4. Make an oven out of a cardboard box if needed.

5. Encourage the toddlers to bake "tasty treats" for each other. Teacher involvement and modeling the use of the baking supplies may be necessary at first.

6. Talk to the children about the names of the items, their uses and the goodies they can make. Emphasize safety with the items, such as using a hot pad with the pans.

7. Enjoy all the freshly made "toddler treats."

To do again

Before introducing this activity, you may wish to do an actual baking project, such as making simple cookies or muffins, with the toddlers' help, or just in their presence, so that they can see how the baking equipment is used.

Teaching hints

The toddlers may at first just enjoy experimenting with the baking equipment and making sounds rather than actually pretending to bake. Allow for this experimentation.

Boxes and More Boxes

Toddlers love exploring boxes of all sizes and shapes. As boxes are often used during holidays and birthdays, they are an easy-to-obtain, inexpensive play item.

To do

1. Send a note home to parents to ask for help collecting boxes.

2. Put out boxes for the toddlers to explore. Observe what they do on their own and follow their discoveries.

3. Talk with them about the sizes, colors, types, uses, etc of the boxes.

4. Encourage the toddlers to get inside large boxes.

5. Have the toddlers put a toy or other object inside a box and close the top for a "peek-a-boo" type game or for pretending to give each other presents.

6. Encourage the toddlers to stack the boxes on top of each other and use them for building. They will probably enjoy crashing them down more than building elaborate structures.

7. Use empty food boxes in the home living area for "cooking."

8. Take larger boxes out onto the playground.

9. Use your imagination and follow the toddlers' lead for more ways to use the boxes.

10. Read *Inside, Outside Upside Down* by Stan and Jan Berenstain.

To do again

Make nesting games with three or four different sizes of boxes with tops that will fit inside each other. Talk with the children about putting the "small" box inside the "medium" box and the "medium" box inside the "largest" box, etc.

Skills encouraged

fine motor
gross motor

Language to use with toddlers

boxes
big
medium
little
huge
inside
close
top
cardboard
build
crash
stack
present
surprise

Materials

all kinds of boxes

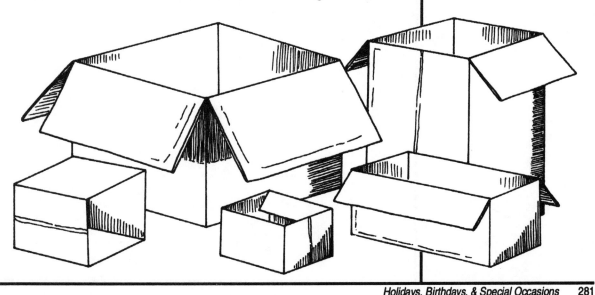

Full-Filling Play

Toddlers have an innate desire to "dump and fill," often to the frustration of their parents and teachers. Yet, dumping and refilling is a prerequisite skill to shape sorting activities. Boxes and other reusable containers provide for loads of dumping and "full-filling" play.

Skills encouraged

fine motor

Language to use with toddlers

empty
full
fill
dump
put inside
take out
box
container
one by one
count

Materials

boxes with removable lids
plastic containers
objects

To do

1. Collect shoe and other types of boxes with easily removable lids. Diaper wipe packages and other plastic containers with tops work well also.

2. Place a variety of objects in the boxes or containers. Any object will do provided it passes the choke test. Suggestions include plastic curlers, ping-pong balls, juice can lids, spray can tops and jar lids. Use your imagination and check the size.

3. Have the toddlers empty the boxes and then fill them up. They will enjoy repeating this process often.

4. If the container has a top, encourage them to put the top back on and then shake to make a noise.

5. Turn the "dump and fill" activity into a counting activity by counting the objects. It can also be a time to see how the child follows simple directions, such as "next put the purple one in the box."

6. Change the objects for variety and to relate to other themes.

Teaching hints

Use counting and other similar games (for example, "I do one and then you do one") to encourage the toddlers to help put away blocks and other multiple item materials they have taken out. Keep in mind that toddlers do love to "dump and fill" so encourage them to use the materials and then turn the cleaning process into a game.

Shape Sorters

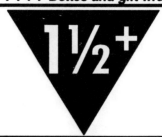

Store bought shape sorters often have too many different pieces for most toddlers. Make simple shape sorting games appropriate for the abilities of your toddlers from shoe boxes or coffee cans.

To do

1. Obtain two or three shoe boxes, boxes with sturdy removable lids and/or coffee cans or similar cans with plastic lids.

2. With coffee cans, smooth the inside edge with a spoon and cover with electrical or duct tape to eliminate any rough edges.

3. Collect multiple items of the same size and shape that pass the choke test, such as wooden blocks, jar tops, juice can lids, oval covers to pump soap dispensers or shapes from incomplete or too advanced store bought shape sorters.

4. For the youngest toddlers, use the boxes or containers as a "dump and fill" game first (see Full-Filling Play, page 282) to introduce shape sorter type games.

5. For the first stage of shape sorting with young toddlers, choose objects of only one shape. Cut the shape into the top of the box top or lid. Circular objects are the easiest to begin with since they fit through the hole at any angle and the toddlers achieve success easily.

6. Show the toddlers how to fit the objects through the hole.

7. For the next stage, provide two different shapes to sort. Cut the shapes in the lid or box top.

8. Continue to make advancing levels of shape sorters to match the ability of the group of toddlers.

Teaching hints

With any manipulative toy, it is best to start out with ones that offer the children success and then build on that beginning level to provide some challenge. Toddlers do become easily frustrated with manipulatives that are too advanced. If the teacher is continually picking up the pieces to shape sorters or similar types of toys, it may be above the groups' level and/or they may need to have someone work with them to learn the appropriate use of the item.

Skills encouraged

fine motor
eye-hand coordination
visual discrimination

Language to use with toddlers

box
can
shape
circle
oval
square
put inside
drop
object
take out

Materials

shoe boxes
coffee cans
spoon
electrical or duct tape
similar shaped objects

Box Expressions

Toddlers express their creativity by using boxes with art materials.

Skills encouraged

fine motor
creative expression

Language to use with toddlers

box
decorate
color
paint
markers
print
box top
squares
rectangles

Materials

plain cardboard or white
  boxes
butcher paper
tape
markers and/or crayons
paint
paintbrushes
scraps of gift wrap, bows
  and/or ribbons

To do

1. Collect a variety of plain cardboard or white boxes. Or cover printed boxes with butcher paper.

2. Provide markers and/or crayons for the toddlers to color on the boxes. For larger boxes, let the children work together as a group to cover all the sides, even over a period of days.

3. Older toddlers can paint on boxes with paintbrushes. Shoe polish bottles filled with paint work well for younger toddlers (see All Polished, page 145).

4. Provide scraps of gift wrap, bows and/or ribbons for the toddlers to glue on boxes.

5. Print with the lids from small boxes to make squares and rectangles. Match the color of the paint to the box.

6. Use the decorated boxes in the classroom or on the playground. Or let each child make his own "treasure box" to take home.

Teaching hints

The coloring, painting and collage activities can be done on separate boxes or on the same box over a period of days with older toddlers.

Pull Toy Boxes

Toddlers are challenged by walking backwards. Using pull toys encourages this skill.
Simple pull toys can be made from boxes.

To do

1. Collect shoe boxes and other types of similar sized boxes.

2. Insert thick rope or macrame string through one of the ends of the box for the child to pull.

3. Leave the top off and allow the toddlers to fill their boxes with blocks, dolls, stuffed animals and other items as they choose. If used outside, the children can fill their boxes with sand, leaves, twigs, etc.

4. Encourage the toddlers to pull their boxes around the room or playground.

5. Fill shoe boxes with items of different weights. For example, fill one box with a few blocks and one with many blocks. Leave a few empty too. Secure the top of the box with tape so that the toddlers will not know what is inside. Encourage the toddlers to pull the "heavy" and "light" boxes.

6. Put on marching music and have a parade of "box floats."

To do again

Decorate the box floats over a period of days. Older toddlers can help paint the boxes with sponge brushes or large paintbrushes if desired. Or decorate the tops of shoe boxes with collage type items, such as curling ribbon, scraps of gift wrap, plastic flowers, wallpaper, bows, etc. Secure the top of the box so that it doesn't fall off when the child pulls the float.

Skills encouraged

gross motor
fine motor
creative expression

Language to use with toddlers

pull
backwards
box
behind
heavy
light
decorate
box
fancy
colors
parade

Materials

shoe boxes
small boxes
thick rope

All Wrapped Up

Wrapping paper with its many colors, patterns and textures makes for festive collage and sensory activities.

Skills encouraged

sensory exploration
fine motor
creative expression

Language to use with toddlers

gift wrap
designs
colors
paper
box
glue
stick
give
present

Materials

used gift wrap
scissors
glue
construction paper
shirt or shoe box or basket

To do

1. Collect a variety of used gift wrap. Parents are an excellent resource for this.

2. Cut the gift wrap into strips or simple shapes that are large enough for the patterns to be visible.

3. Put the pieces of gift wrap into a large box or basket for the toddlers to explore.

4. Talk to the children about the colors, patterns, textures, etc.

5. Encourage the toddlers to practice tearing some of the paper.

6. Let the toddlers make collages with the scraps of gift wrap on construction paper, cardboard and/or a box. Be sure to use the pieces they have used for tearing practice. With older toddlers, add ribbons and old bows.

7. Separately cover the lid and bottom of a shoe or shirt box so that it stays wrapped when opened. Encourage older toddlers to put special objects inside to "give" presents to each other. Model saying "thank you" for the children.

Teaching hints

Gift wrap, with its distinct colors and patterns, is wonderful for making matching and lotto-type games for toddlers .

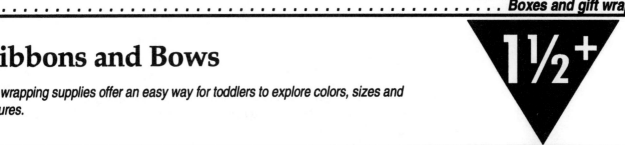

Ribbons and Bows

Gift wrapping supplies offer an easy way for toddlers to explore colors, sizes and textures.

To do

1. Collect old ribbons and bows. Parents are an excellent resource for these items.

2. Put the ribbons and bows out in a large basket or box for the toddlers to explore on their own.

3. Talk with the children about the colors, textures, lengths of ribbons, etc.

4. Let the older toddlers glue some of the ribbons and bows on to paper, cardboard or a box for a collage. Have the toddlers "dip" the bows and ribbons into glue in a pie tin. This will help with the heavier bows that may require more glue.

To do again

Provide two or three different colors or sizes of bows for the toddlers to sort into separate boxes or bowls.

Skills encouraged

fine motor
sensory exploration

Language to use with toddlers

bows
ribbon
curling
silky
colors
long
short
bows
sticky
present
package
attach

Materials

ribbons
bows
large basket or box
glue
pie tin
paper or cardboard

Pull It Up!

As they develop their pincher grasp, toddlers enjoy picking up tiny things—often to the dismay of their caregivers! Pulling up tape provides a challenging opportunity to practice this fine motor skill.

Skills encouraged

fine motor

Language to use with toddlers

tape
sticky
masking
colored
table
floor
Pull it up!
pattern
shape
piece
clothes
fingers

Materials

masking tape or colored
    tape

To do

1. Place strips of masking or colored tape on a table or floor.

2. Encourage older toddlers to remove the tape.

3. When they succeed at pulling up the tape, they can explore the sticky side or put it back down to pull up again.

4. For younger toddlers, put the tape on their clothing. This will be easier for them to pull off than from a hard surface.

5. Place the tape down in various patterns and shapes for variety.

6. Let the toddlers experiment with different types of tape or even duct tape.

To do again

Provide seasonal or regular stickers for the toddlers to explore sticking and un-sticking on a table top or floor.

Teaching hints

This is a good activity to redirect toddlers' attempts to take pictures off the wall. Tell the child, "I can't let you pull down the pictures but you can pull this tape off the floor."

Ring the Bells

1+

Celebrations and holidays are an ideal time to explore musical instruments with toddlers. Bells are a simple, gratifying instrument.

To do

1. Display a variety of non-breakable bells for the toddlers to explore, such as jingle bells, cow bells, leather strands of sleigh bells, children's toys with bells. Be sure they pass the choke test.

2. Thread smaller bells on a key chain or ribbon or in clear plastic containers, such as an empty peanut butter jar for the children to use as a shaker.

3. Let the children freely explore the bells during their play. Talk about the different types and sounds of the bells.

4. Show the toddlers other items that have bells, such as Christmas decorations, busy boxes, toy telephones, etc.

5. Encourage the toddlers to shake the bells while singing the following to the tune of "Row, Row, Row, Your Boat."

> *Ring, ring, ring, your bell,*
> *Ring it just like me.*
> *It will ding-a-ling-a-ling,*
> *And share with us your glee!*

To do again

Securely attach small bells to a wide piece of elastic. Sew the ends together into a small circle to fit the toddlers' ankles. Place the bells on the child's wrist or ankle to use for dancing and stamping.

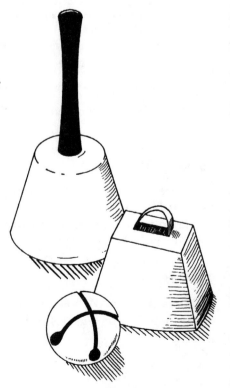

Skills encouraged

sensory exploration
fine motor

Language to use with toddlers

jingle bells
cow bells
sleigh bells
small
large
loud
soft
ring
music
shake

Materials

different kinds of bells
key chain, ribbon or clear
    plastic containers

Play the Drum

Exploring the variety of sounds resulting from hitting two objects together is rewarding for toddlers as they make their own kind of music! Drums also allow the children to experiment with their own internal rhythm.

Skills encouraged

sensory exploration
fine motor

Language to use with toddlers

drum
play
pound
sound
music
tins
loud
hard
soft
quiet
beat

Materials

metal tins with lids
wooden spoon
cans with plastic lids
oatmeal cartons
glue
contact paper

To do

1. Have a variety of metal gift/cookie tins for the children to explore.

2. Encourage the toddlers to play the drums using their hands, a wooden spoon or other similar object. Show the younger toddlers how to pound the tin drum if needed.

3. Chant "pound, pound, pound" with a steady rhythm as you beat on a tin to model the action for the toddlers. Say the chant fast and slow.

4. As the children make music, chant the following to their rhythm.

    > *Play the drum with Alan today.*
    > *Play the drum with Alan today.*
    > *Play the drum with Alan today.*
    > *This is the way. This is the way.*

5. Use the "drums" while saying nursery rhymes or other chants, always emphasizing the rhythm.

6. Or use the drum with the following, sung to the tune of "Row, Row, Row Your Boat."

    > *Pound, pound, pound your drum,*
    > *Pound your drum with me.*
    > *Pound it always to the beat,*
    > *And it will share your glee. (substitute a child's name if desired)*

7. Make different types of drums from cans with plastic lids and oatmeal containers. Secure the lid with glue and cover with contact paper.

8. Talk to the older toddlers about the varying sounds the different drums produce.

To do again

Make shakers from gift tins and containers (see Shaker Maker, page 55). Explore the different characteristics of music with the shakers and drums (see Loud and Soft, page 51 , Slowly and Quickly, page 52, Shake Shake Shake, page 56 and Shh or Not, page 54).

Teaching hints

Toddlers love to make noise. Provide opportunities for them to bang on drums or pound on benches and similar objects to fulfill their need to make noise.

Easy Tambourines

Using tambourines with music helps toddlers gain a sense of rhythm and provides an opportunity to explore the sounds they can make with the object.

To do

1. Show the toddlers a real tambourine. Let them explore making music with the instrument by shaking it or hitting the middle.

2. Use the tambourine with songs and chants to emphasize the rhythm.

3. Make simple tambourines for the toddlers to use. Punch six to eight holes with a hole punch around the edge of the plastic top from a coffee can or similar type can.

4. Thread thick yarn or ribbon through the holes stringing a jingle bell onto the yarn between each hole.

5. When the circle is complete, tie the yarn or ribbon in a double knot. There should be six to eight jingle bells around the edge.

6. The toddlers can decorate the tambourines with stickers or markers if desired.

7. Leave the lid-tambourines out for the toddlers to explore on their own.

To do again

Make small and large tambourines for comparison. Attach small jingle bells to small lids and larger bells to larger lids. Listen to the different sounds of the smaller and larger bells. Ask the toddlers to find you a "big" tambourine or a "small" one.

Skills encouraged

fine motor
sensory exploration

Language to use with toddlers

tambourine
bells
music
shake
hit
sound
listen
loud
soft
big
small

Materials

tambourine
round plastic tops
hole punch
thick yarn or ribbon
jungle bells
stickers

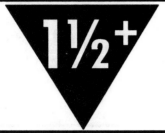

Let's Have a Parade

Toddlers often walk or run around the room as they practice and refine their developing gross motor skills. Marching provides an opportunity for the children to move about the room in a purposeful manner and still practice their motor skills.

Skills encouraged

gross motor

Language to use with toddlers

music
rhythm
march
step
stamp
bend knees
tiptoe
clap
around the room
follow
hat
float
instruments

Materials

recorded
music
hats
ribbons or scarves
box float
pull toy

To do

1. Play marching music or music with a steady rhythm.

2. Encourage the toddlers to follow you as you march around the room or playground. Emphasize bending their knees up high.

3. Wear hats and have a "hat parade."

4. Clap to the rhythm or wave ribbons and/or scarves while marching.

5. Other possibilities for parade additions include pulling a pull toy or a box float (see Pull Toy Boxes, page 285), using a push toy, making music with shakers, bells, tambourines, etc.

Teaching hints

Find any reason to celebrate with a parade, such as a "Pet Parade" with stuffed animals, a "Parade of Green" (or any other color), a "Parade of Tennis Shoes" or even a "Parade of Friends." Toddlers love to celebrate and find joy in even the simplest things, so themes for parades are easy to come by. Channel their enthusiasm with lots of marching fun.

Like a Teddy Bear

Teddy bears are popular with all ages and at times seem to be the "mascot" of holidays and special occasions. Any activity with stuffed bears is sure to be a hit with toddlers, especially if it involves a nursery rhyme with ticklish play.

To do

1. Ask to hold the child's hand.

2. Chant this traditional rhyme in a singsong fashion.

    Round and round the garden, (rub your finger in a circle on the child's palm)
    Like a teddy bear.
    One step, two step, ("walk" two fingers up the child's arm)
    Tickle you under there (gently tickle the child under the arm)

3. Repeat as often as the child shows interest. Do on the other hand, their knee, back, tummy, etc.

4. Encourage older toddlers to do the rhyme on your hand, a friend's hand or even on a doll or stuffed animal.

To do again

Have a little stuffed bear help you do the rhyme and tickling.

Teaching hints

Be sensitive to each child's cues. Some children do not want to be tickled. Yet, most toddlers will be anxiously awaiting their turn. This rhyme also works well on tummies after diaper changes and can help some toddlers be more agreeable to having their diaper changed.

Skills encouraged

language
fine motor

Language to use with toddlers

around
garden
like
teddy bear
one
two
tickle
under
hand

Materials

none needed

Fuzzy Wuzzy

A favorite word of toddlers is "No!" Let them have fun saying it with a familiar rhyme turned into a fingerplay.

Skills encouraged

language
fine motor

Language to use with toddlers

bear
fuzzy
fur
hair
no
fingers
arm
crawl
hide
please

Materials

none needed

To do

1. Say the traditional rhyme of "Fuzzy Wuzzy" with the following hand actions.

   Fuzzy Wuzzy was a bear. (walk two fingers up arm)
   Fuzzy Wuzzy had no hair. (touch hair and shake head no)
   Fuzzy Wuzzy wasn't fuzzy, was he? (walk fingers down arm)
   No! (say loudly, shake head no and hide "bear fingers" behind back)

2. Tell the hiding bear-fingers that "It is okay you don't have any hair. We still love you so please come out." Encourage the children to say "please" too.

3. Bring bear-fingers back out. Give the "bear" a kiss and hug as though comforting a sad friend.

4. With older toddlers, repeat the rhyme for a closing verse with the following changes.

   Fuzzy wuzzy was a bear. (walk two fingers up arm)
   Fuzzy wuzzy had no hair. (shake head no and touch head)
   Fuzzy wuzzy wasn't fuzzy, (walk fingers back down arm, smile)
   And we don't care, do we?
   No! (say emphatically and hug bear-fingers)

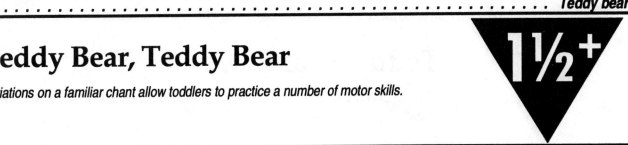

Teddy Bear, Teddy Bear

Variations on a familiar chant allow toddlers to practice a number of motor skills.

To do

1. Say the following chant and perform the actions with the toddlers.

> *Teddy bear, teddy bear,*
> *Spin around.*
> *Teddy bear, teddy bear,*
> *Jump up and down.*
> *Teddy bear, teddy bear,*
> *Pound the ground.*
> *Teddy bear, teddy bear,*
> *Now sit down.*

2. Repeat the chant again, but this time end with:

> *Now lay down.*

3. Substitute other actions for variety. Just use your imagination and try to use rhyming words if possible.

   For example, the following activities can be done while sitting down.

> *Teddy bear, teddy bear,*
> *Wave your hand. (wave)*
> *Teddy bear, teddy bear,*
> *Touch your head. (touch head)*
> *Teddy bear, teddy bear,*
> *Play the drum for the band. (pound legs)*
> *Teddy bear, teddy bear,*
> *Go to bed. (rest head on hands and close eyes)*

To do again

Say the chant while moving a stuffed bear or puppet according to the actions. The teddy bear words in the rhyme can also be changed to other kinds of bears for fun such as brown bears, panda bears, etc. Show the toddlers pictures of the other bears. Other animals can also be used in the chant, just follow the toddlers interests..

Skills encouraged

language
gross motor

Language to use with toddlers

teddy bear
move
follow me
spin around
jump up and down
pound
sit down
wave
touch
play
bed

Materials

none needed

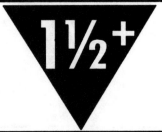

Teddy Bear Cave

Filling an area of the room with all kinds of stuffed bears is sure to bring beary-cozy times!

Skills encouraged

sensory exploration
language

Language to use with toddlers

teddy bear
panda bear
koala bear
polar bear
brown bear
fur
soft
paws
big
huge
forest
hungry
fish
berries
sleep
warm

Materials

a variety of stuffed bears
felt
scissors
empty plastic honey
  bottles
sheet
bath mat or rug
books and pictures of
  bears

To do

1. Place a furry rug or thick bath mat in a corner of the room. Turn the area into a "cave" if desired by hanging a sheet from the wall and/or ceiling to create the effect of a semi-enclosed space. Make sure that there are also open spaces to allow for good supervision.

2. Put a variety of stuffed bears in the "cave."

3. Hang pictures of teddy and real bears on the wall. Old calendars are an excellent source of teddy bear pictures.

4. Add some of the following items: large fish shapes cut out of different colors of felt to "feed" the bears; large circles from dark blue felt for "berries" for the bears; empty plastic honey bottles to feed baby bears; small fabric pieces for bear blankets; and books about bears and teddy bears. Use your imagination for additional items.

5. Play in the cave with the toddlers. Encourage them to play with, feed and take care of the bears in the cave.

6. Talk with the children about different kinds of bears, the soft fur, the foods bears like, etc. Sing songs and read books about bears, and look at pictures of different kinds of bears.

To do again

Read *Sleepy Bear* by Lydia Dabcovich.

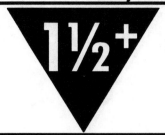

Teddy Bear Picnic

Emphasize the love and warm feelings of holidays and family celebrations with a special day to honor each child's favorite bear.

To do

1. Send a note home inviting each child's special bear to a "Teddy Bear Picnic." On the day of the picnic, have extra bears on hand in case someone forgets to bring their bear.

2. Talk with each child about their special bear, the name, the color, clothing, eyes., etc.

3. Politely ask a child if you can hold her bear. This provides correct language for the children to model when asking to hold another child's bear.

4. Gather together finger foods, such as graham cookies shaped like bears and strawberries for a Teddy Bear Picnic, or make honey sandwiches (see Teddy Bear Sandwiches, page 298).

5. Take a blanket and the finger foods outside to the playground or to another location on the school's grounds. Have each child bring their bear with them for the picnic.

6. Enjoy a snack under a tree with the toddlers and bears. Sing songs about bears during the picnic.

To do again

Read *Teddy Bear Picnic* or listen to a taped version of the song. Dance to the music with the teddy bears.

Skills encouraged

sensory exploration
self-esteem

Language to use with toddlers

teddy bear
picnic
outside
blanket
eat
special
love
hug
care for
unique

Materials

blanket
finger foods

Teddy Bear Sandwiches

Toddlers can help make honey bear-shaped sandwiches for a Teddy Bear Picnic.

Skills encouraged

sensory exploration
fine motor

Language to use with toddlers

bread
sandwich
cookie cutter
shape
honey
sweet
spread
knife
yummy

Materials

loaf of bread
bear cookie cutter
plastic knife
honey

To do

1. Have the toddler wash his hands with you.

2. Cut two bear shapes out of the bread with a cookie cutter.

3. Allow him to help spread the honey on the bread with a plastic knife.

4. Put the two pieces of bread together.

5. Let the toddler taste a little bit of the honey on his finger. Tell him bears love honey!

6. Enjoy the teddy bear sandwiches on a picnic. Yum!

To do again

Make other shaped sandwiches using different cookie cutters to relate to a theme or activity. Pimento cheese, peanut butter, cream cheese, jelly, tuna fish, etc. can also be used as fillings.

Please, Feed the Bears

Toddlers explore colors, sizes and textures in a matching game as they pretend to feed fish and honey to bears.

To do

1. Cut two to three bear shapes out of posterboard.

2. Use the same pattern to cut bears out of different colors of craft fur. Attach the posterboard shape to the back of the fur with glue.

3. Save the scraps from the craft fur for the toddlers to feel and/or use for a collage at another time.

4. Cut a fish shape out of felt in the same color as each bear. Honey pots can be cut out in addition to or instead of the fish.

5. Encourage the toddlers to "feed" the bears the same color of fish or honey.

6. Talk with the toddlers about the colors, the textures, feeding the bears, etc.

7. Store the pieces in a large envelope or small box.

To do again

Cut big and little bears out of one color of craft fur. Cut big and little fish and/or honey pots out of felt of the same color. Encourage the toddler to feed the bears according to size.

Skills encouraged

sensory exploration
visual discrimination

Language to use with toddlers

bear
fur
furry
soft
color
feel
touch
match
same
different
fish
honey pot
size
big
medium
little
feed

Materials

craft fur
scissors
posterboard
glue
felt
large envelope or small
 box

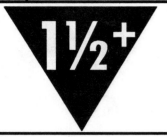

Beary Fun

Pretending to move like bears allows toddlers to crawl, stretch and move in other creative ways while also learning more about the animals.

Skills encouraged

gross motor
creative movement

Language to use with toddlers

bear
move
straight leg
hands
water
fish
paw
honey
tree
curl up
sleep

Materials

none needed

To do

1. Show the toddlers how to move like a bear on all fours with straight legs.

2. Move around the room like bears singing the following verses to the tune of "The Farmer in the Dell."

   The bears move all around,
   The bears move all around.
   Always looking for honey,
   The bears move all around.

   Pretend to find honey in a tree. Stretch up high to reach it and then eat it.

   The bears go to the stream,
   The bears go to the stream.
   They are going to catch a fish,
   The bears go to the stream.

   Pretend to drink water from the stream and to catch a fish with one "paw." Eat the fish and rub your tummy.

   The bears go to their cave,
   The bears go to their cave.
   They need to go to sleep,
   The bears go to their cave.

   Crawl in a circle, curl up and pretend to sleep like a bear.

3. Make up other verses to have the bears look for berries, scratch their backs against the wall, roll over, etc. Use your imagination and change the words of the song to fit the actions.

To do again

Look at pictures and books about specific types of bears, such as panda, polar, brown, etc. Use the specific names in the verses.

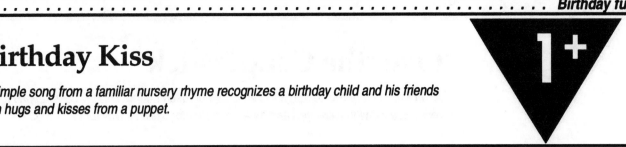

Birthday Kiss

A simple song from a familiar nursery rhyme recognizes a birthday child and his friends with hugs and kisses from a puppet.

To do

1. Find any type of animal puppet.

2. Sing the following verse using the puppet to the tune of "Baa, Baa, Black Sheep."

   > *Baa, baa black sheep, (or substitute sounds and name of the puppet being used)*
   > *Have you any kisses?*
   > *Yes sir, yes sir, I sure do.*
   > *One for the teacher, (have puppet give you a pretend kiss)*
   > *And one for the friends, (have puppet give the children kisses)*
   > *And one for (child's name) who is turning (two) today. (puppet gives a loud*
   >   *smack kiss to birthday child)*

3. Use the verse and puppet with any group of children during their play. Say the children's names in place of teacher, friends and birthday child in the song.

4. Have the puppet give hugs instead of kisses. Change the words and actions of the rhyme accordingly.

Teaching hints

Toddlers who may be hesitant about touch when they are new to the group will often let a puppet give them a hug or kiss. Use this verse with the puppet to help welcome a new child to the group.

Skills encouraged

language
social-emotional

Language to use with toddlers

birthday
kisses
hugs
friend
teacher
puppet
sheep

Materials

an animal puppet

Over the Candlestick

A familiar nursery rhyme about a candle can be used during birthday celebrations to recognize individual children and as a simple motor skills activity for older toddlers.

Skills encouraged

language
gross motor
self-esteem

Language to use with toddlers

birthday
candle
color names
wax
hot
Be careful!
jump over
step over
line
rhyme

Materials

candles

To do

1. Show the toddlers a variety of candles. Talk with them about the different colors, sizes, etc. Emphasize that they must be careful with candles because they can be hot.

2. Chant the following nursery rhyme with the toddlers:

   Jack be nimble,
   Jack be quick,
   Jack jump over the candlestick.

3. Substitute the individual children's names for Jack. Tap to the rhythm while saying the rhyme with their name.

4. With older toddlers, encourage them to jump or step over a candle on the floor. Use the child's name and the color of the candle in the rhyme.

   Ellie be nimble,
   Ellie be quick,
   Ellie steps over the green candlestick.

5. Have the toddlers march together in place to the rhyme and jump at the end over a pretend candlestick.

   We can be nimble,
   We can be quick,
   We can jump over the candlestick. (repeat as the toddlers show interest)

Have Your Cake and Eat It Too

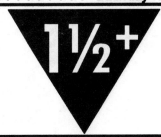

Older toddlers become more aware of birthdays as they start to see others having birthdays around them and will make "cakes" out of almost anything.

To do

1. Encourage the toddlers to make "birthday cakes" when playing with wet sand and buckets outside. Or add wet sand to a dish tub or sensory table with small containers for the toddlers to make "cakes" in the classroom.

2. Provide small twigs for the children to use as candles.

3. Encourage them to also make "birthday cakes" with playdough using craft sticks for candles.

4. Peg board type toys can also be used as birthday cakes.

5. With the toddlers' help, count the candles on the different cakes.

6. Cover a large styrofoam block with contact paper to look like a cake. Stick a few craft stick "candles" in the cake. Let the children take out and replace the candles.

7. Pretend to blow out the candles and taste the cake with the toddlers. Talk with the children about what kind of cake it is and how good it tastes.

8. Encourage the toddlers to give some "cake" to their friends.

9. Sing "Happy Birthday" with the children. Let them tell you who to sing to and how old they are!

Skills encouraged

sensory exploration
fine motor
social interaction

Language to use with toddlers

birthday cake
chocolate
vanilla
taste
candles
sing
Happy Birthday!
bake
hot

Materials

playdough
sand
dish tub or sensory table
styrofoam block
twigs
craft sticks
contact paper

Make a Wish

Toddlers practice visual discrimination skills with a matching game by putting candles on the same color, pattern or size cake.

Skills encouraged

fine motor
visual discrimination

Language to use with toddlers

cake
candle
match
same
different
color
pattern
Happy Birthday!
one
two

Materials

construction paper
scissors
posterboard
gift wrap
wallpaper samples
glue
utility knife
contact paper
resealable bags
double-faced tape

To do

1. Depending on the ability of the children, use two to four different colors of construction paper. Cut a cake and a matching candle out of each color. Gift wrap or wallpaper samples can also be used for matching patterns.

2. Glue the cake pieces to the posterboard with the middle of the top edge of each cake unattached.

3. Laminate or cover the candles and the posterboard with clear contact paper for durability.

4. Slice an opening along the middle of the top edge of each cake with a utility blade so the candles can be slipped inside.

5. Attach a resealable freezer bag for storing the candles on the back of the posterboard with double-faced tape.

6. Encourage the toddlers to match the color or pattern of the candle to each cakes by inserting the candle inside the opening on the top of the cake.

7. Talk with the toddlers about the colors and patterns. Sing "Happy Birthday" while playing the game.

8. Older toddlers will enjoy the challenge of matching two candles to each cake.

To do again

Cut out a large cake, large candle, small cake and small candle for matching sizes.

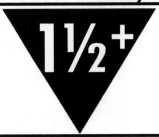

You're Invited

Toddlers enjoy special events, even pretend ones! Have a pretend party with all the fixings and allow the toddlers to celebrate with their friends.

To do

1. Decorate the home living area with party streamers.

2. Add some of the following party props to the area for the toddlers' party: paper cups, paper plates, empty, unbreakable juice container, tablecloth, old cards and envelopes, hats, dress-up clothes.

3. Make a pretend cake out of a styrofoam block covered with contact paper (see Have Your Cake and Eat It Too, page 303).

4. Add pretend ice cream if desired (see Ice Cream Social, page 233).

5. Provide old gift bags and boxes so the toddlers can give each other presents. Cover some of the tops and bottoms of shirt or shoe boxes separately so that they stay wrapped when opened (see All Wrapped Up, page 286).

6. Take pretend pictures with an old camera.

7. Join the toddlers at their party. **Celebrate the wonderful age of toddlerhood!**

Teaching hints

Balloons do present a choking hazard for young children so if any are used make sure they are out of the reach of the children.

Skills encouraged

imaginative play
social interaction

Language to use with toddlers

birthday party
celebrate
Happy Birthday!
special day
invite
friends
cake
cups
plates
juice
present
Thank you!
camera
Smile!

Materials

paper party supplies
styrofoam block
contact paper
hats
boxes
old camera

Books for Toddlers

A mixture of old favorites and soon-to-be favorites.

Asch, Frank. (1989). *Baby in the Box*. New York: Holiday House. (18 months and up)

Aruego, José and Dewey, Ariane. (1989). *Five Little Ducks*. New York: Crown. (18 months and up)

Bailey, Debbie. (1991). *Shoes*. Ontario: Annick Press. (12 months and up). Additional titles by this author: *Clothes, Hats, My Mom* and *My Dad*.

Bang, Molly. (1983). *Ten, Nine, Eight*. New York: Greenwillow. (18 months and up)

Berenstain, Stan and Jan. (1968). *Inside Outside Upside Down*. New York: Random House. (18 months and up)

Berenstain, Stan and Jan. (1970). *Old Hat, New Hat*. New York: Random House. (18 months and up)

Beylon, Cathy. (1992). *Hush Little Baby*. New York: Checkerboard Press. (12 months and up). Additional titles by this author: *The Mulberry Bush* and *Old MacDonald*.

Brown, Margaret (1947). *Goodnight Moon*. New York: HarperCollins. (18 months and up)

Carle, Eric. (1968). *1, 2, 3 to the Zoo*. New York: Putnam. (12 months and up)

Carl, Eric. (1987). *The Very Hungry Caterpillar*. New York: Philomel Books. (18 months and up)

Carl, Eric (1984). *The Very Busy Spider*. New York: Putnam. (18 months and up)

Crews, Donald. (1978). *Freight Train*. New York: Greenwillow. (24 months and up)

Crozat, Francois. (1989). *I Am a Little Duck*. New York: Barron's Educational Series. (18 months and up). Additional titles by this author: *I Am a Little Bear, I Am a Little Cat, I Am a Little Dog, I Am a Little Elephant, I Am a Little Lion, I Am a Little Pony* and *I Am a Little Rabbit*.

Dabcovich, Lydia (1982). *Sleepy Bear*. New York: Penguin. (18 months and up)

Day, Alexandra (1991). *Carl's Afternoon in the Park*. Canada: HarperCollins Canada. (12 months and up). Additional titles by this author: *Carl Goes to Day Care, Carl Goes Shopping , Carl's Christmas* and *Good Dog, Carl*.

Degen, Bruce. (1983). *Jamberry*. New York: HarperCollins. (18 months and up)

Dyer, Jane. (1986). *Moo, Moo, Peekaboo!*. New York: Random House (12 months and up). Additional titles by this author: *Where's Baby?* and *The Fuzzytail Friends' Great Egg Hunt*.

Fox, Mem. (1993). *Time For Bed*. San Diego: Harcourt Brace Jovanovich. (18 months and up)

Galdone, Paul. (1986). *Three Little Kittens*. New York: Clarion. (18 months and up)

Ginsburg, Mirra. (1982). *Across the Stream*. New York: Mulberry Books. (18 months and up)

Hill, Eric. (1985). *Spot Goes to the Beach*. New York: Putnam. (12 months and up). Additional titles by this author: *Spot's First Walk, Spot Goes to the Farm, Spot Goes to the Circus, Spot Goes to School* and *Where's Spot?*

Hutchins, Pat. (1968). *Rosie's Walk*. New York: Macmillian. (18 months and up)

Isaacs, Gwunne and Mott, Evelyn (1994). *Baby Face*. New York: Random House. (12 months and up)

Johnson, Audean. (1982). *Soft as a Kitten*. New York: Random House. (12 months and up)

Kalan, Robert. (1978). *Rain*. New York: Mulberry Books. (18 months and up)

Kline, Suzy. (1989). *Ooops*. New York: Puffin Books. (24 months and up)

Kozikowski, Renate. (1989). *The Teddy Bears' Picnic*. New York: Aladdin Books. (18 months and up)

Lear, Edward. (1991). *The Owl and the Pussy Cat*. New York: Putnam. (12 months and up)

Jones, Carol. (1989). *Old MacDonald*. New York: Houghton Mifflin. (18 months and up)

Lewison, Wendy. (1992). *Where's Baby?* New York: Scholastic. (12 months and up)

Martin, Bill. (1983). Brown Bear, Brown Bear, What Do You See? New York: Henry Holt and Company. (12 months and up). Also by this author: *Polar Bear, Polar Bear, What Do You Hear?*

Moncure, Jane. (1982). *The Look Book*. Chicago: Children's Press. (24 months and up)

Oxenbury, Helen. (1987) *Clap Hands*. New York: Macmillan. (12 months and up). Additional titles by this author: *All Fall Down* and *Tickle Tickle*.

Peek, Merle. (1985). *Mary Wore Her Red Dress and Henry Wore His Green Sneakers*. New York: Clarion Books. (12 months and up)

Pragoff, Fionna. (1987). *Growing*. New York: Doubleday. (12 months and up)

Pragoff, Fionna. (1994). *It's Great to Be Two*. New York: Macmillan. (12 months and up). Also by this author: *It's Great to Be One*.

Ricklen, Neil. (1990). *Baby's Colors*. New York: Simon and Schuster. (12 months and up). Additional books by this author: *Baby's Clothes, Baby's Friends, Baby and Me, Grandpa and Me, Grandma and Me, Baby's Big and Little, Baby's School* and *Baby's Zoo*.

Rockwell, Anne. (1989). *Apples and Pumpkins*. New York: Macmillan. (24 months and up)

Rockwell, Anne. (1993). *Pots and Pans*. New York: Macmillan. (18 months and up)

Rockwell, Anne and Rockwell, Harlow. (1984). *Nice and Clean*. New York: Macmillan. (24 months and up)

Rockwell, Harlow. (1980). *My Kitchen*. New York: Greenwillow. (18 months and up)

Rose, Dorothey. (1993). *Peek-a-boo*. New York: Simon and Schuster. (12 months and up). Additional books by this author: *What Do Lambs Say?* and *Where's Your Nose*.

Sieveking, Anthea. (1991). *Rub a Dub Dub and other Splashy Rhymes*. New York: Barrons. (12 months and up). Additional titles by this author: *Twinkle, Twinkle Little Star* and *Polly Put the Kettle On*.

Slier, Debby. (1989). *Little Babies*. New York: Checkerboard Press. (12 months and up). Additional titles by this author: *Baby's Places, Brothers and Sisters, Busy Baby, Farm Animals* and *Little Animals*.

Stinson, Kathy. (1986). *Bare Naked Book*. Toronto: Annick Press. (18 months and Up). Also by this author: *Big or Little?*

Tafuri, Nancy. (1984). *Have You Seen My Duckling?* New York: Greenwillow. (12 months and up)

Wildsmith, Brian. (1990). *Squirrels*. Oxford: Oxford University Press. (24 months and up)

Williams, Vera. (1990). *More, More, More Said the Baby*. New York: Scholastic. (18 months and up)

Wood, Audrey. (1984). *The Napping House*. San Diego: Harcourt Brace Jovanovich. (18 months and up)

Wood, Audrey. (1990). *Quick as a Cricket*. Singapore: Child's Play. (12 months and up)

Wood, Audrey and Wood, Don. (1991). *The Little Mouse, the Red Ripe Strawberry, and the Big Hungry Bear*. Singapore: Child's Play. (18 months and up)

Ziefert, Harriet. (1992). *Where's Daddy's Car?* New York: HarperCollins. (18 months and up)

Save and Send

Things to save and have parents send from home.
Send notes home periodically to remind parents of suggested items.

From the kitchen...

dish tubs
berry baskets
cookie cutters
egg cartons
canning rings
empty food packages of all kinds
juice can lids (pull tab type)
safe kitchen utensils, such as spatula,
    wire whisk, plastic or metal mixing
    bowls, measuring spoons and cups,
    sifters, tongs, muffin tins, etc.
paper plates
foil pie tins, microwave meal plates, etc.
plastic bottles, jars and containers with
    lids, especially clear ones
resealable bags
scoops
spice containers
flat trays

From the dresser and closet...

hats
mittens and gloves
soft purses, billfolds, wallets
scarves, bandanas
old flat shoes and slippers
shoelaces
skirts with elastic waistbands
old socks
totebags
vests

From the hobby drawer...

old cameras
craft items of all kinds
craft fur
craft sponges
embroidery hoops
fabric, rick rack, lace, ribbon and other
    sewing scraps
feathers
felt
film canisters
macrame beads and string
yarn

From the storage closet...

boxes of all kinds and sizes, especially
    shoe boxes and large boxes
gift wrap
greeting cards
ribbons and bows
tins
tubes from gift wrap rolls

From the cleaning closet and garage...

buckets
laundry soap boxes with handles
clothespins and craft pins
feather dusters
large paintbrushes and rollers
sandpaper
scrub brushes and old toothbrushes
sponges
spray bottles
styrofoam packing blocks
tubes from paper towels and toilet
    paper rolls
wallpaper samples and books

From the office...

old calendars, send a note home re-
    questing them in late December or
    early January
catalogues
computer paper and strips
unopened junk mail
magazines, especially parenting and
    wildlife ones
scrap paper of all kinds

From all over the house...

baby bathtubs
baskets
bathmats
small blankets
dish tubs
pillows
old shower curtains and tablecloths
stuffed animals and puppets
wading pools

Activity and Skills Index

Alphabetical List of Terms and Materials